The Constitutional Canvas: India's Foundational Brushstrokes

OrangeBooks Publication

1st Floor, Rajhans Arcade, Mall Road, Kohka, Bhilai, Chhattisgarh - 490020

Website:**www.orangebooks.in**

© Copyright, 2024, Dhanraj Garwa

All rights reserved. No part of this book may be reproduced, stored in a retrieval system, or transmitted, in any form by any means, electronic, mechanical, magnetic, optical, chemical, manual, photocopying, recording or otherwise, without the prior written consent of its writer.

First Edition, 2024

THE CONSTITUTIONAL CANVAS: INDIA'S FOUNDATIONAL BRUSHSTROKES

DHANRAJ GARWA

FOREWORD BY

Hon'ble Dr. Justice K.G. Balakrishnan,
Former Chief Justice of India

Hon'ble Mr. Justice K.T. Sankaran,
Former Judge, Kerala High Court

OrangeBooks Publication
www.orangebooks.in

Dedication

To my dearest parents

(My Father Shri Omprakash Garwa and my Mother Smt. Anita),

Your unwavering love and steadfast support have been my guiding lights, shaping the contours of my journey. Through life's twists and turns, your belief in my potential has been the driving force behind my achievements.

In the pages of "The Constitutional Canvas: India's Foundational Brushstrokes" I explore the essence of the Basic Structure Doctrine-a doctrine that mirrors the enduring principles shaping our constitutional landscape. Just as this doctrine safeguards the core values of our democracy, your teachings have fortified my moral compass.

Your commitment to fairness and justice has been a constant beacon, motivating me to contribute to a society grounded in equality. This book is a tribute to you, my cherished parents, expressing gratitude for your immeasurable contributions to my growth.

Thank you for being the bedrock of my strength and for instilling in me the values that color my life's canvas with purpose.

With heartfelt appreciation,
Dhanraj Garwa

Preface To The First Edition

In the intricate tapestry of India's constitutional narrative, the contours of its foundational principles are delicately woven into what we understand as the "Basic Structure Doctrine." As I embark on this exploration in the pages of "The Constitutional Canvas: India's Foundational Brushstrokes" my intent is to unravel the profound significance of this doctrine, a guiding thread that intricately binds the constitutional fabric of our nation.

The idea behind this work germinated from a profound curiosity about the principles that form the bedrock of our constitutional order. The Basic Structure Doctrine, as evolved by the Indian judiciary, stands as a sentinel guarding the sanctity and integrity of our Constitution. It delineates the essential features that cannot be amended or altered, ensuring that the spirit of justice, equality, and liberty remains resilient against the winds of change.

Through an in-depth analysis and exploration, this book seeks to illuminate the historical underpinnings, judicial interpretations, and contemporary relevance of the Basic Structure Doctrine. Each chapter endeavours to paint a vivid picture of the constitutional canvas, highlighting the brushstrokes that have shaped our legal landscape and continue to influence our democratic ethos.

As we navigate the intricate terrain of constitutional law, my hope is that readers will find not only a scholarly examination but also a reflective journey into the essence of our constitutional identity. The intention is not merely to dissect legal principles but to foster a deeper understanding of the values that breathe life into our democracy.

"The Constitutional Canvas" is an invitation to engage with the complexities of constitutional jurisprudence and appreciate the nuanced strokes that have defined our legal tapestry. It is my sincere aspiration that this exploration serves as a valuable resource for scholars, practitioners, and enthusiasts alike, contributing to a richer discourse on the constitutional evolution of India.

May this endeavor encourage readers to delve into the constitutional canvas, to scrutinise the foundational brushstrokes that shape our collective destiny, and to ponder the enduring relevance of the Basic Structure Doctrine in India's constitutional journey.

Dhanraj Garwa

Acknowledgements

Embarking on the journey of composing "The Constitutional Canvas: India's Foundational Brushstrokes" has been an intellectually enriching endeavor. It is with profound gratitude that I extend my sincere thanks to those who have played pivotal roles in bringing this work to fruition.

Foremost, I express my deepest appreciation to my esteemed brother Yogesh Garwa and sister Sulbha for their profound understanding of the Basic Structure Doctrine. Their insightful discussions and intellectual contributions have been invaluable, shaping the narrative of this book and adding substantive depth to its analysis.

To my dear friends Aditya Panwar, Harsh Roodra, Mahim Dhingiya, and Lakshay Kainwal, your unwavering support has served as a constant source of inspiration. The countless hours of collaborative brainstorming, spirited debates, and shared enthusiasm for the subject matter have undeniably enriched the journey of crafting this book. Your enduring friendship has added both joy and intellectual vigor to the entire process.

In extending my acknowledgments, I am particularly honoured to recognise the exemplary guidance and mentorship provided by distinguished legal professionals, Senior Advocate S. Wasim A. Qadri and Adv. Dr. Suvesh Kumar, both esteemed practitioners at the Supreme Court of India. Their sage counsel from the inception of this project has been instrumental in shaping my understanding of constitutional law and has significantly enhanced the scholarly content of this book.

I also extend my gratitude to all those who have contributed in various capacities, offering encouragement, feedback, and support throughout this undertaking. The collective influence of these contributors has undoubtedly left an indelible mark on the pages of this work.

Moreover, I wish to acknowledge the unseen hands that have played a crucial role in this endeavor—mentors, colleagues, and well-wishers who have generously provided guidance and encouragement along the way.

Finally, to my family, whose unwavering belief in my academic pursuits has been a steadfast pillar of strength, I offer my deepest thanks. Their enduring love, understanding, and encouragement have served as the solid foundation upon which I have built this exploration of India's constitutional landscape.

This book is as much a testament to their support as it is to my own endeavours, and I am profoundly grateful for the collective effort that has gone into its creation.

With heartfelt appreciation,
Dhanraj Garwa

Prologue

In the labyrinth of legal intricacies that define the constitutional landscape of India, the Basic Structure Doctrine emerges as the linchpin, anchoring the essence of our democratic framework. As we embark on this journey through "The Constitutional Canvas: India's Foundational Brushstrokes" the pages ahead unfold not just a scholarly exploration but an odyssey into the very heart of our constitutional identity.

The canvas upon which we paint our constitutional narrative is vast, each stroke etched with the aspirations of a nation striving for justice, equality, and liberty. The Basic Structure Doctrine, a judicially crafted doctrine that has stood the test of time, serves as a compass, guiding us through the contours of constitutional interpretation.

This prologue serves as an invitation to traverse the intellectual terrain that lies ahead-a terrain shaped by the brilliance of constitutional architects, the wisdom of jurists, and the collective aspirations of a diverse and vibrant democracy. The brushstrokes we will examine are not just legal principles but reflections of societal values, political aspirations, and the evolving nature of governance in India.

Moving beyond the historical tapestry, we engage with the doctrine's contemporary relevance. How does it respond to the challenges of a dynamic and evolving society? What role does it play in shaping the discourse on individual rights, federalism, and the balance of power? These are questions that echo through the corridors of constitutional jurisprudence.

As we navigate through the chapters, we encounter the perspectives of jurists, scholars, and practitioners who have grappled with the intricacies of the Basic Structure Doctrine. Their insights provide a kaleidoscopic view of the doctrine's impact on the legal landscape and its resonance in the broader socio-political context.

"The Constitutional Canvas" is an attempt to capture the spirit of our constitutional journey-a journey marked by the interplay of legal principles, political dynamics, and societal expectations. It is an ode to the resilience of the Basic Structure Doctrine, a testament to its adaptability in the face of evolving challenges.

Let the exploration begin-a journey through the constitutional canvas, where each stroke tells a story, and every chapter unveils another layer of India's foundational brushstrokes.

Dhanraj Garwa

Foreword

JUSTICE K.G BALAKRISHNAN
FORMER CHIEF JUSTICE OF INDIA
FORMER CHAIRPERSON NATIONAL HUMAN RIGHTS COMMISSION

Bungalow No.7, New Moti Bagh, New Delhi-110021
Email: officejusticekgbalakrishnan@gmail.com
Mobile: +919717266700

FOREWORD

It is with great pleasure that I extend my heartfelt appreciation for delving into the pages of "The Constitutional Canvas: India's Foundational Brushstrokes" Authored by Mr. Dhanraj Garwa, this book is a meticulous exploration of the intricate tapestry woven by the basic structure doctrine within the framework of the Indian Constitution.

As we navigate the nuanced landscape of constitutional law, Mr. Dhanraj Garwa expertly guides us through the profound implications and enduring significance of the foundational principles that shape our democratic edifice. Drawing upon years of legal expertise, the author unravels the intricate threads that compose the constitutional fabric, presenting a compelling narrative that resonates with both legal scholars and avid readers.

In these pages, you will find a thought-provoking journey that transcends mere legal analysis; it is an intellectual odyssey that invites contemplation on the very essence of our constitutional democracy. Mr. Garwa's insightful exploration of the basic structure doctrine illuminates the constitutional contours that define the soul of our nation.

I commend the author's dedication to legal scholarship and the meticulous research evident in each chapter. This book serves as a valuable resource for those seeking a profound understanding of the Indian Constitution's core principles.

May "The Constitutional Canvas" find its place among the revered works that contribute to the discourse on constitutional law, inspiring future generations to engage with the constitutional tapestry that binds us as a nation.

Wishing all the best.

Justice K.G Balakrishnan

About: Justice K.G. Balakrishnan

Justice K. G. Balakrishnan made history on January 14, 2007, when he became the first *Dalit* Chief Justice of the Supreme Court. He served on the Supreme Court for ten years, more than three of those years as Chief Justice.

On May 12, 1945, Justice Balakrishnan was born. He attended Government Law College in Ernakulam and earned a bachelor's degree in science after completing his elementary schooling. On March 16, 1968, he became a member of the bar, focusing on civil and criminal cases in Ernakulam. After practicing for five years, on January 10, 1973, he was appointed to the Kerala Judicial Service as a Munsif. He did, however, step down in order to carry on practicing law in the Kerala High Court.

The Kerala High Court appointed Justice Balakrishnan as a judge on September 26, 1985. In 1997, he was moved to the Gujarat High Court following twelve years of service. On July 16, 1998, he was quickly promoted to Chief Justice. One year later, on September 9, 1999, he was appointed Chief Justice of the Madras High Court. On June 8, 2000, the following year, he was named a judge of the Supreme Court.

Justice Balakrishnan wrote 219 decisions and a portion of 787 benches during his ten years on the Supreme Court. Out of all the judges in 2001, he wrote the most: 44.

During his ten years on the Supreme Court, Justice Balakrishnan's work was mostly focused on criminal cases. He was involved in historic instances concerning encroachment, elections, and reservations based on caste.

Foreword

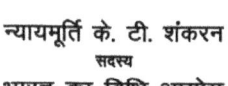

न्यायमूर्ति के. टी. शंकरन
सदस्य
भारत का विधि आयोग
भारत सरकार

Justice K.T. Sankaran
Member
Law Commission of India
Govt. of India

Foreword

"The Constitutional Canvas: India's Foundational Brushstrokes" is a book that explores India's Constitutional landscape and it gives me immense pleasure to pen a few words for the same. The metaphor of "The Constitutional Canvas" aptly captures the intricate design and vibrant hues of our Constitution, which has evolved over the years, reflecting the aspirations and ethos of a diverse and dynamic nation.

This book delves into Constitutional law with a keen eye for detail, offering readers an extensive view of its various facets. From the historical foundation that shaped its inception to the contemporary interpretations that breathes life into its provisions, the author has carefully woven together a narrative that is both informative and engaging. India's Constitutional journey has been marked by significant milestones, each leaving its distinct imprint on the 'canvas', as seen by the author, of our legal framework. Through insightful analysis of key cases and doctrines, this book also highlights the vital role played by the judiciary in shaping the countless features of our Constitution.

One of the main features of this book is the comparative description of the Constitutional law of different nations and the presentation of technology in the Indian scenario, then connecting it with various aspects of the Constitution, making it a complete guide for every reader to have a wholesome view of the highlights of our Constitution and its ongoing journey.

I am aware of the complexities inherent in the interpretation and application of the Constitution of India, therefore, "The Constitutional Canvas" serves as a valuable resource for legal practitioners and students seeking clarity and understanding in topics ranging from the preamble, judicial review, basic structure doctrine and to the latest judicial decisions.

I commend Dhanraj for his scholarly contribution to the field of Constitutional law at such a young age. His dedication and intellect is evident in the pages of this book, which I am confident will find a rightful place in the shelves of all those passionate about India's Constitutional journey. May "The Constitutional Canvas: India's Foundational Brushstrokes" serve as a guiding light for all those who seek to unravel India's Constitutional heritage.

New Delhi
8th January, 2024

Justice K.T Sankaran (Retd.)

कमरा नं. 407, चतुर्थ तल, 'बी' विंग, लोक नायक भवन, खान मार्किट, नई दिल्ली–110003
Room No. 407, 4th Floor, 'B' Wing, Lok Nayak Bhawan, Khan Market, New Delhi-110003
Tel. : 011-24654954, Email : justicektsankaran@gmail.com

About: Justice K.T. Sankaran

Justice K.T. Sankaran was a judge of the Kerala High Court from February 2005 - December 2016.

He was born in Thalakkasseri, near Pattambi, Palakkad, Kerala on 25 December 1954. He completed his education from S.B.S Thanneercode, Government High School, Kumaranellur, St. Thomas College, Thrissur and Sree Krishna College, Guruvayoor, Saraswathy Law College, Mercara, Coorg, Karnataka. He enrolled as an Advocate in 1979. He started practice in Magistrate Court Pattambi in 1979 and shifted his practice to Kerala High Court in 1982. On 2 February 2005, he was appointed as an additional judge of Kerala High Court and became a permanent judge on 22 November 2006. He retired from service upon attaining superannuation on 25/12/2016. He also served as the Director of Kerala Judicial Academy and Professor at NUALS, Kochi.

Currently, he is serving as the Full-Time Member of 22nd Law Commission of India.

Index

Chapter 1 1

Introduction 1
- 1.1 The Tapestry of Diversity 5
- 1.2 Justice, Liberty, Equality, and Fraternity 7
- 1.3 Constitutional Philosophy and Global Influences 10
- 1.4 Anticipating Challenges and Aspirations 13
- 1.5 Global Perspectives and Constitutional Borrowings 15
- 1.6 Dynamic Evolution in Response to Social Challenges 18
- 1.7 Balancing Tradition and Progress 20
- 1.8 Foundational Principles in Action 23
- 1.9 Conclusion of the Contextualization Journey 25
- 1.10 Liberty: A Cultural Ethos 28
- 1.11 Equality: A Dynamic Commitment to Inclusivity 28
- 1.12 Fraternity: The Unseen Thread Binding Diversity 28
- 1.13 Preamble: A Guiding Light in Governance 29
- 1.14 Federal Structure: Unity in Diversity 29
- 1.15 Democratic Principles: The Pulse of Governance 29
- 1.16 Socio-Economic Justice: Transformative Aspirations 30
- 1.17 Dynamic Nature: Amendments and Evolution 30
- 1.18 Culmination of Introduction: The Unfinished Symphony 30

Chapter 2 32

Building Blocks of the Constitution 32
- 2.1 Preamble : The Guiding Light 32
- 2.2 Fundamental Rights : Safeguarding Individuals Freedoms 37
- 2.3 Directive Principles of State Policy : Socio-Economic Justice 43
- 2.4 Judicial Interpretation : Expanding the Canvas of Rights 48
- 2.5 Global Perspectives on Constitutional Principles 53

Chapter 3 63

Basic Structure Doctrine Unveiled 63
- 3.1 Societal Impact of Basic Structure Doctrine 63
- 3.2 Interplay with Fundamental Rights 66
- 3.3 Influence on Legislative Process 69
- 3.4 Comparative Constitutional Case Studies 72
- 3.5 Public Interest Litigation (PIL) and the Doctrine 75
- 3.6 Constitutional Amendments as Challenges 79
- 3.7 Jurisprudential Philosophy Behind the Doctrine 83
- 3.8 Role in Safeguarding Minority Rights 86
- 3.9 Role in Environment Jurisprudence 90
- 3.10 Temporal Dynamics 94
- 3.11 Role in Economic Reforms 97
- 3.12 Innovations in Judicial Interpretation 101
- 3.13 Public Perception and Judicial Legitimacy 104
- 3.14 International Perspective on Basic Structure 108
- 3.15 Educational Initiatives and the Doctrine 112

Chapter 4 119

Essential Features of The Basic Structure 119
- 4.1 Constitutional Amendments as Social Contracts 122
- 4.2 Impact on Governance Structure 125
- 4.3 Environmental Jurisprudence and the Basic Structure 129
- 4.4 Technology and Constitutional Essentials 132
- 4.5 Role in Addressing Economic Injustices 136
- 4.6 Basic Structure as a Shield Against Populism 139
- 4.7 Global Constitutional Trends and Basic Structure 142
- 4.8 Essential Features in Plural Societies 145
- 4.9 Citizen Activism and the Basic Structure 148
- 4.10 Basic Structure and Intergenerational Equity 151
- 4.11 Alternative Dispute Resolution and Constitutional Essentials 154
- 4.12 Role of Legal Education in Understanding Essential Features 157

Chapter 5 161

Landmark Cases Shaping The Doctrine 161
- 5.1 Introduction to the Landmark Cases 161
- 5.2 Kesavananda Bharati v. State of Kerala (1973) 164

   5.3   *Indira Gandhi v. Raj Narain (1975)* 167
   5.4   *Minerva Mills Ltd. v. Union of India (1980)* 170
   5.5   *Waman Rao v. Union of India (1981)*... 172
   5.6   *SR Bommai v. Union of India (1994)* 175
   5.7   *L. Chandra Kumar v. Union of India (1997)*.............................. 177
   5.8   *I.R. Coelho v. State of Tamil Nadu (2007)* 179
   5.9   *Justice K.S. Puttaswamy (Retd.) v. Union of India (2017)* 182
   5.10 *Post-2017 Cases and Developments* 184
   5.11 *Comparative Analysis*.. 186
   5.12 *Critiques and Debates* 189
   5.13 *Conclusion*.. 192

Chapter 6 196
Contemporary Relevance and Challenges.. 196
   6.1   *Technological Advancements and Privacy Concerns*............. 197
   6.2   *National Security vs. Civil Liberties* 199
   6.3   *Equality and Social Justice* 201
   6.4   *Environmental Law and Constitutional Rights*....................... 203
   6.5   *Global Perspectives on Constitutionalism*................................. 205
   6.6   *Crisis Response and Constitutional Governance*.................... 207
   6.7   *Intersectionality and Identity Politics*... 209
   6.8   *Conclusion*.. 211

Chapter 7 214
Comparative Perspectives..214
   7.1   *Introduction to Comparative Analysis*..214
   7.2   *Historical Development of Constitutional Doctrines*............ 216
   7.3   *Basic Structure Doctrine in Different Jurisdictions* 218
   7.4   *Impact on Legal Systems*.. 221
   7.5   *Divergence and Convergence*... 223
   7.6   *Judicial Activism and Restraint* 226
   7.7   *Comparative Case Studies* 228
   7.8   *Influence on Constitutional Amendments* 230
   7.9   *Public Perception and Reception*... 232
   7.10 *Future Trends and Comparative Prospects* 235

Chapter 8 240
Future Horizons: The Evolving Canvas..240

8.1 Introduction to Future Trends...240
8.2 Technology and Constitutional Governance..242
8.3 Artificial Intelligence and Legal Systems..244
8.4 Environmental Law in the 21st Century..245
8.5 Globalization and Constitutionalism...248
8.6 Constitutional Responses to Public Health Crises................................250
8.7 Inclusive Constitutionalism...252
8.8 Human Rights in the Digital Age..253
8.9 Constitutional Governance in Times of Crisis.....................................255
8.10 Constitutionalism and Social Justice..257
8.11 Constitutional Challenges Posed by Biotechnology............................258
8.12 The Role of International Law in National Constitutions..................260
8.13 Constitutional Governance in Multi-Cultural Societies......................262
8.14 Education and Constitutional Literacy..263
8.15 The Future of Judicial Activism...265
8.16 Constitutional Amendments and Flexibility..267
8.17 E-Governance and Constitutional Governance...................................268
8.18 Constitutional Rights in the Cyber Age...270
8.19 The Role of Constitutional Courts in Shaping the Future..................271
8.20 Conclusion: Navigating the Evolving Constitutional Landscape........273

Chapter 9...276

Conclusion...276
9.1 Summary of Key Findings..276
9.2 Relevance to Contemporary Challenges..278
9.3 Impact on Governance and Rights...279
9.4 Comparative Insights..281
9.5 Public Perception and Legitimacy..283
9.6 Future Horizons...287
9.7 Educational and Awareness Initiatives...290
9.8 Educational and Awareness Initiatives...292
9.9 Challenges and Opportunities...294
9.10 Closing Thoughts..296
9.11 Call to Action..298

Bibliography..300

Chapter 1

Introduction

In the grand tapestry of nations, few narratives unfold with the intricacy and significance as that of India-a nation born from the crucible of history, forged in the fires of independence, and endowed with a visionary constitution that breathes life into its democratic soul. As the ink dried on the pages of the Constitution of India in 1950, it marked not just the birth of a republic but the crystallization of a profound commitment to justice, liberty, and equality.

To understand the intricacies of this constitutional canvas, we embark on a journey through time, tracing the genesis of the Indian Constitution. From the spirited debates in the Constituent Assembly to the challenges faced in the early years of independence, we delve into the historical underpinnings that set the stage for the emergence of a doctrine tasked with preserving the very essence of the Constitution. As India emerged from the shadows of colonial rule, the framers of the Constitution faced the monumental task of crafting a document that would not only serve as a legal instrument but as a moral compass for a diverse and dynamic nation. The debates within the Constituent Assembly resonate through the ages, echoing the voices of visionaries who envisioned a society built on the principles of justice, liberty, equality, and fraternity. The constitutional text, therefore, became more than a legal framework; it became a covenant, a promise to every citizen, irrespective of caste, creed, or gender.

Introduction

To grasp the true essence of India's constitutional journey, it is imperative to immerse ourselves in the historical currents that shaped the canvas upon which the Constitution was sketched. The post-independence period was marked not only by the euphoria of newfound freedom but also by the weight of responsibility to construct a nation that encapsulated the aspirations of its diverse populace.

The Constituent Assembly, a gathering of visionaries, jurists, and leaders from varied backgrounds, convened to deliberate upon the foundational principles that would form the bedrock of the nation. As we traverse back to that pivotal moment in history, the echoes of impassioned debates and reasoned discourses resonate-a chorus of voices contributing to the intellectual mosaic that is the Indian Constitution.

The Constituent Assembly debates were not mere legislative discussions; they were philosophical reflections on the nature of democracy, justice, and the delicate equilibrium between individual rights and societal obligations. The framers, cognizant of the weight of their decisions, sought inspiration from various constitutional models, ancient Indian philosophy, and the collective wisdom of humanity's political experiments.

The adoption of a federal structure, the enshrinement of fundamental rights, and the commitment to a democratic form of governance-all these decisions were deliberate strokes on the canvas, reflecting a conscious choice to forge a unique path that honored India's rich cultural tapestry while embracing modern democratic ideals.

Moreover, the Constitution was envisioned not as a static document but as a living, breathing entity capable of adapting to the evolving needs of society. The framers acknowledged the impermanence of legal provisions and, in their wisdom, embedded mechanisms for amendments, ensuring that the constitutional edifice could weather the storms of time while retaining its foundational principles.

The context of partition, the scars of communal violence, and the socio-economic disparities prevalent in post-colonial India were all imprints on this canvas, influencing the framers to address not only immediate challenges but also to anticipate the demands of an uncertain future. The Constitution, therefore, emerged as a dynamic response to historical exigencies, a testament to the resilience of a nation determined to chart its destiny.

The debates on drafting the Directive Principles of State Policy, the discussions on reservations, and the commitment to a secular and inclusive society-all these facets of the constitutional tapestry bear witness to the framers' conscious efforts to create a document that was not just a legal framework but a moral covenant.

As we embark on this exploration of the contextual roots of India's constitutional canvas, we recognize that understanding the nuances of the Constituent Assembly debates is akin to deciphering the artist's preliminary sketches before the grand masterpiece takes shape. The chapters that follow will delve deeper into these foundational deliberations, examining how they set the stage for the emergence of the Basic Structure Doctrine-an essential element in our constitutional narrative.

Within the hallowed halls of the Constituent Assembly, the air was thick with the promise of a nascent democracy, as diverse voices resonated with the urgency of crafting a constitution that would be both a legal compass and a moral guide for the new nation. It was a collective endeavor to mold the aspirations of a people into a constitutional framework that not only withstood the test of time but reflected the spirit of a free and egalitarian India.

In contextualizing the constitutional canvas, one must delve into the unique historical circumstances that shaped the contours of the Indian Constitution. The scars of partition, etched into the collective memory, compelled the framers to fashion an inclusive document that sought to heal rather than exacerbate societal wounds. The preamble, echoing the values of justice, liberty, equality, and fraternity, became a poignant declaration of intent-an invocation for a just and compassionate society.

The debates within the Constituent Assembly were not merely legal deliberations; they were intellectual wrestling matches, where ideologies clashed and congealed to form the foundational principles of the Constitution. Drawing inspiration from the Magna Carta, the American Constitution, and the French Revolution, the framers were acutely aware of the need to weave global democratic ideals into the fabric of India's unique socio-cultural tapestry.

Moreover, the framers confronted the specter of social inequality and sought to address historical injustices through affirmative action. The canvas of the Constitution, therefore, became a space for redressal- a pledge to uplift the marginalized and create a society where every citizen could participate in the nation's growth without the shackles of discrimination.

The federal structure, carefully calibrated, was another stroke on the canvas-an acknowledgment of India's linguistic and cultural diversity. The framers recognized that governance needed to be not only effective but also sensitive to the unique challenges faced by different regions, and thus, the Constitution became a covenant that preserved the unity of the nation while celebrating its rich diversity.

As we delve into the Constituent Assembly debates, it becomes evident that the framers were not merely drafting a legal document; they were sculpting a vision of a just society. The Directive Principles of State Policy, inspired by socio-economic justice ideals, reflected a commitment to address poverty, inequality, and disparities in a nation emerging from centuries of colonial rule.

The contextual roots of the constitutional canvas, therefore, extend beyond legal intricacies to encompass the socio-political milieu of post-independence India. The strokes on this canvas were not arbitrary; they were deliberate, guided by a profound sense of responsibility towards future generations. The resulting Constitution was not a static monument but a living testament to the ideals of a people charting their destiny.

In the chapters that follow, we will navigate through these historical underpinnings, deciphering the intent behind each stroke on the canvas. This exploration sets the stage for a deeper understanding of the Basic Structure Doctrine-an indispensable chapter in the constitutional narrative, one that guards the sanctity of the canvas against the passage of time.

1.1 The Tapestry of Diversity

Diversity became a defining thread in this constitutional tapestry. As the framers deliberated, they grappled with the complex task of harmonizing conflicting interests, ideologies, and aspirations. The recognition of linguistic and cultural diversity was not a mere acknowledgement but a celebration-a commitment to a federal structure that recognized the autonomy of states while maintaining the unity of the nation. The Seventh Schedule, which delineates the powers and responsibilities of the Union and the States, was woven into the constitutional fabric as a testament to this delicate balance.

The debates within the Constituent Assembly were not merely legal deliberations; they were intellectual wrestling matches, where ideologies clashed and congealed to form the foundational principles of the Constitution. Drawing inspiration from the Magna Carta, the American Constitution, and the French Revolution, the framers were acutely aware of the need to weave global democratic ideals into the fabric of India's unique socio-cultural tapestry.

In the grand narrative of India's constitutional journey, diversity emerges as a vibrant and essential thread, intricately woven into the fabric of the nation's identity. As we explore the pages of this constitutional saga within the context of our book, "The Constitutional Canvas: India's Foundational Brushstrokes," it becomes evident that the framers, seated in the Constituent Assembly, were not mere architects of a legal document but artisans crafting a masterpiece that reflected the rich tapestry of India's linguistic, cultural, and regional diversity.

The choice of a federal structure was more than a pragmatic response to administrative challenges; it was a deliberate decision to recognize and embrace the diverse needs and identities of India's regions. The Seventh Schedule, an essential component of this federal framework, becomes a brushstroke on the constitutional canvas. It delineates powers and responsibilities between the Union and the States, symbolizing the delicate balance between national unity and regional autonomy.

As we delve into this aspect, we uncover the nuanced approach adopted by the framers. They sought to grant states a level of autonomy that would allow for governance tailored to local needs, fostering a sense of ownership and identity among diverse communities. The federal model, inspired by global examples, became a cornerstone in addressing the complexities of governance in a vast and culturally diverse nation. This wasn't just a legal provision; it was an ode to the unity found in acknowledging and respecting diversity.

Beyond the federal structure, language played a pivotal role in shaping the constitutional mosaic. The linguistic reorganization of states in the post-independence period was a testament to the commitment to linguistic diversity. This transformative process addressed historical grievances, giving linguistic communities the right to education and governance in their mother tongues. It was a recognition that language isn't merely a means of communication but a repository of culture, history, and identity.

Cultural pluralism found expression in constitutional provisions that protected the rights of religious and ethnic minorities. The framers, drawing inspiration from India's historical traditions of coexistence, enshrined the principle of secularism in the Constitution. This commitment to secular ideals aimed not at erasing religious identities but at fostering an environment where all religions could flourish in harmony. The constitutional canvas thus becomes a reflection of a conscious effort to weave a narrative where diversity is not just tolerated but celebrated.

Another critical strand in the tapestry of diversity is the affirmative action policies aimed at addressing historical social inequalities. Recognizing that certain communities had been historically marginalized, the framers embedded provisions for reservation in education and public employment. This wasn't a departure from the principle of meritocracy but a conscious effort to level the playing field, acknowledging that true equality necessitated redressal of historical injustices.

The reservation policies, as part of the constitutional canvas, were designed not as permanent fixtures but as transitional measures. They sought to provide an initial thrust to historically disadvantaged communities, intending to create a society where affirmative action would become obsolete as true social equity took root. As we unfold this chapter of the constitutional narrative, we witness the framers grappling with the complexities of social justice, seeking not just to draft laws but to create a societal shift towards inclusivity.

The constitutional canvas also incorporated the age-old principles of decentralized governance, as reflected in the adoption of Panchayati Raj. Inspired by the Gandhian vision of self-sufficient village republics, this constitutional amendment empowered local communities to take charge of their governance. The recognition of local self- government was a nod to the diversity of rural India, where different regions had distinct needs and aspirations.

In essence, the Panchayati Raj system was more than just a legal provision; it was a manifestation of the constitutional philosophy that governance should be attuned to the unique needs of local communities. As we navigate through this aspect, we uncover how decentralization was not merely an administrative strategy but a brushstroke that emphasized the strength found in the diverse identities of India's villages.

As we unravel the constitutional tapestry, the recognition of diversity isn't confined to legal provisions alone. It permeates the very ethos of the Constitution, reflecting the framers' intent to create a document that resonates with the myriad identities and aspirations of the Indian populace. Each provision, whether related to federalism, linguistic diversity, cultural pluralism, or social justice, is a testament to the framers' commitment to unity in diversity.

In the constitutional canvas, diversity isn't a challenge to be overcome but a source of strength to be embraced. The framers, in their wisdom, sought to create a constitutional order where every thread of diversity contributes to the vibrant tapestry of a united and resilient nation. As we navigate through this chapter, we discover that the framers didn't view diversity as a cacophony of conflicting voices but as a symphony that enriches the constitutional melody, making it uniquely Indian and enduring.

1.2 Justice, Liberty, Equality, and Fraternity

These guiding principles, enshrined in the preamble, became the North Star for the framers-an unwavering guide in the creation of a just and inclusive society. Justice, in its manifold forms-social, economic, and political-became the touchstone against which laws and policies were to be measured. Liberty was not just a legal concept but a promise of freedom from oppression, and equality, an assurance that every citizen, irrespective of caste, creed, or gender, would have an equal stake in the nation's progress.

Moreover, the framers confronted the specter of social inequality and sought to address historical injustices through affirmative action. The canvas of the Constitution, therefore, became a space for redressal-a pledge to uplift the marginalized and create a society where every citizen could participate in the nation's growth without the shackles of discrimination.

In our exploration of "The Constitutional Canvas: India's Foundational Brushstrokes," a profound chapter unfolds as we delve into the core principles that form the bedrock of the Indian Constitution-Justice, Liberty, Equality, and Fraternity. These aren't just lofty ideals etched into the text; they are the guiding stars that illuminate the path toward a just and egalitarian society. As we navigate through this constitutional landscape, we witness the framers, seated in the Constituent Assembly, imbuing each stroke with the spirit of these principles.

The concept of justice permeates every facet of the constitutional canvas. Social justice, economic justice, and political justice are not mere buzzwords but foundational principles that echo through the Constitution. As we scrutinize this aspect, we uncover the nuanced approach of the framers who recognized that justice wasn't a one-size-fits-all concept. They sought to balance the scales, ensuring that the vulnerable and marginalized found protection under the umbrella of the law.

The Preamble, the poetic prelude to the Constitution, declares India's commitment to securing justice, social, economic, and political. It reflects a conscious decision to create a society where fairness isn't a privilege but a right. The framers, with their collective wisdom, embedded justice as a cornerstone in the constitutional narrative, acknowledging that a just society is a prerequisite for any meaningful democratic order.

As we peer into the canvas, we discern how justice, as envisaged by the framers, is not static but a dynamic principle that evolves with the changing needs of society. The introduction of Public Interest Litigation (PIL), for instance, became a significant brushstroke in the pursuit of justice. It empowered citizens to seek judicial redressal for societal issues, ensuring that justice wasn't confined to individual grievances but extended to the broader collective. This evolution illustrates the framers' foresight in crafting a Constitution that adapts to the evolving landscape of justice.

Liberty, the second pillar, stands tall in the constitutional edifice, representing the freedom of thought, expression, belief, and action. It is a principle that resonates through the Constitution, creating a space where individual freedoms are protected against arbitrary state interference. As we navigate through this aspect, we observe how liberty isn't absolute but carefully balanced with the needs of a democratic society.

The framers, mindful of the delicate balance between individual freedom and societal welfare, ensured that liberty wasn't a license for anarchy but a responsibility. The restrictions placed on free speech in the interest of public order, the reasonable restrictions on fundamental rights, and the delicate dance between personal freedoms and the collective good all underscore the framers' nuanced approach to liberty.

Equality, the third pillar, manifests as a commitment to creating a society where every citizen is afforded equal opportunities and treatment. As we scrutinize this constitutional facet, we unravel the framers' intentional efforts to address historical injustices. The affirmative action policies, enshrined in the Constitution, become a powerful brushstroke, leveling the playing field for marginalized communities and redressing centuries-old social inequities.

The framers didn't conceptualize equality as a mere legal provision but as a transformative principle capable of reshaping societal structures. The constitutional mandate for equal pay for equal work, the abolition of untouchability, and the reservation policies were all strokes on the canvas, painting a vision of an egalitarian society.

Fraternity, the fourth pillar, represents the spirit of brotherhood and a commitment to fostering unity among India's diverse communities. As we delve into this aspect, we discover that fraternity isn't a passive sentiment but an active principle that calls for the elimination of discrimination and the promotion of a harmonious society.

The framers, cognizant of India's diversity, enshrined secularism in the Constitution, emphasizing the equal treatment of all religions. The commitment to fraternity was a deliberate choice to celebrate India's pluralism, where different communities could coexist in peace. The constitutional canvas, therefore, becomes a testament to the framers' vision of a nation where diversity is not a source of division but a strength that binds communities together.

In conclusion, the principles of Justice, Liberty, Equality, and Fraternity are not abstract ideals but the essence of India's constitutional identity. As we traverse the intricate details of these principles within the constitutional canvas, we witness the framers' intent to craft a document that goes beyond legal provisions-a document that reflects a vision of a just, free, equal, and fraternal society. Each stroke, carefully placed, contributes to the masterpiece that is the Indian Constitution, a living testament to the enduring values that shape the nation's democratic ethos.

1.3 Constitutional Philosophy and Global Influences

The deliberations were not confined to the national sphere alone. The framers were keenly aware of the global political landscape and drew inspiration from constitutional philosophies worldwide. Ideas of justice and democracy from Western political thought, coupled with elements from India's ancient past, forged a unique blend that sought to encapsulate the spirit of the nation.

The framers were intentional in their approach, recognizing that the Constitution was not a static entity but a living document capable of evolving with the changing needs of society. The canvas, therefore, wasn't merely a depiction of the present but a projection into the future-an acknowledgment that the ideals engraved would resonate across generations.

The constitutional philosophy of India, shaped within the crucible of the Constituent Assembly, bears the imprints of diverse global influences. As we delve into this aspect within the pages of "The Constitutional Canvas: India's Foundational Brushstrokes," we encounter a profound narrative that transcends national boundaries. The framers, immersed in a wealth of constitutional ideas from around the world, undertook a delicate balancing act, blending global wisdom with India's unique socio-cultural fabric.

The deliberations of the Constituent Assembly were not confined to the geographical contours of the subcontinent; they drew inspiration from the broader spectrum of human experience in constitutional governance. The framers, acutely aware of the challenges and opportunities presented by the global political landscape, sought to create a constitutional philosophy that would resonate both nationally and internationally.

In this exploration, we unravel the threads of influence from various constitutional traditions. The Westminster model, inherited from the British, left an indelible mark on India's parliamentary system. The adoption of a bicameral legislature, the Prime Minister's role, and the concept of a parliamentary democracy were strokes on the canvas that reflected the framers' recognition of the functional efficacy of the British constitutional system.

Yet, the framers were not confined to a singular influence. The American experiment in democracy, with its emphasis on individual rights and a written constitution, also played a pivotal role. Fundamental rights, enshrined in Part III of the Constitution, were a direct reflection of the American Bill of Rights. The framers, by incorporating these rights, sought to anchor the Indian Constitution in a commitment to safeguarding individual liberties.

The French Revolution, with its clarion call for liberty, equality, and fraternity, echoed through the Constituent Assembly debates. These principles found a home in the preamble of the Indian Constitution, becoming the guiding stars that illuminate the nation's democratic journey. The framers, through this global borrowing, crafted a constitutional philosophy that aspired not just for legal structure but moral and ethical values.

Introduction

Furthermore, the framers drew from India's own historical legacy, infusing the constitutional canvas with elements from ancient texts like the Arthashastra and Manusmriti. This unique synthesis of global and indigenous influences reflects a conscious effort to harmonize the modern with the traditional, creating a constitutional philosophy that is deeply rooted in India's cultural heritage.

The choice of a federal structure, inspired by the experiences of federations like the United States and Canada, showcased the framers' understanding of the need to balance centralized power with regional autonomy. The Seventh Schedule, mirroring the distribution of powers, was a stroke on the canvas that acknowledged India's linguistic and cultural diversity.

Moreover, the framers were intentional in recognizing the need for socio-economic justice, drawing from socialist principles to address the vast economic disparities inherited from colonial rule. The Directive Principles of State Policy, though not legally enforceable, became a guiding philosophy for future governance, reflecting the framers' commitment to building a just and equitable society.

As we traverse the global influences on India's constitutional philosophy, we discern that the framers were not engaged in a mere copy-paste exercise. Instead, they undertook a careful curation, selecting principles and values that resonated with India's aspirations. The constitutional canvas thus became a mosaic, each piece contributing to a unique vision that transcends time and space.

The framers, in their sagacity, understood that the Constitution was not a static document but a living testament to the evolving ideals of a nation. By drawing from global influences, they ensured that the constitutional philosophy remained adaptable, capable of responding to the changing needs of society. This dynamic approach, evident in the incorporation of amendments and the evolution of judicial interpretations, underscores the framers' commitment to a living, breathing constitution.

In conclusion, the constitutional philosophy of India, shaped by global influences, is a testament to the foresight and wisdom of the framers. The constitutional canvas, enriched by ideas from various corners of the world, stands as a beacon of democratic governance, reflecting not only the framers' intellectual prowess but their deep-seated commitment to crafting a constitution that would stand the test of time. Each stroke on this canvas is a reflection of the framers' belief in a constitutional order that would resonate globally while remaining distinctly Indian.

1.4 Anticipating Challenges and Aspirations

As the debates unfolded, the framers weren't just responding to immediate challenges but were anticipating the aspirations of a future India. Questions of gender equality, socio-economic justice, and the balance between individual rights and societal welfare were all part of this intricate tapestry. The Constitution, thus, became a dynamic instrument, reflecting not just the realities of 1950 but the envisioned progress of a nation.

In contextualizing the constitutional canvas, we recognize that each stroke, each provision, was a deliberate choice-a brushstroke on a canvas that depicted the dreams and aspirations of a nation emerging from the shadows of colonialism. This exploration sets the stage for a deeper understanding of the Basic Structure Doctrine-an indispensable chapter in the constitutional narrative, one that guards the sanctity of the canvas against the passage of time.

As we delve deeper into "The Constitutional Canvas: India's Foundational Brushstrokes," the nuanced chapter of anticipating challenges and aspirations unfurls with a resonance that echoes through the corridors of the Constituent Assembly. The framers, seated at the precipice of India's nascent democracy, were not just architects of a legal document; they were visionaries sculpting a constitutional edifice that would stand resilient in the face of challenges and rise to meet the aspirations of a burgeoning nation.

Foreseeing the multifaceted challenges that an independent India would confront, the framers approached the constitutional task with a strategic foresight. The scars of colonial rule were still fresh, and the specter of social inequality loomed large. Yet, the framers envisioned a democratic fabric that could not only withstand these challenges but also lay the foundation for a society rooted in justice, liberty, equality, and fraternity.

The question of women's rights, for instance, was a challenge that was not only acknowledged but addressed within the constitutional framework. The framers recognized the historical injustices faced by women and sought to rectify them through provisions that safeguarded their rights. While the journey towards gender equality would be a long and evolving one, the framers laid the groundwork for a constitutional canvas that could adapt to the changing contours of societal expectations.

The caste system, deeply entrenched in the socio-cultural fabric, posed another formidable challenge. The framers, cognizant of the historical injustices perpetuated by this system, envisioned a constitutional order that would actively work towards dismantling caste-based discrimination. The affirmative action policies, encapsulated in reservations, were not just reactive measures but proactive strokes on the canvas, a commitment to reshape societal structures for the betterment of marginalized communities.

Economic disparities inherited from colonial exploitation were yet another challenge. The framers, recognizing the need for socio-economic justice, embedded within the constitutional philosophy the Directive Principles of State Policy. These principles, though not immediately enforceable, reflected the framers' anticipation of a future where the state would actively work towards mitigating economic inequalities and uplifting the socio-economically disadvantaged.

In the realm of religious diversity, the framers confronted the potential for inter-communal tensions. Their response was to enshrine the principles of secularism in the Constitution, reinforcing the idea that the state would not favor any particular religion. This constitutional stroke was not just a reaction to historical animosities but a proactive vision for a nation where all religious communities could coexist harmoniously.

Beyond anticipating challenges, the framers were keenly attuned to the aspirations of a new India. The Constitution was not just a response to historical grievances; it was a forward-looking document that sought to provide a roadmap for the nation's progress. The framers envisioned a society where the dignity of the individual was paramount, where every citizen had the opportunity to contribute to the nation's growth unencumbered by social or economic constraints.

The introduction of fundamental rights, enshrined in Part III of the Constitution, exemplified this aspiration. These rights were not just legal provisions but a clarion call for the protection of individual liberties. The framers, in carving these rights into the constitutional framework, were articulating a vision where citizens could live free from arbitrary state interference, where the principles of justice and liberty would guide the nation's trajectory.

Education, as a fundamental right, was another stroke on the canvas that mirrored the framers' aspirations for a society where knowledge and enlightenment would be accessible to all. By emphasizing the importance of education, the framers underscored their belief in the transformative power of knowledge to break the shackles of ignorance and usher in an era of informed citizenry.

In essence, the framers, with remarkable foresight, anticipated the challenges that would beset an independent India and wove into the constitutional fabric provisions that would actively address these challenges. Simultaneously, they articulated a vision for a nation that aspired towards lofty ideals of justice, liberty, equality, and fraternity. The constitutional canvas, thus, becomes not just a reactive response to historical injustices but a proactive manifesto for a democratic experiment that could navigate the complexities of a diverse and dynamic nation. Each stroke on this canvas is a testament to the framers' belief in the resilience of their creation and its capacity to evolve in tandem with the aspirations of generations to come.

1.5 Global Perspectives and Constitutional Borrowings

The framers, far from insulating themselves with in national boundaries, took a global outlook. They drew on constitutional practices from various parts of the world, learning from the successes and failures of other democratic experiments. While the Westminster model influenced the parliamentary system, the concept of fundamental rights found inspiration in the American Bill of Rights. This cross-pollination of ideas marked the Constitution as a product of collective global wisdom, a forward-looking document grounded in the accumulated knowledge of democratic governance.

In essence, the constitutional canvas was not just a reflection of Indian ideals but a nuanced integration of universal democratic principles. The framers, cognizant of India's unique socio-cultural milieu, curated an amalgamation of philosophies that transcended geographical boundaries. The Constitution, therefore, stands as a testament to the fact that the journey toward a just society is a shared endeavor, a universal aspiration binding diverse nations in a common pursuit.

In our exploration of "The Constitutional Canvas: India's Foundational Brushstrokes," the captivating narrative of global perspectives and constitutional borrowings unfolds as a testament to the cosmopolitan vision of the framers. Seated in the Constituent Assembly, the framers were not confined by geographical boundaries; they cast their gaze globally, drawing inspiration from diverse constitutional traditions to craft a document that would encapsulate the universal ideals of democracy and justice.

The framers' engagement with global perspectives was not merely an academic exercise but a conscientious effort to distill the best practices and insights from constitutional experiments around the world. The infusion of global wisdom into the Indian Constitution reflects a profound understanding that the journey toward a just and democratic society is a collective, global endeavor.

The Westminster model, inherited from the British constitutional tradition, was a pivotal influence on the framers. The adoption of a parliamentary system, with a Prime Minister as the head of government, mirrored the British approach to governance. Yet, the framers were discerning in their adaptation, recognizing the need to contextualize these borrowed elements within the socio-cultural milieu of India.

From the American constitutional tradition, the framers borrowed the concept of fundamental rights, echoing the principles enshrined in the U.S. Bill of Rights. The framers, cognizant of the importance of protecting individual liberties, incorporated these rights into the Indian Constitution, marking a departure from the British tradition where such rights were implicit rather than explicitly enumerated.

The French Revolution's ideals of liberty, equality, and fraternity found a reverberating echo in the Preamble of the Indian Constitution. While framing the Preamble, the framers drew inspiration from the French commitment to these universal principles, signaling India's intent to create a society founded on these ideals. The constitutional borrowings from the French Revolution weren't just symbolic; they were foundational strokes that painted the overarching vision of the Indian democratic experiment.

Moreover, the framers embraced the concept of federalism from diverse sources, including the United States, Canada, and Australia. The federal structure, delineating powers between the Union and the States, was a deliberate choice to address India's linguistic and cultural diversity. This constitutional borrowing wasn't a blind replication; it was a judicious adoption, acknowledging the strengths of federalism in fostering regional autonomy within a unified nation.

Intriguingly, the framers' engagement with global perspectives extended beyond the Western constitutional traditions. They delved into India's own historical and philosophical roots, borrowing elements from ancient texts such as the Arthashastra and Manusmriti. This fusion of indigenous and global influences created a constitutional tapestry that was uniquely Indian yet globally informed.

The framers' embrace of constitutional borrowings wasn't a mere homage to external models; it was a strategic adaptation, driven by the pragmatic recognition that no single constitutional tradition could perfectly encapsulate India's diverse reality. The Constitution, thus, became a living document, enriched by a blend of global and indigenous wisdom, attuned to the needs of a dynamic and pluralistic society.

This global perspective was not confined to the constitutional drafting phase; it continued to influence India's constitutional evolution. Judicial decisions often drew on international precedents and human rights principles, expanding the constitutional discourse beyond national boundaries. The framers, in their wisdom, had crafted a document capable of resonating with global democratic ideals while remaining rooted in India's specific historical and cultural context.

In conclusion, the global perspectives and constitutional borrowings that shaped the Indian Constitution are a testament to the framers' intellectual acumen and their commitment to creating a democratic masterpiece. Each borrowed element, whether from the West, the East, or India's own past, was carefully woven into the constitutional fabric. The constitutional canvas, therefore, stands as a dynamic synthesis of global and indigenous influences-a testament to the framers' belief that the pursuit of justice and democracy transcends borders and finds resonance in the shared aspirations of humanity.

1.6 Dynamic Evolution in Response to Social Challenges

The Constitution was conceived not as a rigid structure but as a living organism capable of responding to the evolving needs of society. It was a blueprint for a democratic experiment that recognized the inevitability of change. As the nation grappled with economic disparities, social injustices, and the complexities of cultural pluralism, the framers had the foresight to embed within the constitutional framework mechanisms for adaptation and growth.

The introduction of Directive Principles of State Policy, a set of socio-economic guidelines, exemplifies this dynamic approach. While fundamental rights set the stage for individual liberties, the Directive Principles outlined a socio-economic vision, a commitment to building a just society. The Constitution, viewed through this lens, becomes a document not frozen in time but a framework capable of addressing the ever-evolving challenges and aspirations of a vibrant democracy.

The evolution of the Indian Constitution, captured within the pages of "The Constitutional Canvas: India's Foundational Brushstrokes," is a dynamic narrative in response to the ever-shifting landscape of social challenges. The framers, in their sagacity, crafted a living document capable of adapting to the evolving needs of a society in flux. As we explore this aspect, we encounter a constitutional journey that not only anticipated challenges but responded to them with a resilience that has shaped India's democratic identity.

The framers, seated in the Constituent Assembly, were acutely aware of the impermanence of societal norms and the potential emergence of new challenges. The inclusion of Directive Principles of State Policy exemplifies this foresight. Though not immediately enforceable, these principles served as a compass, guiding future generations in addressing socio-economic challenges. The constitutional canvas, therefore, became a space where aspirations for societal progress were etched, and subsequent generations could draw inspiration to navigate contemporary challenges. Social justice, a foundational principle within the Constitution, has seen dynamic evolution. The reservation policies, initially framed as temporary measures, underwent amendments reflecting an understanding that historical injustices persisted. As societal structures evolved, so did the constitutional responses. The framers' vision wasn't static; it was a call to successive generations to refine and recalibrate responses to social challenges.

The canvas witnessed transformative strokes in response to gender-based challenges. Over the decades, the judiciary interpreted fundamental rights expansively, recognizing the right to life with dignity as encompassing the right to live without violence or discrimination. Amendments reflected societal aspirations for gender equality, revealing the Constitution as a responsive tool, adapting to a collective desire for a more inclusive and just society.

The canvas further expanded to accommodate environmental concerns. While not explicitly present in the original document, environmental jurisprudence evolved as an intrinsic part of constitutional interpretation. The judiciary, recognizing the urgent need for environmental protection, interpreted existing provisions to encompass the right to a healthy environment-a response to a contemporary challenge that transcended traditional boundaries.

The advent of technology brought forth novel challenges to privacy and data protection. The constitutional canvas, ever responsive, witnessed landmark judgments recognizing the right to privacy as a fundamental right. This acknowledgment was a brushstroke that underscored the framers' foresight-creating a constitutional space adaptable to challenges emerging in the digital age.

The canvas also embraced the LGBTQ+ community's struggle for equal rights. The judiciary, reflecting a broader societal acceptance, overturned colonial-era laws criminalizing same-sex relationships. This transformation wasn't merely a legal adjustment; it was a reflection of the constitutional canvas mirroring the evolving societal attitudes toward inclusivity and diversity.

Moreover, economic challenges spurred constitutional responses. Economic liberalization in the 1990s prompted a reevaluation of the state's role in the economy. Constitutional interpretations evolved, reflecting a shift toward a more market- oriented economic framework- a nuanced brushstroke in response to the demands of a changing global economic landscape.

The framers' dynamic approach is epitomized in the amendment process. The Constitution, far from being a static manuscript, is an evolving text, responsive to the zeitgeist. Amendments have addressed issues ranging from land reforms to the reorganization of states, demonstrating a constitutional adaptability that reflects the framers' intent to respond to the evolving needs of a diverse nation.

In essence, the constitutional canvas is a testament to the framers' commitment to creating a document that would not be confined by its original strokes. It is a living masterpiece, constantly evolving in response to the ever-changing colors of societal challenges. Each stroke, whether an amendment, judicial interpretation, or societal shift, contributes to the rich tapestry of India's constitutional journey. The dynamic evolution encapsulated within this canvas is an enduring legacy, an invitation for each generation to pick up the brush and contribute to the ongoing narrative of justice, liberty, equality, and fraternity.

1.7 Balancing Tradition and Progress

Embedded within the constitutional canvas is the delicate dance between tradition and progress. The framers, steeped in the rich tapestry of India's cultural heritage, sought to preserve its essence while embracing the winds of change. Fundamental rights, derived from the Constitution, were not seen as revolutionary departures but as a natural extension of age-old principles of justice and righteousness.

The canvas, therefore, reflects a conscious effort to strike a balance between continuity and innovation. The framers, guardians of tradition and pioneers of progress, sculpted a constitutional narrative that embraced the ancient roots of Dharma and Nyaya while laying the groundwork for a modern, egalitarian society.

The delicate dance between tradition and progress, intricately woven into the fabric of the Indian Constitution, unfolds as a nuanced chapter within "The Constitutional Canvas: India's Foundational Brushstrokes." The framers, architects of a nation's destiny, faced the formidable task of crafting a constitutional order that harmonized the rich tapestry of India's cultural traditions with the imperative for progress and modernity.

In embracing tradition, the framers drew inspiration from India's ancient heritage. References to ancient texts like the Arthashastra and Manusmriti underscored the acknowledgment of historical wisdom. The constitutional canvas, thus, became a vessel for the continuity of India's cultural ethos, a bridge connecting the past with the present. This conscious homage to tradition was not a mere nod to antiquity but a deliberate effort to ground the Constitution in the roots of Indian civilization.

However, this reverence for tradition did not equate to a blind adherence. The framers, keenly aware of the imperatives of progress, imbued the constitutional canvas with a forward-looking vision. The emphasis on fundamental rights, the commitment to social justice, and the adoption of a democratic framework were strokes that signaled a break from feudal legacies, signaling a desire for a progressive and inclusive society.

In navigating this delicate balance, the framers sought to weave a constitutional tapestry that was not frozen in time but capable of evolving with the aspirations of a changing society. The Directive Principles of State Policy, while drawing on traditional values, were framed as aspirational goals, providing a flexible framework for governance that could adapt to emerging challenges without forsaking foundational principles.

The question of personal laws encapsulates this intricate balancing act. The framers, cognizant of India's diverse religious and cultural traditions, refrained from imposing a uniform civil code. Instead, they entrusted the task of reform to future generations. This approach, far from a concession to conservatism, reflected a nuanced understanding of the complex interplay between tradition and societal evolution.

As India progressed, constitutional interpretations reflected an ongoing dialogue between tradition and progress. Landmark judgments on issues like gender equality, environmental protection, and LGBTQ+ rights demonstrated a commitment to upholding constitutional values while challenging regressive practices rooted in tradition. The judiciary, as a custodian of the constitutional spirit, became a vital player in navigating this delicate equilibrium.

Economic liberalization in the 1990s provided another canvas for this balance. The framers' commitment to socialism was reinterpreted to accommodate a more market-oriented economy, showcasing an adaptability that didn't discard tradition but allowed it to coexist with modern economic principles.

The notion of secularism, enshrined in the Constitution, embodies this balancing act. It does not imply a rejection of religious traditions but a commitment to equal treatment of all religions. The constitutional canvas, in this regard, becomes a space where diverse religious beliefs coexist without impinging on the principles of justice, liberty, equality, and fraternity.

The framers' approach to language and cultural diversity also exemplifies this delicate equilibrium. While recognizing Hindi as the official language, they ensured the protection of linguistic and cultural rights. The constitutional canvas, therefore, accommodates the multiplicity of languages and cultures, fostering a sense of unity without stifling diversity.

In essence, the constitutional canvas is a testament to the framers' wisdom in navigating the complex interplay between tradition and progress. It reflects an acknowledgment that tradition, when not ossified, can serve as a guiding force, providing a cultural anchor in the face of rapid change. At the same time, the canvas is a dynamic space, inviting progress and evolution in response to the evolving needs of a society in flux.

The delicate balancing act, as depicted on the constitutional canvas, is an ongoing process. It invites each generation to participate in the dialogue between tradition and progress, ensuring that the constitutional order remains not just a relic of the past but a living, breathing document that resonates with the pulsating heartbeat of a nation charting its course through the currents of history.

1.8 Foundational Principles in Action

The adoption of the Gandhian philosophy of village self-governance, known as Panchayati Raj, further exemplifies the integration of traditional wisdom into constitutional principles. This nod to traditional governance structures was not a romanticized return to the past but a pragmatic recognition of the efficacy of decentralized decision-making in a diverse and sprawling nation.

In essence, the constitutional canvas captures not only the foundational principles but also the subtle interplay between tradition and progress, a dynamic equilibrium that defines the constitutional experiment in India.

The foundational principles embedded within the Indian Constitution come to life as we observe them in action, dynamically shaping the contours of the nation's democratic journey. "The Constitutional Canvas: India's Foundational Brushstrokes" captures the essence of these principles as they unfold in the intricate tapestry of governance, law, and societal interactions.

Justice, as a foundational principle, is not a theoretical abstraction but a living reality manifested in the legal framework and judicial proceedings. The judiciary, as the custodian of justice, interprets and applies the law to ensure fairness and equity. Landmark decisions addressing social injustices, protecting individual liberties, and upholding the rule of law are brushstrokes that bring the principle of justice to life.

Liberty, another cornerstone, resonates in the democratic ethos of the nation. Citizens exercise their freedom of speech, expression, and belief, contributing to a vibrant public discourse. The constitutional canvas provides the space for individuals to pursue their aspirations, fostering a society where liberty isn't merely a legal provision but a palpable force shaping everyday lives.

Equality, deeply ingrained in the constitutional framework, unfolds in societal structures that seek to dismantle historical discriminations. Affirmative action policies, reservations, and anti-discrimination laws are instrumental strokes on the canvas that translate the principle of equality into tangible measures, fostering inclusivity and social harmony.

Fraternity, representing the spirit of brotherhood and unity, is evident in the coexistence of diverse communities. The constitutional commitment to secularism ensures that individuals of different religions, castes, and ethnicities share a common civic space. The constitutional canvas becomes a mosaic of cultural diversity, where different threads interweave to create a cohesive societal fabric.

The Preamble, a poetic prologue to the Constitution, encapsulates these foundational principles and serves as a guiding light for the nation. It is more than words on paper; it is a declaration of intent that reverberates in every corner of governance. The constitutional canvas, as it unfolds in administrative decisions, legislative debates, and executive actions, reflects a commitment to the ideals enshrined in the Preamble. The federal structure, another foundational principle, is not a mere structural choice but a dynamic arrangement that allows for the accommodation of diverse regional aspirations. The Seventh Schedule, delineating powers between the Union and the States, is a brushstroke on the canvas that reflects a delicate balance between national unity and regional autonomy.

Democratic principles find expression in the electoral process, where the voice of the people shapes the course of governance. Elections, a vibrant ritual in the democratic narrative, are more than procedural; they are strokes on the constitutional canvas, illustrating the people's exercise of their sovereign right to choose their representatives.

The commitment to socio-economic justice, reflected in the Directive Principles of State Policy, is not a distant ideal but an ongoing endeavor. Policies addressing poverty, education, healthcare, and rural development are the brushstrokes that transform constitutional principles into actionable initiatives aimed at uplifting the marginalized and underprivileged.

The constitutional canvas is not static; it evolves through amendments that respond to societal needs. The inclusion of new fundamental rights, changes in the Directive Principles, and adaptations to economic policies demonstrate the Constitution's dynamic nature-a living document that breathes life into foundational principles.

In essence, the foundational principles of justice, liberty, equality, and fraternity are not theoretical musings but practical guides shaping the trajectory of the nation. The constitutional canvas, with its intricate strokes, captures the vibrancy of India's democratic spirit, where the principles articulated by the framers are not distant ideals but living realities, influencing the collective conscience of the nation.

1.9 Conclusion of the Contextualization Journey

In traversing the contextual roots of India's constitutional canvas, we unravel a narrative that goes beyond legal intricacies. It is a story of a nation's collective endeavor to carve out a democratic identity, a testament to the foresight of visionaries who, in framing the Constitution, sought to capture the spirit of an emerging India. Each stroke on this canvas, whether inspired by global philosophies, rooted in historical challenges, or molded by cultural ethos, contributes to the richness and complexity of the constitutional narrative.

The journey of contextualization through "The Constitutional Canvas: India's Foundational Brushstrokes" concludes as we stand at the intersection of history, philosophy, and governance. This exploration has been a traverse through the intricate details of India's constitutional journey-a journey that mirrors the complex and dynamic nature of the nation it seeks to govern.

In contextualizing the canvas, we have delved into the foundational principles that serve as the bedrock of the Indian Constitution. Justice, liberty, equality, and fraternity, once abstract ideals, have been unveiled as living, breathing forces shaping the everyday realities of Indian society. These principles are not distant aspirations but tangible benchmarks against which the nation measures its progress.

Introduction

The canvas, adorned with the brushstrokes of tradition and progress, reflects the delicate balance struck by the framers. It is a testament to their foresight, as they navigated the interplay between ancient wisdom and modern imperatives, creating a constitutional order that bridges the gap between tradition and progress.

Global perspectives and constitutional borrowings have added layers of richness to the canvas, illustrating the cosmopolitan vision of the framers. The Constitution is not an isolated document but a product of dialogues with diverse constitutional traditions, both from the West and India's own historical legacy. It stands as a testament to the framers' belief that the pursuit of justice, liberty, equality, and fraternity is a universal endeavor that transcends borders.

The canvas, dynamically evolving in response to social challenges, showcases the resilience and adaptability of the constitutional order. Whether in addressing gender disparities, environmental concerns, or the advent of the digital age, the Constitution is not a static relic but a responsive tool that adjusts its strokes to meet the demands of a changing society.

Balancing tradition and progress has been an ongoing theme in our exploration. The constitutional canvas, as a space for this delicate dance, invites each generation to contribute to the narrative. The framers, in their wisdom, crafted a document that respects the cultural heritage of the past while embracing the imperatives of a forward-looking society.

Foundational principles, in action, reveal themselves not as lofty ideals confined to the pages of a legal document but as dynamic forces shaping governance, law, and societal interactions. The Preamble, a poetic declaration, echoes through the corridors of governance, guiding administrative decisions and legislative debates. The federal structure, the electoral process, and socio-economic policies are not mere abstractions but concrete manifestations of constitutional principles.

As we conclude this contextualization journey, we recognize that the constitutional canvas is an ongoing masterpiece. It invites participation, interpretation, and adaptation. Amendments, judicial decisions, and societal shifts contribute to the ever- evolving narrative of India's constitutional journey. The canvas, far from being a static portrait, is a dynamic space where the aspirations, challenges, and progress of the nation are continually painted and repainted.

The contextualization journey, therefore, is not a finite exploration but an ongoing dialogue with the constitutional spirit. It is an acknowledgment that the canvas will continue to capture the essence of India's democratic experiment, reflecting the collective dreams and aspirations of its people. As the journey concludes, it marks not an endpoint but a pause-a moment to reflect on the rich tapestry that is the Indian Constitution and its enduring significance in shaping the destiny of a diverse and dynamic nation.

As we reach the culmination of this introductory chapter, we stand at the threshold of a profound journey-a journey that promises to unravel the intricacies and unveil the living mosaic that is "The Constitutional Canvas: India's Foundational Brushstrokes." In traversing the pages of this chapter, we have embarked on a nuanced exploration, peeling back the layers of India's constitutional tapestry to reveal a dynamic and living document that echoes the aspirations, challenges, and collective spirit of a diverse nation.

This introductory chapter serves not merely as a prelude but as an invitation to delve deeper into the essence of the Indian Constitution-a document that encapsulates the dreams and ideals of a nation emerging from the shackles of colonialism to embrace the promises of democracy. We have embarked on a journey through the foundational principles of justice, liberty, equality, and fraternity, witnessing how these ideals are not mere abstract concepts but living forces shaping the course of governance, law, and societal interactions.

Justice Unveiled: Beyond Courts and Statutes

Justice, our first exploration, goes beyond the confines of courtrooms and legal statutes. It is a living force that resonates through every decision taken by the state. The constitutional canvas becomes a space where justice is not just punitive measures but a dynamic concept that adapts to rectify historical wrongs, protect individual rights, and ensure a fair and equitable society. The strokes on this canvas paint a narrative of justice seeking to level the playing field and respond to the evolving needs of a society in flux.

1.10 Liberty: A Cultural Ethos

Liberty, our second stroke on the canvas, reverberates far beyond legal frameworks. It is a cultural ethos that permeates the very soul of democratic governance, allowing citizens the freedom to express, believe, and live without undue interference. As we traverse the constitutional canvas, we uncover not just the absence of legal restrictions but the promotion of a culture that values individual freedoms. The canvas tells tales of free speech, artistic expression, and a society where the diversity of thought flourishes—a testament to the framers' belief in the inviolability of individual liberties.

1.11 Equality: A Dynamic Commitment to Inclusivity

Equality, deeply ingrained in the constitutional fabric, is not a static ideal but a commitment to dismantling historical discriminations. The canvas, adorned with strokes on affirmative actions, reservations, and anti-discrimination laws, comes alive with the pursuit of inclusivity and social harmony. Our journey into equality reveals a nuanced approach, acknowledging the diverse social fabric of India. The framers envisioned a canvas where equality is a dynamic principle, adapting to the specific needs and challenges of different communities.

1.12 Fraternity: The Unseen Thread Binding Diversity

Fraternity, though often overlooked, emerges as an unseen thread binding the diverse tapestry of India. It goes beyond legal provisions, weaving through the very essence of a nation that celebrates diversity. The constitutional canvas becomes a living testimony to the framers' commitment to secularism-a mosaic of cultural richness where different threads interweave to create a cohesive societal fabric. As we explore fraternity, we uncover instances where the constitutional vision fosters an environment of understanding, respect, and unity.

1.13 Preamble: A Guiding Light in Governance

The Preamble, our poetic prologue to the Constitution, encapsulates the foundational principles and serves as a guiding light for the nation. It is more than words on paper; it is a declaration of intent that reverberates in every corner of governance. The constitutional canvas, as it unfolds in administrative decisions, legislative debates, and executive actions, reflects a commitment to the ideals enshrined in the Preamble. Our exploration of the Preamble reveals it not as a mere formality but a living document, a compass that directs the nation towards the ideals of justice, liberty, equality, and fraternity.

1.14 Federal Structure: Unity in Diversity

The federal structure, another foundational principle, is not a mere structural choice but a dynamic arrangement that allows for the accommodation of diverse regional aspirations. The Seventh Schedule, delineating powers between the Union and the States, is a brushstroke on the canvas that reflects a delicate balance between national unity and regional autonomy. Our journey through the federal structure unfolds as a narrative of unity in diversity. The framers envisioned a nation where regional aspirations are not stifled but embraced-a constitutional order that recognizes the unique cultural, linguistic, and historical diversity within the broader framework of a united India.

1.15 Democratic Principles: The Pulse of Governance

Democratic principles find expression in the electoral process, where the voice of the people shapes the course of governance. Elections, a vibrant ritual in the democratic narrative, are more than procedural; they are strokes on the constitutional canvas, illustrating the people's exercise of their sovereign right to choose their representatives. As we traverse the democratic landscape, we encounter a canvas pulsating with the energy of citizen participation. It's not just about casting votes but an engagement with the very essence of democratic governance. The constitutional canvas becomes a living testimony to the people's role in shaping the destiny of the nation.

1.16 Socio-Economic Justice: Transformative Aspirations

The commitment to socio-economic justice, reflected in the Directive Principles of State Policy, is not a distant ideal but an ongoing endeavor. Policies addressing poverty, education, healthcare, and rural development are the brushstrokes that transform constitutional principles into actionable initiatives aimed at uplifting the marginalized and underprivileged. Our journey into socio-economic justice reveals the canvas as a space where constitutional aspirations are not confined to lofty rhetoric but translated into transformative measures. The framers envisioned a nation where economic disparities are addressed, and opportunities for growth and development are accessible to all.

1.17 Dynamic Nature: Amendments and Evolution

The constitutional canvas is not static; it evolves through amendments that respond to societal needs. The inclusion of new fundamental rights, changes in the Directive Principles, and adaptations to economic policies demonstrate the Constitution's dynamic nature-a living document that breathes life into foundational principles.

In essence, the foundational principles of justice, liberty, equality, and fraternity are not theoretical musings but practical guides shaping governance, law, and societal interactions. The constitutional canvas, with its intricate strokes, captures the vibrancy of India's democratic spirit, where the principles articulated by the framers are not distant ideals but living realities, influencing the collective conscience of the nation.

1.18 Culmination of Introduction: The Unfinished Symphony

As we conclude this introduction, we recognize that our journey has just begun. The canvas unveiled here is but a glimpse, a prelude to the intricate patterns and vivid colors that will emerge as we navigate through the subsequent chapters. "The Constitutional Canvas" beckons-a canvas that is expansive, dynamic, and alive with the pulsating energy of a democratic nation charting its course through the currents of history.

As we turn the page from introduction to exploration, we carry with us the echoes of foundational principles, the resonance of global influences, the lessons from challenges and aspirations, and the delicate balance between tradition and progress. The constitutional canvas awaits, inviting us to participate in the ongoing narrative-a narrative that is not just about laws and governance but about the very soul of a nation and its ceaseless quest for a more perfect union. It is an unfinished symphony, and as we immerse ourselves in its melodies, we become not just observers but active participants in the grand tapestry of India's constitutional journey.

Chapter 2

Building Blocks of the Constitution

In this chapter, we delve into the foundational elements that provide the structural integrity to the Indian Constitution. These building blocks, intricately designed, fortify the principles outlined in the introduction, shaping the framework for India's democratic governance.

2.1 Preamble : The Guiding Light

The Preamble of the Indian Constitution is more than a mere introduction; it serves as the foundational philosophy that sets the tone for the entire constitutional framework. In its concise yet profound language, the Preamble articulates the aspirations, ideals, and principles that guide the democratic journey of the nation. With "We, the people of India" echoing as a powerful proclamation, the Preamble becomes a living testament to the collective will and determination of a diverse and dynamic populace.

Justice: A Cornerstone of Democracy

The first pillar, "Justice," is not just a legal concept; it is a moral imperative engrained in the very essence of the Constitution. The Preamble pledges to secure justice in all its dimensions-social, economic, and political. This commitment reflects a deep-seated resolve to eradicate inequalities and create a society where fairness prevails. The framers envisioned a judicial system that not only interprets the law but also becomes a catalyst for positive societal change.

Social Justice

The concept of social justice embedded in the Preamble reflects a commitment to creating a society free from discrimination, where each individual, regardless of caste, creed, or gender, is treated with dignity and respect. The Constitution acknowledges historical injustices and seeks redressal through affirmative action and inclusive policies.

Economic Justice

Economic justice, as envisaged in the Preamble, is a call to bridge the gap between the privileged and the marginalized. It underscores the need for equitable distribution of resources and opportunities, aiming to uplift the economically weaker sections and create a more balanced socio-economic landscape.

Political Justice

Political justice signifies equal participation and representation in the democratic process. The Preamble articulates a vision where every citizen has an equal voice in shaping the destiny of the nation. It reinforces the idea that political power must be accessible to all, fostering a participatory democracy.

Liberty: The Bedrock of Individual Autonomy

The second pillar, "Liberty," represents the core freedoms that form the bedrock of individual autonomy. The Preamble commits to securing for every citizen the liberty of thought, expression, belief, faith, and worship. This overarching commitment to freedom reflects an understanding that a vibrant democracy thrives on the diversity of perspectives and the unrestricted flow of ideas.

Freedom of Thought

The Preamble recognizes the intrinsic value of independent thought and expression. It champions the right of every citizen to form opinions, challenge norms, and contribute to the intellectual tapestry of the nation. This freedom serves as a safeguard against intellectual stagnation and promotes a culture of innovation and progress.

Freedom of Expression

The freedom of expression is a cornerstone of democratic societies. The Preamble acknowledges the importance of an open discourse, enabling citizens to articulate their views without fear of reprisal. This liberty fosters a society where diverse opinions coexist, contributing to a robust democratic dialogue.

Freedom of Belief and Worship

Respecting the diversity of faiths and beliefs, the Preamble guarantees the freedom of religion and worship. It ensures that individuals have the right to practice their chosen faith without interference, fostering a pluralistic society where religious coexistence is not just tolerated but celebrated.

Equality: A Commitment to Inclusivity

The third pillar, "Equality," is a commitment to building a society where all individuals, irrespective of their background or circumstance, stand on an equal footing. The Preamble recognizes that true equality goes beyond formal recognition; it requires addressing historical injustices and dismantling systemic barriers.

Equal Opportunities

The concept of equality in the Preamble extends beyond the idea of equal treatment; it encompasses the provision of equal opportunities. The framers envisioned a society where each individual, regardless of their social or economic background, has an equal chance to succeed and prosper.

Eradication of Discrimination

The Preamble condemns discrimination based on caste, creed, gender, or any other grounds. It heralds a society where biases are challenged, and prejudices dismantled. The commitment to equality serves as a constant reminder that the nation's progress is intrinsically linked to the eradication of systemic discrimination.

Fraternity: Fostering Unity in Diversity

The final pillar, "Fraternity," encapsulates the spirit of brotherhood and unity among the people of India. It moves beyond the legal and political dimensions of democracy, emphasizing the need for a cohesive and harmonious society.

Beyond Divisions

Fraternity, as articulated in the Preamble, calls for transcending barriers of caste, creed, religion, or gender. It envisions a society where individuals look beyond their differences, embracing a shared identity as citizens of a diverse yet united nation.

Shared Responsibility

The notion of fraternity implies a shared responsibility towards each other. It emphasizes the idea that the well-being of one is intricately connected to the well- being of all. The Preamble fosters a sense of collective responsibility, urging citizens to contribute to the common good.

Unity in Plurality

India's diversity is both its strength and its challenge. The Preamble acknowledges this diversity but also highlights the importance of unity. It envisions a nation where the rich tapestry of cultures, languages, and traditions coexists harmoniously, creating a mosaic that reflects the beauty of unity in plurality.

Adapting to Changing Realities: The Preamble in Action

As a living document, the Preamble is not frozen in time; it is a dynamic covenant that adapts to the changing realities of the nation. The framers, in their wisdom, recognized the need for flexibility and foresight, allowing the Constitution to remain relevant across generations.

Constitutional Amendments

The process of constitutional amendments, as outlined in the Preamble, reflects the foresight of the framers. While the Constitution provides a stable framework, amendments allow for adaptation to changing social, political, and economic realities. Key amendments, such as those related to the Goods and Services Tax (GST) and reservations, showcase the responsiveness of the Constitution.

Socio-Economic Evolution

The Preamble's commitment to justice and equality acknowledges the evolving nature of societal challenges. It provides a foundation for addressing emerging issues, from technological advancements to shifts in global economics. The Constitution, guided by the principles of the Preamble, remains a tool for shaping India's responses to contemporary realities.

Case Law: The Preamble in Judicial Interpretation

The Preamble is not a mere preamble to the Constitution; it is a substantive part that informs and illuminates the interpretation of the document. Judicial decisions play a pivotal role in shaping and refining the principles articulated in the Preamble.

Golaknath v. State of Punjab

In the landmark case of Golaknath v. State of Punjab, the Supreme Court grappled with the scope of amending fundamental rights. The court, in its judgment, reaffirmed the supremacy of the Preamble and the essential principles embedded within it. This case underscored the Preamble's significance in interpreting the broader constitutional framework.

Mabo v. Queensland (No 2)

Internationally, the Preamble has influenced legal perspectives. In the Australian case of Mabo v. Queensland (No 2), the High Court acknowledged the importance of a preamble in recognizing the rights of Indigenous peoples. This case demonstrates how the Preamble can resonate beyond national borders, inspiring legal thought worldwide.

Conclusion: The Eternal Flame of Democracy

In conclusion, the Preamble of the Indian Constitution stands as the eternal flame that lights the path for the nation's democratic journey. It is a solemn covenant, a living philosophy that resonates through every article, section, and amendment. The Preamble's commitment to justice, liberty, equality, and fraternity is not a static ideal but an ever-evolving aspiration, urging the nation to strive for a more perfect union.

As we reflect on the Preamble's guiding light, it becomes clear that its principles are not confined to the pages of a legal document; they are embedded in the collective consciousness of a nation. The Preamble is not a relic of the past but a beacon that continues to illuminate the way forward. In its words, we find the inspiration to build a society that is just, free, equal, and fraternal - a society that embodies the true spirit of democracy.

2.2 Fundamental Rights : Safeguarding Individuals Freedoms

Embedded within the intricate tapestry of the Indian Constitution lies a cornerstone that upholds the essence of individual liberty – the Fundamental Rights. These rights, enshrined in Part III of the Constitution, stand as sentinels guarding against arbitrary state actions and ensuring that every citizen enjoys the core freedoms essential for a vibrant and thriving democracy.

The Foundational Bedrock
Origins and Significance

The genesis of Fundamental Rights in the Indian Constitution can be traced back to the struggle for independence and the collective yearning for a society that respects the dignity and autonomy of its citizens. The framers, cognizant of the historical injustices and the need to build a democratic nation, meticulously crafted a set of rights that would serve as the bedrock for individual freedoms.

Pivotal Role in the Constitutional Scheme

Fundamental Rights occupy a unique position in the constitutional hierarchy, acting as a bulwark against any encroachment on the inherent liberties of citizens. They are not mere privileges granted by the state; instead, they are inherent rights, essential for the holistic development of an individual and the flourishing of a democratic society.

The Rich Tapestry of Rights
Right to Equality
Equality Before the Law

The Constitution, through Article 14, ensures that every person is equal before the law. This principle of equality prohibits discrimination and mandates that the state shall not deny to any person equality before the law or the equal protection of the laws.

Prohibition of Discrimination

Article 15 reinforces the commitment to equality by prohibiting discrimination on grounds of religion, race, caste, sex, or place of birth. This provision aims to eliminate social prejudices and ensures that all citizens have equal access to opportunities and resources.

Equality in Public Employment

Article 16 extends the principle of equality to public employment, guaranteeing equal opportunities for all citizens in matters of employment under the state. The framers envisaged a meritocratic system that transcends considerations of caste, creed, or gender in public service.

Right to Freedom

Freedom of Speech and Expression

Article 19, often hailed as the cornerstone of democratic governance, guarantees the freedom of speech and expression. This fundamental right empowers citizens to articulate their thoughts, opinions, and dissent, fostering a vibrant marketplace of ideas essential for a democratic society.

Right to Assemble Peacefully and Without Arms

Article 19 (1)(b) recognizes the right of citizens to assemble peacefully and without arms. This right serves as a foundation for collective expression and public protest, allowing citizens to voice their concerns and grievances in a democratic manner.

Right to Form Associations or Unions

Article 19 (1)(c) ensures that citizens have the right to form associations or unions. This right is fundamental for the formation of civil society organizations and interest groups, enabling collective action for various social, economic, and political causes.

Right to Move Freely Throughout the Territory of India

Article 19 (1)(d) guarantees the right of citizens to move freely throughout the territory of India. This freedom, essential for the integration and unity of the nation, ensures that citizens can travel and reside in any part of the country without restrictions.

Right to Reside and Settle in Any Part of the Territory of India

Article 19 (1)(e) complements the right to move freely by ensuring that citizens have the right to reside and settle in any part of the territory of India. This provision reinforces the principle of a unified and integrated nation.

Right to Practice Any Profession, or to Carry on Any Occupation, Trade or Business

Article 19 (1)(g) safeguards the right of citizens to practice any profession, carry on any occupation, trade, or business. This economic freedom is vital for individual self-determination and the pursuit of livelihoods without unjust restrictions.

Right against Exploitation

Abolition of Untouchability

Article 17 takes a historic stride by abolishing the practice of untouchability, declaring it to be an offense punishable by law. This provision reflects the constitutional commitment to eradicate social evils and promote a more inclusive and egalitarian society.

Prohibition of Traffic in Human Beings and Forced Labor

Article 23 reinforces the commitment against exploitation by prohibiting traffic in human beings and forced labor. This right ensures the protection of human dignity and integrity, prohibiting any form of forced servitude.

Right to Freedom of Religion

Freedom of Conscience and Free Profession, Practice, and Propagation of Religion

Article 25 guarantees every citizen the freedom of conscience and the right to freely profess, practice, and propagate their religion. This provision acknowledges the diverse religious fabric of the nation, ensuring that individuals have the autonomy to follow their chosen faith.

Freedom to Manage Religious Affairs

Article 26 further secures the freedom to manage religious affairs. It recognizes the autonomy of religious institutions to govern themselves, preserving the diversity of religious practices within the constitutional framework.

Freedom from Payment of Taxes for Promotion of Any Particular Religion

Article 27 ensures that citizens are not compelled to pay taxes for the promotion of any particular religion. This provision underscores the secular character of the Indian state, safeguarding citizens from any financial burden related to religious activities.

Cultural and Educational Rights

Protection of Interests of Minorities

Article 29 safeguards the cultural and educational rights of minorities. It ensures that minorities have the right to establish and administer educational institutions of their choice, preserving their unique cultural identity.

Right of Minorities to Establish and Administer Educational Institutions Article 30 reinforces the rights of minorities by granting them the freedom to establish and administer educational institutions. This provision recognizes the importance of preserving linguistic, religious, and cultural diversity in the education system.

Right to Constitutional Remedies

Article 32, often referred to as the 'Heart and Soul' of the Constitution, empowers citizens to directly approach the Supreme Court for the enforcement of Fundamental Rights. This provision serves as a constitutional guarantee that ensures the protection and enforcement of individual freedoms.

Judicial Interpretation: Expanding the Canvas of Rights

Landmark Cases

Kesavananda Bharati v. State of Kerala

The landmark case of Kesavananda Bharati v. State of Kerala (1973) marked a turning point in constitutional jurisprudence. The Supreme Court, through the doctrine of the basic structure, affirmed that while Parliament has the power to amend the Constitution, it cannot alter its basic structure. This decision acted as a safeguard, protecting the essential features of the Constitution, including Fundamental Rights, from arbitrary changes.

Maneka Gandhi v. Union of India

In the case of Maneka Gandhi v. Union of India (1978), the Supreme Court expanded the scope of the right to life and personal liberty under Article 21. The court held that the procedure established by law must be fair, just, and reasonable, and it cannot be arbitrary, oppressive, or unjust.

Vishakha v. State of Rajasthan

The Vishakha case (1997) addressed the issue of sexual harassment at the workplace. The Supreme Court, recognizing the violation of the right to gender equality and the right to life and liberty, laid down guidelines to combat sexual harassment, creating a landmark precedent for gender justice.

Navtej Singh Johar v. Union of India

In the historic Navtej Singh Johar case (2018), the Supreme Court decriminalized homosexuality, recognizing the rights of LGBTQ+ individuals. The judgment emphasized the principles of equality, dignity, and personal liberty, underscoring the evolving nature of Fundamental Rights in response to changing societal norms.

Challenges and Evolving Realities

Balancing Rights and Responsibilities

The exercise of Fundamental Rights is not absolute; it comes with certain limitations. The Constitution recognizes the need to balance individual freedoms with the requirements of public order, morality, and the rights of others. This delicate balance ensures that the enjoyment of rights does not infringe upon the well-being of society as a whole.

Addressing Emerging Issues

As society evolves, new challenges emerge that require a nuanced understanding of Fundamental Rights. Issues such as privacy in the digital age, challenges to free speech in the era of social media, and the intersectionality of rights pose novel questions that demand thoughtful judicial consideration.

Ensuring Access to Justice

While Fundamental Rights provide a robust framework for the protection of individual freedoms, ensuring access to justice remains a critical concern. Disparities in legal literacy, economic constraints, and procedural complexities often pose barriers to the effective enforcement of these rights.

Conclusion: Upholding the Pillars of Democracy

Fundamental Rights, as articulated in the Indian Constitution, are not static principles but dynamic ideals that evolve with the changing contours of society. They serve as the bulwark against tyranny, ensuring that the promise of justice, liberty, equality, and fraternity is not just a distant ideal but a living reality for every citizen.

As we navigate the complexities of a modern democratic society, the significance of Fundamental Rights becomes increasingly apparent. They are the compass that guides us towards a more inclusive, just, and egalitarian future. In the canvas of democracy, Fundamental Rights are the vibrant colors that paint the portrait of a nation where individual freedoms are cherished, protected, and celebrated.

2.3 Directive Principles of State Policy : Socio-Economic Justice

Nestled within the constitutional framework of India, the Directive Principles of State Policy (DPSP) stand as a testament to the nation's commitment to socio-economic justice. Enshrined in Part IV of the Constitution, these principles outline the moral and social obligations of the state, serving as a guiding compass for governance. While not enforceable by the courts, the DPSP form an integral part of the constitutional ethos, embodying the vision of the framers for an equitable and just society.

Ideals of Socio-Economic Justice
Preamble to the DPSP
The Preamble to the DPSP sets the tone, emphasizing the commitment to secure social, economic, and political justice to all citizens. It envisions a society free from exploitation, where opportunities are not confined to a privileged few but are accessible to every stratum of society.

Gandhian Principles
Embedded within the DPSP are Gandhian principles that advocate a decentralized and self-sufficient economy. These principles draw inspiration from Mahatma Gandhi's vision of Gram Swaraj, emphasizing the empowerment of rural communities and the equitable distribution of resources.

Socialist Aspirations
The DPSP also reflects socialist aspirations, aiming to reduce economic inequalities and ensure the welfare of all citizens. It envisions a society where the concentration of wealth is tempered by measures that uplift the economically marginalized sections.

Economic Justice: A Constitutional Mandate
Equal Pay for Equal Work
Article 39(d) directs the state to ensure that there is equal pay for equal work for both men and women. This principle seeks to eliminate gender-based wage disparities, promoting workplace equality and contributing to overall socio-economic justice.

Ownership and Control of Material Resources
Article 39(b) and (c) emphasize that the ownership and control of material resources of the community are distributed to serve the common good. These provisions underscore the constitutional mandate to prevent

the concentration of wealth in a few hands and promote the well-being of the entire community.

Right to Adequate Means of Livelihood

Article 39(a) declares that the state shall direct its policy towards securing the right to an adequate means of livelihood for all citizens. This principle recognizes the fundamental importance of economic well-being and ensures that every individual has the opportunity to lead a dignified life.

Social Justice: Empowering Marginalized Sections

Promotion of Educational and Economic Interests of Scheduled Castes, Scheduled Tribes, and Other Weaker Sections

Article 46 directs the state to promote the educational and economic interests of the Scheduled Castes, Scheduled Tribes, and other weaker sections. This provision is a cornerstone for affirmative action, acknowledging historical injustices and advocating for the upliftment of marginalized communities.

Equal Justice and Free Legal Aid

Article 39A stresses the state's commitment to providing equal justice and free legal aid, ensuring that justice is not a privilege but a right accessible to all, regardless of socio-economic status.

Cultural and Educational Rights: Preserving Diversity

Promotion of Education and Economic Interests of Scheduled Tribes

Article 46A emphasizes the state's responsibility to promote the educational and economic interests of Scheduled Tribes, recognizing their unique cultural identity and the need for targeted development measures.

Promotion of Educational and Economic Interests of Other Backward Classes

Article 46B extends a similar commitment to promoting the educational and economic interests of Other Backward Classes (OBCs), acknowledging the diversity within the Indian social fabric and the necessity of inclusive development.

Challenges and Implementation
Balancing Socio-Economic Goals

The DPSP present a delicate balancing act for the state, requiring a nuanced approach to harmonize socio-economic goals with the practical challenges of governance. The tension between ideals and implementation necessitates a pragmatic and evolving policy framework.

Resource Constraints

While the DPSP outline ambitious socio-economic objectives, resource constraints often pose challenges to their effective implementation. Striking a balance between the ideal and the feasible remains a constant challenge for policymakers.

Ensuring Inclusivity

The DPSP call for inclusive development, but ensuring that the benefits of policies reach the grassroots level and marginalized communities requires a concerted effort. Implementation strategies must address systemic barriers to inclusivity.

Evolving Paradigms: New Avenues for Socio-Economic Justice
Technological Advancements

In the contemporary landscape, technological advancements open new avenues for socio-economic justice. Digital inclusion, access to information, and leveraging technology for skill development become crucial in uplifting marginalized sections.

Sustainable Development

The DPSP, rooted in the idea of intergenerational equity, align with the global push for sustainable development. Balancing economic growth with environmental sustainability becomes a key consideration for policymakers.

Social Entrepreneurship

Encouraging social entrepreneurship aligns with the DPSP's vision of distributive justice. Fostering a culture of social innovation and enterprise can contribute to sustainable and inclusive economic development.

Judicial Interpretation: Navigating the Constitutional Landscape

Expanding Horizons

While not legally enforceable, the principles enshrined in the DPSP often find expression in judicial pronouncements. Courts, cognizant of the socio-economic imperatives outlined in the DPSP, have used these principles to interpret constitutional provisions and guide policy decisions.

Right to Education

The judiciary, drawing inspiration from the DPSP, recognized the right to education as a fundamental right under Article 21. This landmark decision marked a significant step towards realizing the constitutional vision of socio-economic justice.

Environmental Jurisprudence

In cases related to environmental protection, the judiciary has invoked the DPSP's principles to emphasize the state's duty to protect and improve the environment. This reflects a holistic approach, recognizing the interconnectedness of socio-economic and environmental well-being.

Global Perspectives on Socio-Economic Justice

United Nations Sustainable Development Goals (SDGs)

The DPSP resonate with the global commitment to sustainable development, as reflected in the United Nations SDGs. Aligning national policies with international benchmarks becomes imperative for realizing the constitutional vision of socio- economic justice.

Lessons from Comparative Constitutionalism

Studying socio-economic justice provisions in the constitutions of other nations provides valuable insights. Comparative constitutionalism allows policymakers to learn from successful models and adapt strategies that align with India's unique socio- economic context.

Conclusion: Charting the Path Forward

The Directive Principles of State Policy, with their vision of socio-economic justice, represent the moral compass that guides the nation towards a more equitable and inclusive future. As India navigates the complexities of a rapidly changing world, the DPSP offer a roadmap for policymakers, urging them to craft policies that prioritize the welfare of all citizens.

In the canvas of constitutional governance, socio-economic justice becomes the brushstroke that paints a picture of a nation where every individual has the opportunity to lead a dignified life. The ideals enshrined in the DPSP, though aspirational, fuel the collective endeavor to build a society that transcends economic disparities and upholds the principles of justice, liberty, equality, and fraternity.

2.4 Judicial Interpretation : Expanding the Canvas of Rights

The Constitution of India, often hailed as the supreme law of the land, serves as the bedrock for protecting the rights and liberties of its citizens. While the document itself articulates the fundamental rights and directive principles, the interpretation of these provisions by the judiciary plays a pivotal role in shaping their scope and impact. This section delves into the rich tapestry of judicial interpretation, exploring landmark cases and the evolving dynamics of constitutional rights.

Constitutional Adjudication: The Judicial Imperative
Role of the Judiciary in a Democracy

In a constitutional democracy, the judiciary assumes the crucial responsibility of interpreting the Constitution. This role extends beyond a mere legal function; it involves safeguarding the principles of justice, upholding individual freedoms, and ensuring the checks and balances that form the essence of democratic governance.

The Doctrine of Judicial Review

The power of judicial review, implicit in the Constitution, empowers the judiciary to examine the constitutionality of legislative and executive actions. This doctrine forms the cornerstone of constitutional adjudication, enabling the courts to strike down laws inconsistent with the fundamental rights or other constitutional provisions.

Fundamental Rights in Focus

Expanding the Horizon of Right to Life and Personal Liberty

Maneka Gandhi v. Union of India (1978)

In the watershed case of Maneka Gandhi v. Union of India, the Supreme Court expanded the interpretation of the right to life and personal liberty under Article 21. The court held that the procedure established by law must be fair, just, and reasonable, broadening the scope of protection for individual freedoms.

Right to Privacy: Justice K.S. Puttaswamy v. Union of India (2017)

In a landmark judgment, the Supreme Court recognized the right to privacy as a fundamental right, deriving from the right to life and personal liberty. This decision set a precedent for acknowledging the intrinsic value of individual privacy in the digital age.

Freedom of Speech and Expression: A Dynamic Paradigm

Romesh Thappar v. State of Madras (1950)

In the early years of the Republic, the Supreme Court, in the case of Romesh Thappar v. State of Madras, asserted the expansive scope of freedom of speech and expression. The court emphasized that restrictions on free speech must be narrowly construed to preserve the democratic ethos.

Landmark Decisions on Internet Freedom

As the digital landscape evolved, the judiciary grappled with defining the contours of freedom of speech in the online realm. Cases such as *Shreya Singhal v. Union of India (2015)* and *Anuradha Bhasin v. Union of India (2020)* marked significant milestones in establishing and protecting internet freedom.

Right to Equality: Striking Down Discrimination

State of West Bengal v. Anwar Ali Sarkar (1952)

The Supreme Court, in the early years of its existence, confronted issues related to discriminatory laws. In the case of State of West Bengal v. Anwar Ali Sarkar, the court struck down a provision that gave unbridled power to the state government, emphasizing the need for non-arbitrary exercise of authority.

Navtej Singh Johar v. Union of India (2018)

In a historic decision, the Supreme Court decriminalized homosexuality, recognizing the right to equality and the right to life and personal liberty for LGBTQ+ individuals. This judgment marked a significant step towards dismantling societal prejudices and upholding the principles of inclusivity.

Directive Principles in Action
Balancing Rights and Responsibilities
Right to Education: A Socio-Economic Imperative

In a series of cases, the judiciary addressed the constitutional implications of the right to education. Notable cases include *Mohini Jain v. State of Karnataka (1992)* and *Unni Krishnan v. State of Andhra Pradesh (1993)*, where the court underscored the significance of education as a fundamental right and a directive principle.

Environmental Jurisprudence: Protecting the Common Good

Cases such as *M.C. Mehta v. Union of India (1987)* and *Vellore Citizens Welfare Forum v. Union of India (1996)* exemplify the judiciary's commitment to environmental protection. The court, drawing from the directive principles, emphasized the state's duty to safeguard the environment for present and future generations.

Social Justice and Inclusive Development
Reservation Policies: Balancing Equality and Equity

The courts have often grappled with the constitutionality of reservation policies aimed at uplifting marginalized communities. Cases like *Indra Sawhney v. Union of India (1992)* and *M. Nagaraj v. Union of India (2006)* shed light on the delicate balance between ensuring social justice and preventing reverse discrimination.

Right to Food: Expanding the Ambit of Social Rights

In the Public Interest Litigation (PIL) era, the judiciary played a proactive role in addressing socio-economic issues. Cases like *People's Union for Civil Liberties (PUCL) v. Union of India (2001)* emphasized the right to food as an integral facet of the right to life under Article 21.

Global Perspectives on Judicial Activism
Comparative Constitutionalism: Lessons from Across Borders

Examining judicial activism in other democracies provides valuable insights for India. Comparative constitutionalism allows for a nuanced understanding of how different judiciaries navigate constitutional interpretation and protect individual rights.

Human Rights Jurisprudence: A Global Dialogue

Engaging with international human rights jurisprudence enriches the domestic discourse on rights protection. The evolving nature of human rights, as reflected in global conventions and treaties, informs the judiciary's interpretation of constitutional rights.

Challenges and Critiques

Judicial Overreach or Activism?

Critics often question the judiciary's role in shaping policy and governance, arguing that certain decisions infringe upon the separation of powers. Evaluating the fine line between judicial activism and overreach becomes imperative in assessing the legitimacy of judicial decisions.

Enforcement and Implementation Hurdles

While the judiciary plays a crucial role in interpreting constitutional rights, the effective enforcement and implementation of these rights often face practical challenges. Issues such as delays in legal proceedings, resource constraints, and administrative hurdles can impede the realization of constitutional guarantees.

Evolving Notions of Justice

The judiciary must grapple with evolving notions of justice in a dynamic society. Cases related to emerging issues like data privacy, artificial intelligence, and environmental sustainability present novel challenges that require the judiciary to adapt and innovate.

Future Trajectories: Navigating a Changing Landscape

Technology and the Constitution

The intersection of technology and constitutional rights poses novel challenges. Cases related to digital privacy, surveillance, and online expression highlight the need for the judiciary to navigate uncharted territories in the digital age.

Environmental Concerns and Sustainable Development

As the global community grapples with environmental challenges, the judiciary's role in balancing developmental needs with environmental sustainability becomes crucial.

Cases related to environmental clearances, conservation efforts, and climate change litigation shape the trajectory of environmental jurisprudence.

Access to Justice in the 21st Century

Advancements in technology provide new avenues for enhancing access to justice. The judiciary's embrace of digital courts, online dispute resolution mechanisms, and technology-driven legal services can potentially revolutionize the justice delivery system.

Conclusion: A Dynamic Constitutional Discourse

In the ever-evolving tapestry of judicial interpretation, the judiciary emerges as a dynamic force shaping the constitutional discourse. While navigating the complexities of a changing society, the judiciary serves as the guardian of individual rights, ensuring that the canvas of constitutional guarantees continues to expand and adapt.

As India looks towards the future, the role of judicial interpretation remains integral to upholding the ideals of justice, liberty, equality, and fraternity. The interplay between constitutional principles and judicial decisions forms the essence of a living constitution that reflects the evolving aspirations of a democratic nation.

2.5 Global Perspectives on Constitutional Principles

Constitutional governance transcends national boundaries, and examining global perspectives on constitutional principles provides a nuanced understanding of diverse legal systems and their impact on democratic institutions. This section delves into the constitutional frameworks of various nations, exploring shared values, divergent approaches, and the evolving nature of constitutionalism on the international stage.

Constitutional Pluralism: A Comparative Lens
Understanding Constitutional Pluralism
Constitutional pluralism acknowledges the coexistence of multiple legal orders within a state, such as national, regional, and international laws. Exploring how different jurisdictions navigate this complexity offers insights into the adaptability and resilience of constitutional systems.

European Union: A Supranational Experiment
The European Union (EU) stands as a unique experiment in constitutional pluralism. The interplay between EU law and the constitutional frameworks of member states raises questions about sovereignty, legal hierarchy, and the harmonization of legal norms across diverse jurisdictions.

Federalism in Action: The United States and Germany
Comparing federal systems provides a rich landscape for understanding constitutional principles. Examining the cooperative federalism of the United States and the cooperative federalism of Germany offers perspectives on the distribution of powers, the role of states, and the impact on individual rights.

Comparative Constitutionalism: Lessons from Across Borders
The Indian Experience in a Global Context
Placing the Indian Constitution in a global context allows for a comparative analysis of constitutional principles. Learning from the experiences of other nations enhances India's constitutional discourse, providing valuable insights for addressing contemporary challenges.

Common Law and Civil Law Traditions
Distinguishing between common law and civil law traditions unveils distinct approaches to legal reasoning, judicial precedent, and the role of legal scholars. Analyzing countries within each tradition, such as the United Kingdom (common law) and France (civil law), highlights the impact of historical legal legacies.

Constitutional Rights: A Global Dialogue

International Human Rights Instruments

Engaging with international human rights instruments, such as the Universal Declaration of Human Rights (UDHR) and international covenants, reveals shared principles that transcend national boundaries. Examining how nations incorporate and implement these rights contributes to a global human rights discourse.

Comparative Freedom of Expression

Exploring freedom of expression in various jurisdictions, including the United States, Canada, and Germany, provides insights into the balance between protecting individual liberties and addressing societal interests. Analyzing landmark cases reveals evolving standards and interpretations.

Right to Privacy: A Global Concern

The right to privacy, recognized by many constitutional systems and international agreements, has become a global concern in the digital age. Comparative analysis of privacy laws in the European Union, the United States, and India sheds light on different approaches to safeguarding personal information.

Constitutional Courts: Guardians of Rights

The Role of Constitutional Courts in Democracy

Constitutional courts play a pivotal role in upholding constitutional principles. Examining the functions and powers of constitutional courts across the world, including the United States Supreme Court, the German Federal Constitutional Court, and the South African Constitutional Court, provides insights into the judiciary's role as a guardian of rights.

Comparative Judicial Activism

Judicial activism varies across jurisdictions, reflecting different legal cultures and approaches to constitutional interpretation. Comparative analysis of landmark decisions and the judiciary's engagement with social issues illuminates the dynamics of judicial activism in diverse constitutional contexts.

Constitutional Challenges: Global Responses

National Security and Constitutional Rights

Balancing national security imperatives with constitutional rights poses a universal challenge. Comparative examination of responses to terrorism and the impact on individual freedoms in countries like the United States, the United Kingdom, and India highlights the complexities of safeguarding both security and rights.

Immigration and Citizenship Policies

The constitutional implications of immigration and citizenship policies differ across nations. Comparative analysis of how countries address issues of migration, citizenship, and the rights of non-citizens sheds light on evolving norms and challenges related to diversity and inclusion.

Constitutional Responses to Public Health Crises

The COVID-19 pandemic has tested the resilience of constitutional systems worldwide. Exploring how different countries have responded to public health emergencies provides insights into the balance between protecting public health and preserving individual liberties.

Constitutional Evolution: Navigating Change

Constitutional Amendments: A Global Perspective

Comparative analysis of constitutional amendments reveals how nations adapt to changing circumstances. Studying the amendment processes in countries like the United States, South Africa, and Japan offers insights into the flexibility and stability of constitutional frameworks.

Constituent Assembly Experiences

The process of constitution-making, as witnessed in various countries, shapes the foundational principles of a nation. Examining the experiences of constituent assemblies in countries like India, South Africa, and Brazil provides perspectives on the aspirations, debates, and compromises inherent in shaping a constitution.

Constitutional Borrowings and Inspirations

Influence of Foreign Jurisprudence

Nations often draw inspiration from foreign jurisprudence when crafting or amending their constitutions. Analyzing how constitutional principles travel across borders, as seen in the influence of American constitutionalism in post-war Japan, illustrates the global exchange of legal ideas.

Constitutional Borrowings in the Commonwealth

The Commonwealth nations share historical ties and, in many cases, similar constitutional frameworks. Exploring how Commonwealth countries adapt constitutional principles, as observed in Canada, Australia, and India, unveils the interconnectedness of constitutional traditions.

Challenges and Opportunities in Comparative Constitutionalism

Cultural Context and Legal Pluralism

The cultural context significantly influences legal norms and practices. Understanding how cultural diversity intersects with legal pluralism, as exemplified in countries like India and Indonesia, provides insights into the challenges and opportunities of harmonizing diverse legal traditions.

Globalization and Legal Harmonization

Globalization has facilitated increased legal harmonization, but it also poses challenges to national sovereignty. Examining the tensions between international legal norms and domestic constitutional frameworks sheds light on the evolving dynamics of legal harmonization.

Addressing Global Injustices: The Role of Constitutional Principles

Constitutional principles serve as a tool for addressing global injustices. Exploring how nations incorporate principles of justice, equality, and human rights into their constitutional frameworks provides a lens for understanding the global pursuit of a just and equitable world.

Conclusion: Towards a Common Constitutional Discourse

In a world interconnected by constitutional principles, the global dialogue on constitutionalism contributes to a shared understanding of democratic governance. While each nation's constitution reflects its unique historical, cultural, and social

context, the universal aspirations for justice, liberty, equality, and fraternity create common ground for a collective constitutional discourse.

As nations grapple with contemporary challenges, the exchange of constitutional ideas and experiences becomes paramount. The global perspectives on constitutional principles enrich the constitutional discourse, offering a reservoir of knowledge for nations to draw upon in navigating the complexities of a rapidly changing world.

Peroration

The odyssey through the foundational elements of the Indian Constitution, encompassing the evocative Preamble, the bedrock of Fundamental Rights, the aspirational Directive Principles of State Policy, the dynamic realm of Judicial Interpretation, and the enlightening panorama of Global Perspectives on Constitutional Principles, culminates in a profound understanding of the constitutional edifice that underpins the democratic tapestry of India.

The Preamble, often hailed as the soul of the Constitution, serves as an evocative prologue to the epic constitutional narrative. Its resonant words-"We, the People of India"-evoke a collective consciousness, a covenant between the citizens and their democratic aspirations. The Preamble is not a mere ornamental preface but a solemn declaration of the foundational values that echo through the corridors of constitutional governance.

In declaring India as a sovereign, socialist, secular, democratic, and republican state, the Preamble sketches the contours of the nation's character. Sovereignty, the assertion of India's independent identity on the global stage, is accompanied by the commitment to socialism-a promise to bridge the socio-economic disparities that persist. The secular ethos embedded in the Preamble underscores the pluralistic fabric of

Indian society, celebrating diversity and inclusivity. Democracy, enshrined as a cardinal principle, positions the people at the epicenter of governance, while republicanism envisages a state where elected representatives serve as custodians of public trust.

As we contemplate the Preamble, it is evident that its words are not static; they resonate with the evolving aspirations of a dynamic society. The Preamble is both a reflection and a projection-a reflection of the constitutional values inherited and a projection of the ideals yet to be fully realized. It serves as a guiding light, illuminating the path towards a more perfect union, where justice, liberty, equality, and fraternity are not just lofty ideals but lived realities.

The Fundamental Rights, etched into Part III of the Constitution, stand as sentinels guarding the individual against the potential excesses of the state. These rights, bestowed upon citizens, are not mere legal entitlements but the essence of a democratic ethos. As the custodian of these rights, the Constitution positions itself as a bulwark against tyranny, ensuring that the rights and dignity of individuals are inviolable and sacrosanct.

In the intricate mosaic of Fundamental Rights, the right to equality emerges as a fulcrum upon which the entire structure pivots. It goes beyond the narrow confines of formal equality, transcending to substantive equality that seeks to address historical injustices and societal imbalances. The right to life and personal liberty, enshrined in Article 21, is not a mere procedural safeguard but a profound affirmation of the intrinsic worth and dignity of every individual. The right to freedom of speech and expression, often considered the lifeblood of a vibrant democracy, empowers citizens to participate in the democratic discourse, fostering an informed and engaged citizenry.

Yet, these rights are not absolute; they are subject to reasonable restrictions in the interest of the sovereignty and integrity of the nation, the security of the state, friendly relations with foreign nations, public order, decency, or morality. The delicate balance between individual freedoms and societal interests is a perennial challenge that the judiciary, as the ultimate arbiter, must navigate with sagacity.

Moreover, the Fundamental Rights are not solitary islands but interconnected strands weaving a comprehensive tapestry. The right to freedom of religion, a testament to India's secular fabric, recognizes the individual's autonomy in matters of faith. The right against exploitation underscores the constitutional commitment to eradicating forms of forced labor and human trafficking, addressing the social malaise that undermines the principles of justice and liberty.

As we reflect on the Fundamental Rights, it becomes apparent that they are not static pronouncements but dynamic principles that must adapt to the evolving needs of society. Judicial interpretation, as seen in landmark cases, breathes life into these rights, expanding their scope and ensuring their relevance in the contemporary landscape. The judiciary, in its role as the sentinel on the qui vive, is tasked with striking a delicate balance between individual freedoms and collective welfare.

The Directive Principles of State Policy, enshrined in Part IV of the Constitution, unfold as a roadmap for the state to realize socio-economic justice. These principles, though not legally enforceable, are nonetheless the moral imperatives that guide the state in its pursuit of creating a just and equitable society.

Economic justice, as envisaged in the Directive Principles, encompasses the equitable distribution of resources and the prevention of concentration of wealth. The state is mandated to direct its policies towards securing not only the right to an adequate means of livelihood but also to ensure that the ownership and control of material resources are not concentrated in a few hands.

Social justice, another cornerstone, calls for the elimination of inequalities and the protection of marginalized sections. The reservation policies, rooted in the principle of affirmative action, aim to uplift historically disadvantaged communities and ensure their integration into the mainstream. The state is entrusted with the responsibility to promote the welfare of the people by securing and protecting, as effectively as it may, a social order in which justice-social, economic, and political-shall inform all the institutions of national life.

However, the implementation of these Directive Principles necessitates a delicate balancing act. The state must harmonize its socio-economic policies with the imperatives of individual rights, recognizing that the pursuit of collective welfare should not infringe unduly on individual freedoms. The synergy between the Fundamental Rights and Directive Principles represents the constitutional architecture's attempt to reconcile individual aspirations with the broader goals of societal welfare.

Judicial interpretation, as exemplified in landmark cases, plays a pivotal role in delineating the contours of socio-economic justice. The judiciary, while respecting the separation of powers, serves as the final arbiter in disputes arising from the interplay between individual rights and directive principles. Cases such as *Minerva Mills v. Union of India (1980)* underscore the judiciary's commitment to ensuring that socio-economic justice remains a guiding principle in governance.

As we reflect on the Directive Principles, it is imperative to recognize that they embody the constitutional philosophy of a welfare state-one that transcends the traditional notion of the state as a mere arbiter and enforcer of rights. The Directive Principles envision an activist state, driven by a commitment to creating conditions for the realization of socio-economic justice. The challenge lies in translating these visionary principles into tangible policy frameworks that uplift the marginalized, eliminate disparities, and foster an inclusive society.

The realm of Judicial Interpretation, as elucidated in the annals of constitutional jurisprudence, unfolds as a dynamic process that breathes life into the constitutional text. The judiciary, vested with the solemn duty of interpreting the Constitution, plays a pivotal role in shaping the contours of justice, liberty, equality, and fraternity.

The doctrine of judicial review, implicit in the Constitution, empowers the judiciary to scrutinize legislative and executive actions for their conformity with constitutional norms. This power, though not explicitly enumerated, emerges as a necessary corollary to ensure the supremacy of the Constitution. Landmark cases such as *Kesavananda Bharati v. State of Kerala (1973)* cement the doctrine of judicial review, affirming the judiciary's authority to strike down laws that violate the basic structure of the Constitution.

The canvas of judicial interpretation extends beyond the confines of legality; it encompasses a nuanced understanding of constitutional morality. In cases like *Navtej Singh Johar v. Union of India (2018)*, where the Supreme Court decriminalized homosexuality, the judiciary ventured beyond legalistic considerations to address societal prejudices and uphold the principles of equality.

Chapter 3

Basic Structure Doctrine Unveiled

3.1 Societal Impact of Basic Structure Doctrine

The societal impacts of the Basic Structure Doctrine extend deeply into the fabric of Indian society, leaving an indelible mark on how constitutional principles are perceived and internalized. This profound influence is not confined to legal circles but permeates the collective consciousness, shaping societal attitudes towards governance, justice, and the foundational ethos of the nation.

The constitutional bedrock of India, as protected by the Basic Structure Doctrine, serves as a guiding light for the citizenry. It goes beyond the legal nuances, becoming a cultural touchstone that resonates with the ideals enshrined in the Preamble of the Constitution. The doctrine, in essence, is a reflection of the collective vision that the framers of the Constitution had for an inclusive, just, and democratic society.

As the Basic Structure Doctrine safeguards the core principles of the Constitution, it acts as a beacon for educational outreach and awareness. The impact is most pronounced in legal education, where students grapple with the intricacies of constitutional law. However, the influence extends beyond law schools, seeping into broader educational curricula. From civics classes to political science discussions, the Basic Structure

Doctrine becomes a pivotal topic, fostering an early understanding of constitutional values.

This educational outreach contributes significantly to the democratization of constitutional awareness. As citizens gain a nuanced understanding of the Basic Structure Doctrine, they are empowered to critically assess the actions of the state. This awareness forms the bedrock of an informed citizenry, capable of holding the government accountable to the constitutional principles that underpin the nation's governance.

Furthermore, the doctrine plays a pivotal role in shaping public discourse. As legal cases invoking the Basic Structure Doctrine garner attention, they become touchpoints for discussions on constitutional morality, governance, and the delicate balance between individual rights and collective welfare. Media outlets, academic forums, and public debates become arenas where the societal impacts of the doctrine unfold in real-time.

In the public sphere, the Basic Structure Doctrine becomes a tool for advocacy and activism. Civil society organizations and grassroots movements leverage its principles to challenge legislation or government actions that are perceived to violate the foundational tenets of the Constitution. In this way, the doctrine becomes a catalyst for social change, offering a legal framework through which societal grievances can be addressed.

One of the significant societal impacts is evident in the heightened consciousness of individual rights. The Basic Structure Doctrine, by safeguarding fundamental principles, reinforces the idea that certain rights are immutable, forming the bedrock of a democratic society. This awareness seeps into the collective psyche, fostering a culture where citizens are cognizant of their rights and liberties, and are willing to defend them when necessary.

Importantly, the Basic Structure Doctrine acts as a bulwark against potential authoritarian tendencies. In a diverse and pluralistic society like India, the doctrine becomes a unifying force, preventing any single entity from undermining the democratic and secular foundations of the nation. It fosters a culture of constitutionalism, where allegiance to the principles of the Constitution is seen as a shared responsibility.

The doctrine's societal impacts are also manifested in the realm of social justice. As citizens become more aware of the Constitution's commitment to egalitarian principles, there is a heightened sensitivity to issues of discrimination and injustice.

Movements advocating for the rights of marginalized communities often draw inspiration from the Basic Structure Doctrine, framing their struggles within the broader constitutional narrative.

In the cultural sphere, the Basic Structure Doctrine becomes part of the national identity. It is invoked in discussions about the soul of the nation, reflecting not only legal intricacies but a shared understanding of what it means to be Indian. The doctrine, in this context, becomes a source of unity, transcending regional, linguistic, and cultural divides.

While the impact of the Basic Structure Doctrine on society is profound, it is not without challenges. Critiques and debates surrounding the doctrine contribute to a dynamic discourse. Some argue that an overreliance on the doctrine could lead to judicial activism, potentially infringing on the separation of powers. Others question whether the doctrine adequately addresses the evolving needs of society and whether it may inadvertently stifle legislative innovation.

Moreover, the doctrine's application in specific cases can be a subject of contention. Different interpretations by the judiciary may give rise to varying societal responses, with some segments expressing satisfaction while others voice dissent. This diversity of perspectives is intrinsic to a democratic society and contributes to the ongoing dialogue about the role of the Basic Structure Doctrine.

As India continues its journey into the 21st century, the societal impacts of the Basic Structure Doctrine will evolve. The ongoing interplay between constitutional principles and societal values will shape the trajectory of the nation's governance. The doctrine, as a living testament to the resilience of constitutional ideals, will remain a dynamic force, influencing not only legal frameworks but the very ethos of the nation it seeks to protect.

3.2 Interplay with Fundamental Rights

The interplay between the Basic Structure Doctrine and Fundamental Rights is a nuanced tapestry woven into the constitutional fabric of India. At the heart of this interplay lies the delicate balance between individual liberties and the overarching principles that define the constitutional identity of the nation.

Fundamental Rights, enshrined in Part III of the Constitution, serve as the bedrock of individual freedoms and protections. The Basic Structure Doctrine, on the other hand, acts as a safeguard for the foundational principles that ensure the very essence of the Constitution is preserved. The intricate relationship between these two facets of constitutional law unfolds in the courtroom, where judges grapple with questions of constitutional interpretation, striking a balance that upholds individual rights without compromising the foundational integrity of the Constitution.

One of the primary dimensions of this interplay is evident in cases where the judiciary is called upon to adjudicate on the validity of laws that may impact Fundamental Rights. The courts, guided by the Basic Structure Doctrine, have often played a crucial role in scrutinizing legislation to ensure that it aligns with the core principles of the Constitution. This involves a meticulous examination of whether the impugned law infringes upon the basic structure, and if so, the court is empowered to strike it down.

The evolution of this interplay can be traced through landmark cases where Fundamental Rights were at the forefront of legal scrutiny. The Kesavananda Bharati case (1973) stands as an epitome of this interplay, as the Supreme Court grappled with the question of whether the Parliament could amend the Constitution in a manner that altered its basic structure. In asserting that there are limitations on the amending power of the legislature, the court underscored the significance of protecting the core values embedded in Fundamental Rights.

Fundamental Rights themselves are not static; they evolve and adapt to the changing needs of society. The judiciary, in its role as the guardian of the Constitution, has the task of interpreting these rights in a manner that aligns with contemporary understandings of justice, equality, and liberty.

The interplay with the Basic Structure Doctrine becomes particularly relevant in cases where the court is asked to reexamine the scope and applicability of Fundamental Rights in light of societal changes.

Moreover, the Basic Structure Doctrine acts as a check against potential legislative overreach that could infringe upon Fundamental Rights. It serves as a guardian against laws that, while ostensibly framed for public welfare, might encroach upon individual liberties. The judiciary, in interpreting the Constitution through the lens of the Basic Structure, ensures that the very foundations of individual freedoms are not compromised even in the pursuit of collective welfare.

The relationship between the Basic Structure Doctrine and Fundamental Rights gains added significance when considering the role of the judiciary in expanding the contours of individual liberties. Landmark cases, such as Maneka Gandhi v. Union of India (1978), have seen the judiciary interpreting Fundamental Rights expansively, bringing new dimensions to the understanding of personal liberty. In such cases, the Basic Structure Doctrine serves as a guiding principle, ensuring that the expansion of Fundamental Rights aligns with the foundational principles of the Constitution.

In the realm of equality, the interplay between the Basic Structure Doctrine and Fundamental Rights is evident in cases that seek to address historical injustices and societal imbalances. Affirmative action measures, aimed at uplifting marginalized communities, often face scrutiny, and the court's evaluation requires a delicate balancing act. The Basic Structure Doctrine, by safeguarding the principles of equality and justice, ensures that such measures are in harmony with the larger constitutional framework.

As the judiciary navigates this intricate interplay, it grapples with questions of proportionality and necessity. Fundamental Rights, while sacrosanct, are not absolute, and limitations can be imposed in the interest of the sovereignty and integrity of the nation, among other grounds. The Basic Structure Doctrine provides a framework for the judiciary to assess the reasonableness of such limitations, ensuring that even when Fundamental Rights are curtailed, the core principles of the Constitution remain inviolate.

Furthermore, the interplay between the Basic Structure Doctrine and Fundamental Rights extends into the domain of personal autonomy. Cases related to privacy, dignity, and personal choices bring to the forefront the dynamic nature of individual freedoms. The judiciary, guided by the Basic Structure Doctrine, navigates these complexities, ensuring that while protecting personal autonomy, the broader constitutional values are not compromised.

Fundamental Rights are not isolated islands; their interdependence with the larger constitutional framework is intrinsic. The Basic Structure Doctrine acts as a unifying force, preventing any interpretation of Fundamental Rights that might undermine the very foundations of the Constitution. The judiciary, in interpreting Fundamental Rights, is mindful of the broader constitutional principles that shape the destiny of the nation.

The interplay with Fundamental Rights is also evident in cases where the judiciary, invoking the Basic Structure Doctrine, has struck down laws that were perceived as infringing upon the secular fabric of the nation. The delicate balance between religious freedoms and the larger principles of secularism underscores the complexity of this interplay. The judiciary's role becomes crucial in ensuring that Fundamental Rights, including the right to profess, practice, and propagate religion, coexist harmoniously within the larger constitutional framework.

Importantly, the interplay with Fundamental Rights extends beyond the courtroom. It resonates in the public sphere, shaping societal perceptions of the role of the judiciary in safeguarding individual liberties. Public interest litigations, often invoking Fundamental Rights, become avenues for citizens to seek justice and hold the government accountable. The Basic Structure Doctrine, by guiding the judiciary in such cases, reinforces the belief that the constitutional principles enshrined in Fundamental Rights are not mere legal abstractions but tangible rights that citizens can invoke.

The evolving nature of this interplay is perhaps most visible in cases that deal with emerging challenges and technologies. Issues of data privacy, surveillance, and the impact of technological advancements on individual freedoms present novel challenges for the judiciary. The interplay with the Basic Structure Doctrine requires a forward-looking approach, ensuring that the principles embedded in Fundamental Rights are resilient in the face of technological transformations.

In conclusion, the interplay between the Basic Structure Doctrine and Fundamental Rights forms the essence of constitutional jurisprudence in India. It is a dynamic interrelationship that requires the judiciary to delicately balance individual liberties with the larger principles that define the constitutional identity of the nation. As the courts navigate this intricate tapestry, they play a pivotal role in shaping the destiny of a nation where Fundamental Rights are not mere legal provisions but the very soul of constitutional governance.

3.3 Influence on Legislative Process

The influence of the Basic Structure Doctrine on legislative processes in India is a complex and dynamic interplay that shapes the contours of governance, lawmaking, and the relationship between the executive and the judiciary. This influence is not confined to the courtroom; it extends into the legislative arena, where lawmakers grapple with the constitutional principles articulated by the judiciary through the Basic Structure Doctrine.

At its core, the Basic Structure Doctrine serves as a check on legislative actions that may seek to amend the Constitution in a manner inconsistent with its foundational principles. This inherent tension between the legislative and judicial branches is an essential feature of the constitutional design in India. Lawmakers, while endowed with the authority to frame laws and amend the Constitution, operate within the boundaries set by the judiciary through the Basic Structure Doctrine.

One of the most significant ways in which the Basic Structure Doctrine influences legislative processes is by establishing a threshold beyond which the Parliament cannot amend the Constitution. The Kesavananda Bharati case (1973) stands as a landmark in this regard. The Supreme Court, through this judgment, held that while the Parliament has the power to amend the Constitution, it cannot alter its basic structure. This has profound implications for legislative initiatives that may seek to fundamentally transform the constitutional framework.

The Kesavananda Bharati case set the precedent that certain features of the Constitution, deemed as part of its basic structure, are beyond the reach of the amending power of the Parliament. This has a profound impact on the legislative agenda, requiring lawmakers to navigate the delicate balance between constitutional amendments and the preservation of the Constitution's core values.

The influence of the Basic Structure Doctrine is particularly pronounced in cases where constitutional amendments are challenged in courts. The judiciary, guided by the doctrine, becomes the arbiter in determining whether a proposed amendment infringes upon the basic structure. This legal scrutiny injects an additional layer of accountability into the legislative process, ensuring that constitutional amendments align with the overarching principles of the Constitution.

The doctrine's influence on legislative processes also manifests in the need for a rigorous examination of the implications of proposed amendments. Lawmakers are compelled to consider the constitutional ramifications of their legislative initiatives,

taking into account not only the immediate goals of the legislation but also its long- term impact on the constitutional fabric. This introspection is a direct consequence of the doctrine's assertion that certain elements of the Constitution are immutable.

Furthermore, the influence of the Basic Structure Doctrine extends into the realm of constitutional amendments related to Fundamental Rights. Lawmakers, when contemplating changes to provisions that impact individual liberties, must navigate the constitutional framework set by the doctrine. The judiciary, in turn, assumes the role of a constitutional sentinel, ensuring that the delicate balance between the protection of Fundamental Rights and the authority of the legislature is maintained.

The Kesavananda Bharati case, while establishing the supremacy of the Basic Structure Doctrine, also introduced the concept of the "harmonious construction" of the Constitution. This implies that the judiciary seeks to interpret legislative enactments in a manner that harmonizes with the basic structure. This approach compels lawmakers to be mindful of the constitutional nuances while framing laws, understanding that any ambiguity may invite judicial scrutiny based on the Basic Structure Doctrine.

Another significant influence of the Basic Structure Doctrine on legislative processes is seen in cases where courts, in the course of interpreting statutes, refer to constitutional principles to ascertain legislative intent. The judiciary, acting as the guardian of the Constitution, incorporates the principles enshrined in the Basic Structure Doctrine as part of statutory interpretation. This symbiotic relationship ensures that legislative intent is assessed not in isolation but in alignment with the broader constitutional vision.

The doctrine's influence is not confined to explicit challenges to constitutional amendments. It seeps into the legislative conscience, creating an environment where lawmakers are cognizant of the constitutional implications of their actions. This awareness is a testament to the enduring impact of the Basic Structure Doctrine on

legislative processes, fostering a culture where constitutional values permeate the entire spectrum of lawmaking.

In cases where legislative initiatives may intersect with the principles protected by the Basic Structure Doctrine, the judiciary assumes the role of a constitutional guardian. The doctrine empowers the courts to scrutinize the legislative intent and impact, ensuring that the foundational principles of the Constitution remain inviolate. This judicial oversight adds a layer of accountability to the legislative process, fostering a constitutional dialogue between the branches of government.

Moreover, the influence of the Basic Structure Doctrine extends beyond direct challenges to constitutional amendments. It shapes the broader legislative landscape by instilling a culture of constitutionalism within the legislative process. Lawmakers, conscious of the constitutional principles protected by the doctrine, engage in a nuanced dialogue with the Constitution when framing laws. This not only enriches the legislative discourse but also reinforces the symbiotic relationship between the legislature and the Constitution.

The influence of the Basic Structure Doctrine on legislative processes is particularly pronounced in cases where the judiciary, while upholding the principle of parliamentary sovereignty, ensures that the Constitution remains the ultimate source of authority. This delicate balance between legislative autonomy and constitutional supremacy is a testament to the enduring impact of the Basic Structure Doctrine on the constitutional ethos of India.

In conclusion, the influence of the Basic Structure Doctrine on legislative processes is a testament to the constitutional vision that seeks to balance the powers of the legislature with the foundational principles of the Constitution. The doctrine serves as a dynamic force, ensuring that the legislative agenda aligns with the enduring values enshrined in the Constitution. It acts not as a constraint but as a guide, steering legislative initiatives towards a harmonious coexistence with the constitutional framework. As lawmakers navigate the complexities of governance, the influence of the Basic Structure Doctrine continues to shape the legislative landscape, reaffirming the constitutional commitment to justice, liberty, equality, and fraternity.

3.4 Comparative Constitutional Case Studies

Comparative constitutional case studies provide a fascinating lens through which to examine the diverse approaches that different nations take toward constitutional governance, the protection of rights, and the preservation of their constitutional orders. By juxtaposing the experiences of various countries, we gain valuable insights into the complexities, challenges, and innovations that shape constitutionalism across the globe.

One prominent avenue of comparison lies in the safeguards implemented to protect fundamental rights. Different countries employ distinct mechanisms and doctrines to ensure the protection of individual liberties. For example, the United States, with its Bill of Rights, places explicit limitations on government power to protect citizens' freedoms. In contrast, countries like Germany and South Africa have developed robust systems of constitutional review, allowing their respective constitutional courts to strike down legislation that violates fundamental rights. These comparative studies illuminate the various paths nations take to strike a balance between individual freedoms and the needs of society.

Comparative analysis also sheds light on the intricacies of federalism and the distribution of powers among different levels of government. The constitutional structures of countries like India, the United States, Canada, and Australia offer rich material for examination. While the Indian Constitution establishes a quasi-federal system with a strong central government, the U.S. Constitution delineates clear powers between the federal and state governments. Understanding the nuances of these systems aids in appreciating the diverse approaches nations adopt to address the challenges of governance within federal structures.

Constitutions often reflect a nation's historical context, and comparative case studies allow for a deeper exploration of this relationship. For instance, post-colonial constitutions in Africa, Asia, and Latin America bear the imprints of decolonization struggles and the quest for self-determination. Analyzing how these constitutions grapple with issues of nationhood, identity, and historical injustices provides invaluable insights into the complex interplay between history and constitutional design.

Furthermore, comparative case studies offer a window into how different legal systems approach the separation of powers and checks and balances. While the Westminster system in the United Kingdom fuses the executive and legislative branches, the U.S. Constitution meticulously separates these powers. Similarly, the concept of judicial review is articulated differently in various jurisdictions, with some countries vesting this power exclusively in specialized constitutional courts.

Constitutional amendments and the flexibility of constitutional frameworks represent another compelling dimension for comparative analysis. The contrasting approaches to constitutional amendments in the United States, where amendments require a two-thirds majority in Congress, and in countries like India, where amendments are subject to judicial review, highlight the divergent strategies nations employ to adapt their constitutions to changing circumstances.

Comparative constitutional case studies also delve into the protection of minority rights. The experiences of countries like Canada, which has developed an elaborate system to protect linguistic and cultural minorities, offer important lessons for nations grappling with issues of diversity and inclusion. Similarly, examining how countries address religious freedoms, ethnic rights, and other forms of minority protection enriches our understanding of the global constitutional landscape.

The role of international law in constitutional interpretation is another intriguing facet explored through comparative case studies. Nations may differ in their approach to incorporating international legal norms into their domestic legal systems. Some countries, like Germany, accord constitutional status to international human rights treaties, while others, like the United States, may adopt a more cautious approach, considering international law as a factor in judicial decision-making but not as binding precedent.

Comparative analysis also brings to the fore the evolving nature of constitutionalism in response to contemporary challenges. The impact of globalization, technological advancements, and climate change on constitutional governance varies across jurisdictions. Nations may grapple with similar issues but devise distinct constitutional responses, reflecting their unique historical, cultural, and institutional contexts.

Examining the role of the judiciary in constitutional interpretation provides rich material for comparative constitutional case studies. The varying degrees of judicial activism or restraint, the interpretive methodologies employed by courts, and the relationship between the judiciary and other branches of government offer a kaleidoscopic view of the diverse approaches to constitutional adjudication.

The interplay between formal and informal constitutional norms is another dimension explored in comparative constitutional case studies. While some countries may rely heavily on written constitutional provisions, others may place significant weight on unwritten conventions and practices. This interplay reflects the dynamic nature of constitutionalism and the ways in which different societies navigate the tension between written and unwritten constitutional norms.

Comparative constitutional case studies are also instrumental in understanding the influence of cultural and historical factors on constitutional interpretation. The experiences of countries with long-standing constitutional traditions, such as the United Kingdom, and those with relatively recent constitutional developments, like post-Soviet states, highlight the enduring impact of history on constitutional structures and practices.

Moreover, the study of constitutional crises and moments of constitutional change provides a unique vantage point for comparative analysis. How nations respond to challenges such as political transitions, armed conflicts, or social movements offers valuable insights into the resilience and adaptability of constitutional systems.

In conclusion, comparative constitutional case studies offer a panoramic view of constitutionalism, providing a nuanced understanding of the diverse ways in which nations grapple with issues of governance, rights protection, and constitutional design. By examining the experiences of different countries, scholars and policymakers gain valuable perspectives that enrich the ongoing discourse on constitutional theory and practice. The global conversation on constitutionalism benefits immensely from the insights gleaned through these comparative explorations, fostering a more comprehensive and nuanced appreciation of the complexities inherent in constitutional governance across the world.

3.5 Public Interest Litigation (PIL) and the Doctrine

Public Interest Litigation (PIL) and the associated doctrine represent a transformative force in the realm of legal activism and access to justice. Emerging as a legal innovation in the mid-20th century, particularly in India, PIL has evolved into a powerful instrument for addressing public grievances, promoting social justice, and ensuring governmental accountability. The doctrine underlying PIL has resonated globally, influencing legal systems in various jurisdictions and becoming a crucial component of constitutional governance.

PIL fundamentally departs from traditional litigation models by allowing public-spirited individuals and non-governmental organizations (NGOs) to initiate legal action on behalf of the marginalized, oppressed, or those unable to seek redress for themselves. It democratizes access to the judiciary, enabling citizens to act as "private attorneys general" to safeguard public interests. The doctrine, in essence, expands the locus standi (standing) traditionally required for filing a lawsuit, transcending narrow legalistic constraints to embrace a broader conception of justice.

The origins of PIL can be traced to the United States, where the Warren Court's expansive interpretation of standing and the liberalization of procedural rules facilitated a more inclusive approach to public interest litigation. However, it was in India that PIL found its most influential expression. The Indian Supreme Court, in a series of landmark cases in the 1970s and 1980s, developed the doctrine to address systemic issues affecting the marginalized and underprivileged.

The doctrine's underpinnings lie in the constitutional ethos of justice, equality, and the rule of law. PIL operates as a bridge between constitutional principles and the lived realities of citizens, allowing the judiciary to step in as the ultimate protector of fundamental rights. It aligns with the constitutional imperative to ensure justice not only in form but also in substance, breaking down procedural barriers to access the courts.

The procedural innovation introduced by PIL is characterized by relaxed rules of standing, liberal interpretation of the adversarial process, and a broad scope for court intervention. The doctrine recognizes that traditional legal procedures may not be well-suited to address systemic injustices or issues affecting large sections of society. As such, it empowers the judiciary to take suo motu cognizance of matters and act in the absence of a formal petition, marking a departure from the traditional adversarial model.

In its application, PIL encompasses a vast array of issues, ranging from environmental protection and human rights to corruption, gender justice, and administrative accountability. The flexibility of the doctrine allows it to adapt to the evolving needs of society, making it a dynamic tool for addressing emergent challenges. Notably, PIL often involves the interpretation and enforcement of socio- economic rights, expanding the traditional conception of civil and political rights.

Environmental protection has been a prominent domain of PIL, with citizens and environmental activists utilizing the doctrine to challenge policies and practices detrimental to the ecological balance. Landmark cases such as MC Mehta v. Union of India in India and the development of environmental jurisprudence globally exemplify the role of PIL in addressing transboundary environmental issues and holding governments accountable for sustainable development.

PIL also plays a pivotal role in the protection of human rights, often acting as a catalyst for social justice. Cases related to bonded labor, child rights, and prison reform have been championed through PIL, providing a platform for marginalized communities to seek redress and assert their fundamental rights. In this context, the doctrine acts as a counterbalance to systemic inequalities and offers a forum for the articulation of rights-based claims.

Gender justice is another area where PIL has made significant contributions. Landmark cases addressing issues such as sexual harassment at the workplace, dowry-related violence, and the rights of transgender individuals underscore the transformative potential of PIL in challenging deeply entrenched social norms and fostering a more inclusive and egalitarian society.

Administrative accountability and the fight against corruption have been central themes in PIL, with citizens leveraging the doctrine to demand transparency and accountability from public officials. PIL cases challenging corrupt practices, demanding the investigation of high-profile cases, and advocating for the autonomy of anti-corruption bodies showcase the doctrine's role in promoting good governance and upholding the rule of law.

The success of PIL is inherently tied to the activism of the judiciary. In embracing the PIL doctrine, the judiciary assumes a proactive role in addressing societal concerns, often functioning as a co-manager of public affairs. The concept of "judicial activism" associated with PIL refers to a judiciary willing to intervene, innovate, and sometimes even legislate in the pursuit of justice. This proactive stance has garnered both praise and criticism, with proponents lauding the judiciary's responsiveness to social issues and detractors expressing concerns about the potential overreach of judicial powers.

Critics argue that the expansive nature of PIL, coupled with the judiciary's proactive role, may lead to an imbalance in the separation of powers. They contend that the doctrine could blur the boundaries between the judiciary and the executive, potentially encroaching on the policymaking domain traditionally reserved for elected representatives. Concerns about the potential for judicial overreach have sparked debates about the appropriate scope and limits of the PIL doctrine.

Additionally, the impact of PIL may vary depending on the institutional context and the receptiveness of the legal system to judicial activism. In countries where the judiciary has a strong tradition of activism and enjoys public trust, PIL has been a potent tool for social change. In contrast, in legal systems with a more conservative or restrained judiciary, the impact of PIL may be limited, and the doctrine may face skepticism or resistance.

Despite these critiques, the transformative potential of PIL in promoting social justice cannot be overstated. The doctrine has become an integral part of the constitutional landscape in various countries, shaping legal systems, influencing legislative reforms, and empowering citizens to hold governments accountable. The success of PIL lies in its ability to bridge the gap between legal formalism and the lived experiences of citizens, making justice more accessible, responsive, and inclusive.

The internationalization of the PIL model is another noteworthy development. The principles underlying PIL have inspired legal activism in different parts of the world, contributing to the global discourse on human rights, environmental protection, and access to justice. Transnational networks of activists and NGOs often draw on the strategies and successes of PIL cases from various jurisdictions, creating a shared repertoire of legal strategies for addressing common challenges.

However, the globalization of the PIL model also raises questions about cultural and contextual differences. The transplantation of legal strategies across diverse legal systems requires careful consideration of local norms, traditions, and institutional capacities. The success of PIL in one jurisdiction may not necessarily translate seamlessly to another, and a nuanced understanding of the socio-political context is crucial for the effective implementation of the doctrine.

In conclusion, Public Interest Litigation and the associated doctrine represent a paradigm shift in the dynamics of legal activism, offering a powerful mechanism for citizens to engage with the legal system, hold governments accountable, and champion social justice causes. The doctrine's evolution from a local innovation to a global inspiration underscores its enduring relevance in the pursuit of constitutional values and the protection of fundamental rights. PIL, with its expansive scope and transformative potential, continues to shape legal landscapes, challenge systemic injustices, and contribute to the ongoing discourse on the role of the judiciary in fostering a more just and equitable society.

3.6 Constitutional Amendments as Challenges

Constitutional amendments, while essential tools for adapting a nation's fundamental law to changing circumstances, often present multifaceted challenges that resonate in the political, legal, and societal spheres. The process of amending a constitution is inherently delicate, involving the reevaluation of foundational principles that shape the governance and identity of a nation. The challenges posed by constitutional amendments are intricate and nuanced, touching upon issues of democratic legitimacy, individual rights, and the equilibrium of power among the branches of government.

At the heart of the challenge posed by constitutional amendments lies the tension between the need for adaptability and the imperative of stability in a constitutional order. The constitution, as the supreme law of the land, provides the framework for governance and protects individual rights. Amendments, therefore, represent a critical mechanism for ensuring that the constitution remains a living document capable of responding to evolving societal needs. However, the process of amending the constitution requires careful consideration to prevent hasty or arbitrary changes that could undermine the foundational principles enshrined in the document.

One of the primary challenges associated with constitutional amendments is the potential threat to the basic structure or core values of the constitution. This concern is particularly evident in jurisdictions that recognize the concept of the basic structure doctrine, where certain fundamental principles are considered immutable and beyond the reach of the amendment power. The landmark Kesavananda Bharati case in India established the basic structure doctrine, illustrating the judiciary's role in safeguarding the constitution's foundational tenets from arbitrary or transformative amendments.

The challenge of safeguarding the basic structure is intertwined with questions of constitutional identity. Amendments that seek to alter the fundamental identity of a constitution, such as changes to the preamble or core principles, often provoke intense debates about the essence of the nation and its governance. Such challenges necessitate a careful balance between the imperative of constitutional flexibility and the preservation of a nation's constitutional soul.

Moreover, the process of amending a constitution involves complex negotiations among political actors, necessitating broad consensus and political will. The challenge arises when constitutional amendments become instruments of partisan politics, used to consolidate power or pursue short-term political objectives. In such scenarios, the legitimacy of the amendment process is called into question, as it may be perceived as serving narrow political interests rather than the collective welfare of the nation.

The challenge of democratic legitimacy is accentuated when constitutional amendments are initiated and enacted without sufficient public participation or deliberation. Ensuring that the citizenry has a meaningful role in the amendment process is crucial for upholding democratic principles. When amendments are pushed through without adequate public scrutiny or debate, concerns about transparency, accountability, and the representativeness of the amendment process emerge. The challenge, therefore, is to strike a balance between the need for public participation and the requirement for efficient decision-making.

Another layer of complexity arises when constitutional amendments impact the distribution of powers between different levels of government in federal systems. The challenge here lies in maintaining the delicate equilibrium between federal and state or provincial governments. Amendments that upset this balance can lead to conflicts over jurisdiction, potentially undermining the federal structure and impacting the autonomy of subnational entities. Striking a balance that respects both the unity of the nation and the diversity of its constituent parts is an ongoing challenge in federal systems.

Constitutional amendments may also confront the challenge of aligning with evolving norms of human rights and international law. As societies progress and develop new understandings of human dignity and justice, constitutional amendments may be required to reflect these advancements. The challenge lies in navigating the tension between tradition and progress, ensuring that amendments uphold fundamental rights and align with contemporary standards while respecting the nation's historical and cultural context.

The challenge of intergenerational equity is particularly relevant in the context of constitutional amendments. As amendments shape the legal and political landscape for future generations, the responsibility to ensure that these changes contribute to the long-term welfare of the nation becomes paramount. Striking a balance between meeting the immediate needs of the present and safeguarding the interests of future generations is a nuanced challenge that requires a farsighted approach to constitutional governance.

Moreover, constitutional amendments may encounter challenges related to social cohesion and inclusivity. Amendments that impact the rights and status of particular groups within society, such as ethnic or religious minorities, can raise questions about equality, non-discrimination, and the protection of vulnerable populations. The challenge lies in crafting amendments that foster social harmony and inclusivity, recognizing the diverse tapestry of the nation while upholding the principles of equality and justice.

Constitutional amendments may also pose challenges in terms of implementation and enforcement. Even when amendments are well-intentioned, their effectiveness depends on the ability of the legal and institutional framework to translate constitutional provisions into tangible outcomes. Inadequate mechanisms for enforcement or resistance from entrenched interests can impede the successful implementation of amendments, raising questions about the real-world impact of constitutional changes.

The challenge of judicial review adds another layer of complexity to the landscape of constitutional amendments. Courts, often tasked with interpreting and applying constitutional provisions, play a crucial role in assessing the validity of amendments. Judicial review ensures that amendments adhere to constitutional principles and do not infringe upon individual rights. However, the challenge lies in maintaining a delicate balance between the judiciary's role as a guardian of the constitution and the principle of legislative supremacy.

In some cases, the challenge of constitutional amendments extends beyond the national context to international implications. Amendments that impact a nation's international obligations, treaties, or relationships can have far-reaching consequences. Balancing the nation's sovereign right to amend its constitution with its commitments on the international stage requires careful diplomacy and legal acumen.

Furthermore, constitutional amendments may encounter challenges related to historical injustices and reconciliation. Addressing past wrongs through constitutional changes, such as acknowledging historical atrocities or recognizing the rights of marginalized communities, poses complex challenges. Striking a balance between acknowledging historical injustices and fostering national healing requires a nuanced approach that considers both the demands of justice and the imperatives of reconciliation.

The challenge of constitutional amendments is also intertwined with issues of public trust in institutions. When citizens perceive that constitutional amendments are driven by narrow political interests, lack transparency, or disregard public input, trust in the democratic process may erode. Restoring and maintaining public trust requires a commitment to openness, accountability, and responsiveness to the concerns of the citizenry.

In conclusion, constitutional amendments, while essential for adapting to the evolving needs of society, pose intricate challenges that span the realms of law, politics, and society. Striking the right balance between adaptability and stability, safeguarding the constitution's core principles, upholding democratic legitimacy, and navigating complex issues of identity and equity are among the multifaceted challenges inherent in the process of amending a constitution. Successfully addressing these challenges requires a thoughtful and inclusive approach that engages all stakeholders in the constitutional order, ensuring that amendments contribute to the enduring strength and resilience of the nation's foundational law.

3.7 Jurisprudential Philosophy Behind the Doctrine

The jurisprudential philosophy behind the doctrine represents a profound exploration into the theoretical underpinnings that shape legal thought and influence the development of legal doctrines. This inquiry delves into the philosophical foundations that inform the basic structure doctrine and similar principles, unraveling the complex interplay between legal philosophy and constitutional interpretation. At its core, the jurisprudential philosophy behind the doctrine reflects a commitment to certain fundamental values, constitutionalism, and the protection of essential principles that define the legal and political order.

Central to the jurisprudential philosophy behind the basic structure doctrine is the notion of constitutional supremacy. This foundational principle posits that the constitution is the supreme law of the land, and all other laws, including ordinary legislation, must conform to its dictates. The concept of constitutional supremacy is deeply rooted in the philosophy of legal positivism, which asserts that the validity of law is derived from its source, in this case, the constitution. The basic structure doctrine, by declaring certain principles as immutable, reinforces the idea that even the sovereign power of the legislature is circumscribed by the higher authority of the constitution.

Philosophically, the jurisprudential foundations of the basic structure doctrine also draw from natural law principles. Natural law, with its emphasis on inherent rights and universal justice, underlies the notion that there are certain principles that are so fundamental and inherent that they transcend positive law. The identification of a basic structure reflects a belief in the existence of inherent constitutional values that are integral to the very idea of constitutional governance. These values are seen as part of a transcendent legal order that guides and limits the actions of the state.

Furthermore, the jurisprudential philosophy behind the doctrine reflects a commitment to the principles of justice and fairness. This commitment is grounded in the idea that a just legal system is one that adheres to fundamental principles of equality, non-discrimination, and protection of individual rights. The identification and protection of a basic structure serve as a bulwark against arbitrary or discriminatory state action. In this sense, the doctrine is an expression of the philosophical commitment to justice as a foundational value in constitutional governance.

The principle of constitutionalism, deeply embedded in the jurisprudential philosophy behind the doctrine, underscores the idea that government power must be exercised within the bounds set by the constitution. Constitutionalism is not merely a legal concept but a broader philosophical stance that emphasizes the importance of limiting government authority, protecting individual rights, and ensuring that public power is exercised in accordance with established norms and principles. The identification of a basic structure serves as a manifestation of the commitment to constitutionalism, as it sets certain principles beyond the reach of ordinary legislative action.

A significant aspect of the jurisprudential philosophy behind the basic structure doctrine is the recognition of the constitution as a living document. This philosophy draws inspiration from the dynamic nature of legal realism, asserting that legal principles evolve and adapt to the changing needs and values of society. The identification of a basic structure reflects a belief that the constitution, while providing a stable framework, must also be flexible enough to accommodate evolving societal norms. This dynamic approach to constitutional interpretation aligns with the broader philosophical perspective that law is not static but a living, evolving entity.

The concept of legal reasoning and interpretation also plays a pivotal role in the jurisprudential philosophy behind the basic structure doctrine. The hermeneutic principles that guide constitutional interpretation involve a nuanced understanding of legal texts, historical context, and the underlying values and purposes of the constitution. Legal reasoning, in this context, is not a mechanical exercise but a sophisticated engagement with the complexities of legal language and the broader aims of constitutional governance. The doctrine's jurisprudential philosophy recognizes the interpretive nature of law and the need for judges to engage in principled, value-laden reasoning.

Moreover, the jurisprudential philosophy behind the basic structure doctrine is influenced by principles of legal institutionalism. This perspective emphasizes the role of courts as institutions entrusted with the duty of safeguarding the constitution. Legal institutionalism posits that courts, through judicial review, play a crucial role in upholding constitutional principles and ensuring that the actions of the state conform to the constitution. The basic structure doctrine, by entrusting the judiciary with the responsibility to identify and protect fundamental principles, aligns with the institutionalist perspective that sees courts as guardians of the constitutional order.

The principle of stare decisis, a cornerstone of common law systems, is another aspect of the jurisprudential philosophy behind the basic structure doctrine. Stare decisis, which means "to stand by things decided," reflects the idea that legal decisions, once made, should guide future cases. The doctrine's jurisprudential philosophy recognizes the importance of precedent in maintaining legal consistency and predictability. The identification of a basic structure and the application of the doctrine in subsequent cases demonstrate a commitment to the principle of stare decisis as a stabilizing force in constitutional jurisprudence.

Additionally, the jurisprudential philosophy behind the basic structure doctrine engages with principles of legal realism, acknowledging that judicial decision- making is influenced by factors beyond formal legal texts. Legal realism posits that judges are not mere automatons applying predetermined rules but are influenced by their backgrounds, experiences, and societal context. The doctrine's recognition of a basic structure reflects an understanding that judicial decision-making involves a nuanced appreciation of the broader social and political landscape.

Philosophically, the basic structure doctrine aligns with the concept of constitutional morality. Constitutional morality emphasizes adherence to constitutional values, ethical principles, and the spirit of the constitution. The identification and protection of a basic structure reflect a commitment to constitutional morality by ensuring that the constitution's core principles are not compromised for transient political or social considerations. The jurisprudential philosophy behind the doctrine recognizes that constitutional governance requires not only legal compliance but also a commitment to the underlying moral and ethical principles of the constitution.

Furthermore, the jurisprudential philosophy behind the basic structure doctrine engages with principles of legal pluralism. Legal pluralism recognizes the coexistence of multiple legal systems, including formal state law, customary law, and international law. The doctrine's recognition of a basic structure acknowledges the presence of foundational principles that transcend individual legal sources. This pluralistic perspective underscores the interconnectedness of various legal norms and the need for a holistic understanding of the legal landscape.

In conclusion, the jurisprudential philosophy behind the basic structure doctrine reflects a rich tapestry of legal thought, drawing from constitutionalism, natural law, justice, legal realism, institutionalism, stare decisis, legal pluralism, and constitutional morality. This philosophy underscores the dynamic, evolving nature of constitutional interpretation, recognizing that the law is not a static entity but a reflection of evolving societal values and aspirations. The identification and protection of a basic structure within this jurisprudential framework exemplify a commitment to fundamental principles that transcend the immediate political and legal context, contributing to the enduring resilience of constitutional governance.

3.8 Role in Safeguarding Minority Rights

The role of the basic structure doctrine in safeguarding minority rights represents a critical dimension of constitutional governance, reflecting a commitment to upholding the principles of equality, non-discrimination, and protection of marginalized communities. Minority rights are fundamental to the ethos of a democratic and inclusive society, and the basic structure doctrine serves as a bulwark against potential infringements on these rights. This exploration delves into the jurisprudential underpinnings, historical context, and practical implications of the basic structure doctrine in the context of safeguarding minority rights.

Jurisprudentially, the foundational philosophy behind the basic structure doctrine aligns with principles of constitutionalism, recognizing that the constitution sets the parameters within which the state must operate. In the context of minority rights, this philosophy underscores the idea that certain principles, such as equality and non- discrimination, are so integral to the constitutional order that they form part of the immutable core—the basic structure. The doctrine, by identifying and protecting this core, implicitly safeguards the rights of minorities from arbitrary or discriminatory state action.

A key facet of the basic structure doctrine's role in protecting minority rights lies in its commitment to the principle of non-discrimination. The jurisprudential philosophy underlying the doctrine emphasizes that the constitution mandates equal treatment for all citizens, irrespective of their background, religion, or ethnicity. In the context of minority rights, this commitment to non-discrimination becomes a powerful tool for challenging laws or policies that may disproportionately impact minority communities. By ensuring that discriminatory measures do not become part of the constitutional fabric, the basic structure doctrine contributes to the protection of minority rights.

Historically, the basic structure doctrine has played a pivotal role in addressing challenges related to minority rights in diverse societies. The doctrine emerged at a time when post-colonial nations were grappling with questions of identity, diversity, and the need to reconcile competing interests within a constitutional framework. In India, for example, the basic structure doctrine took root in response to attempts to amend the constitution in ways that could potentially undermine its secular and inclusive character. The judiciary, by invoking the basic structure doctrine, signaled a commitment to preserving the foundational values that safeguard the rights of minority communities.

The protection of minority rights within the ambit of the basic structure doctrine is intricately connected to the broader principles of human rights. The doctrine's role in upholding minority rights aligns with international human rights norms that emphasize the equal worth and dignity of every individual, irrespective of their belonging to a minority group. The judiciary's invocation of the basic structure doctrine, in cases pertaining to minority rights, often draws inspiration from international human rights instruments, creating a symbiotic relationship between domestic constitutionalism and the global human rights framework.

A critical aspect of the basic structure doctrine's role in safeguarding minority rights is its application in cases involving legislative measures that may disproportionately affect minority communities. By subjecting such measures to constitutional scrutiny, the doctrine ensures that laws or policies that target minorities or infringe upon their rights are held to the highest constitutional standards. This judicial scrutiny acts as a check on potential abuses of legislative power that could undermine the rights and interests of minority groups.

The doctrine's protection of minority rights extends to issues of cultural and religious identity. Minority communities often face challenges in preserving and promoting their distinct cultural practices and religious traditions. The basic structure doctrine, by safeguarding the principles of secularism and cultural diversity, provides a constitutional shield against attempts to marginalize or suppress minority cultures. This protection reinforces the constitutional commitment to fostering a pluralistic society where diverse cultural and religious expressions coexist harmoniously.

In the context of religious minorities, the basic structure doctrine assumes particular significance. The commitment to secularism as a part of the basic structure ensures that the state remains equidistant from all religions and does not favor or disfavor any particular faith. This principle is vital for protecting the rights of religious minorities to practice, profess, and propagate their religions freely without facing discrimination or undue interference from the state. The doctrine's role in preserving the secular fabric of the constitution contributes to the broader goal of ensuring religious harmony and coexistence.

The basic structure doctrine's role in safeguarding minority rights is also evident in cases where the autonomy of educational and cultural institutions of minorities is at stake. Recognizing that the preservation of minority languages, traditions, and educational institutions is integral to the protection of their identity, the doctrine acts as a guardian against measures that could undermine such autonomy. By upholding the principle of non-interference in the internal affairs of minority institutions, the doctrine fosters an environment where minority communities can nurture and transmit their distinct cultural and educational heritage.

Landmark cases where the basic structure doctrine has been invoked to protect minority rights include Kesavananda Bharati v. State of Kerala in India. In this case, the Supreme Court of India held that certain basic features of the constitution, including secularism, are beyond the amending power of the legislature. The court's recognition of secularism as a part of the basic structure was instrumental in safeguarding the rights of religious minorities and ensuring that the state remains neutral in matters of religion.

Moreover, the doctrine's role in protecting minority rights intersects with the broader discourse on social justice. Recognizing that minority communities often face historical and systemic disadvantages, the doctrine contributes to a jurisprudence that seeks to rectify imbalances and promote substantive equality. By preventing the dilution of constitutional provisions that uphold the rights of minorities, the basic structure doctrine aligns with the constitutional imperative to foster an inclusive and just society.

The basic structure doctrine's protection of minority rights is not limited to preventing legislative encroachments; it also extends to executive actions and policies. Cases where minority communities are disproportionately affected by government policies, such as those related to affirmative action or social welfare programs, have been subject to constitutional scrutiny under the basic structure doctrine. This scrutiny ensures that well-intentioned policies do not inadvertently perpetuate discrimination or infringe upon the rights of minorities.

Beyond the legal realm, the basic structure doctrine's role in safeguarding minority rights has broader societal implications. The doctrine serves as a beacon of constitutional values, signaling to the public that certain principles are inviolable and form the bedrock of the nation's commitment to justice, equality, and pluralism. This signaling effect has the potential to shape public discourse and foster a culture of respect for minority rights, contributing to the cultivation of a more inclusive and tolerant society.

However, it is essential to acknowledge the limitations and challenges associated with the basic structure doctrine's role in protecting minority rights. The doctrine operates within the broader context of constitutional governance, and its effectiveness relies on the judiciary's commitment to robust judicial review and the protection of constitutional principles. Challenges may arise when there is a lack of judicial independence, political pressures, or societal attitudes that are not conducive to the protection of minority rights.

In conclusion, the basic structure doctrine plays a crucial role in safeguarding minority rights within the framework of constitutional governance. Its jurisprudential foundations, historical context, and practical applications underscore a commitment to principles of equality, non-discrimination, and the protection of marginalized communities. The doctrine's role extends beyond legal scrutiny, signaling a constitutional ethos that upholds the dignity and rights of minorities, contributing to the ongoing quest for a just, inclusive, and pluralistic society.

3.9 Role in Environment Jurisprudence

The role of the basic structure doctrine in environmental jurisprudence marks a significant intersection of constitutional principles and the imperative to address pressing ecological concerns. This exploration delves into the underlying jurisprudential philosophy, historical context, and practical implications of the basic structure doctrine in the context of environmental protection. At its core, the doctrine's role in environmental jurisprudence underscores a commitment to sustainable development, intergenerational equity, and the recognition of environmental rights as integral to constitutional governance.

Jurisprudentially, the basic structure doctrine's role in environmental jurisprudence is anchored in the recognition that certain principles are foundational to the constitutional order and must be preserved to ensure the well-being of present and future generations. Environmental protection, within this framework, emerges as a constitutional imperative that is essential to the basic structure of governance. The doctrine's jurisprudential foundations draw from the broader principles of constitutionalism, recognizing that the constitution sets the limits within which governmental powers must be exercised, and that includes the duty to safeguard the environment.

A key facet of the basic structure doctrine's role in environmental jurisprudence lies in its commitment to the principle of intergenerational equity. This principle acknowledges that the present generation holds the environment in trust for future generations and must act as stewards to ensure the conservation of natural resources and the integrity of ecosystems. By recognizing environmental sustainability as part of the basic structure, the doctrine emphasizes the importance of balancing the immediate needs of the present with the long-term interests of future generations.

Historically, the basic structure doctrine has played a crucial role in shaping environmental jurisprudence in response to the ecological challenges faced by nations. The evolution of the doctrine has mirrored a growing awareness of environmental issues and the need for constitutional mechanisms to address them. In several jurisdictions, the judiciary has invoked the basic structure doctrine to safeguard environmental principles from legislative or executive actions that could compromise ecological integrity. This historical context highlights the doctrine's adaptability to address emerging challenges, including those related to environmental conservation.

The role of the basic structure doctrine in environmental jurisprudence is closely intertwined with the broader global discourse on sustainable development. The doctrine's recognition of environmental principles as part of the basic structure aligns with international commitments to sustainable development, as reflected in documents such as the United Nations Sustainable Development Goals. By embedding environmental considerations within the constitutional framework, the doctrine contributes to a holistic understanding of development that encompasses ecological sustainability, social well-being, and economic prosperity.

A critical aspect of the basic structure doctrine's role in environmental jurisprudence is its application in cases involving legislative measures or executive actions that may impact the environment. By subjecting such measures to constitutional scrutiny, the doctrine ensures that laws or policies that pose a threat to environmental integrity are held to the highest constitutional standards. This judicial scrutiny acts as a safeguard against potential abuses of governmental power that could result in environmental degradation.

The doctrine's role in environmental jurisprudence is particularly evident in cases where the right to a healthy environment is asserted as a fundamental right. Courts, relying on the basic structure doctrine, have recognized the right to a healthy environment as an essential component of the right to life and dignity. This recognition elevates environmental rights to a constitutional pedestal, emphasizing their significance within the broader human rights framework. The doctrine's role in protecting the right to a healthy environment reinforces the interconnectedness of ecological well-being and the enjoyment of fundamental rights.

Moreover, the basic structure doctrine's role in environmental jurisprudence extends to issues of environmental justice. The doctrine recognizes that environmental harms often disproportionately impact marginalized communities and vulnerable populations. By ensuring that environmental principles are integral to the constitutional order, the doctrine contributes to a jurisprudence that seeks to rectify environmental injustices and promotes equitable access to a clean and healthy environment. This commitment aligns with the broader constitutional imperatives of justice, equality, and non-discrimination.

The doctrine's role in environmental jurisprudence also encompasses the protection of biodiversity and the conservation of natural resources. Courts, invoking the basic structure doctrine, have intervened in cases where legislative or executive actions threatened the ecological balance and biodiversity. The doctrine's recognition of environmental sustainability as part of the basic structure emphasizes the importance of preserving the diversity of ecosystems and ensuring the responsible stewardship of natural resources.

The basic structure doctrine's role in environmental jurisprudence is not limited to preventing legislative or executive encroachments; it extends to the formulation of environmental policies and regulations. Courts, in their role as constitutional custodians, may interpret the basic structure to guide the development of environmentally conscious policies. This proactive role ensures that environmental considerations are integrated into the decision-making processes of the state, fostering a culture of environmental responsibility.

The doctrine's role in environmental jurisprudence also intersects with the broader discourse on climate change and the legal responses required to address this global challenge. Courts, relying on the basic structure doctrine, have been called upon to adjudicate cases related to climate change impacts, mitigation measures, and the protection of vulnerable communities. The doctrine's recognition of environmental principles as part of the constitutional order positions it as a valuable tool for addressing the complex and transboundary nature of environmental issues, including climate change.

Beyond the legal realm, the basic structure doctrine's role in environmental jurisprudence has broader societal implications. The doctrine serves as a catalyst for public awareness and discourse on environmental issues. By emphasizing the constitutional importance of environmental protection, the doctrine encourages civic engagement, advocacy, and accountability in matters related to ecological sustainability. This signaling effect has the potential to shape public attitudes, promote environmental stewardship, and foster a culture of sustainability.

However, it is crucial to acknowledge the limitations and challenges associated with the basic structure doctrine's role in environmental jurisprudence. The effectiveness of the doctrine relies on the judiciary's commitment to robust judicial review and the protection of constitutional principles. Challenges may arise when there is a lack of judicial independence, limited expertise in environmental matters, or resistance to recognizing environmental concerns as integral to the constitutional order.

In conclusion, the basic structure doctrine plays a pivotal role in environmental jurisprudence by recognizing the constitutional significance of environmental principles. Its jurisprudential foundations, historical context, and practical applications underscore a commitment to sustainable development, intergenerational equity, and the protection of environmental rights as part of constitutional governance. The doctrine's role extends beyond legal scrutiny, signaling a constitutional ethos that upholds the intrinsic value of the environment and its integral role in ensuring a just, equitable, and sustainable future.

3.10 Temporal Dynamics

Temporal dynamics within the context of the basic structure doctrine unravel a complex interplay between constitutional principles, evolving societal norms, and the need for a dynamic and adaptive legal framework. This exploration delves into the jurisprudential underpinnings, historical context, and practical implications of the temporal dynamics inherent in the basic structure doctrine. At its core, the doctrine's treatment of temporal changes reflects a nuanced understanding of the constitution as a living document that responds to the evolving needs of society across different eras.

Jurisprudentially, the treatment of temporal dynamics within the basic structure doctrine is rooted in the principles of constitutional interpretation. The dynamic nature of the constitution is premised on the recognition that societal values, perspectives, and challenges change over time. The doctrine, by acknowledging the need for adaptability, ensures that the constitution remains relevant and responsive to the evolving aspirations of the people it governs. This jurisprudential foundation draws inspiration from legal realism, which emphasizes the dynamic nature of law and its responsiveness to changing social, economic, and cultural contexts.

The historical context of the basic structure doctrine's engagement with temporal dynamics is intricately tied to the post-colonial period and the framing of constitutions in newly independent nations. Many post-colonial societies sought to establish constitutional orders that reflected their unique histories, cultural identities, and aspirations for self-governance. The doctrine emerged as a response to challenges posed by attempts to amend or alter the constitution in ways that could compromise its foundational values. In this historical context, the doctrine became a safeguard against arbitrary changes that could undermine the constitutional promises made during the transformative period of independence.

The temporal dynamics within the basic structure doctrine are particularly evident in its treatment of fundamental principles that endure across time. The identification of a basic structure implies a recognition that certain constitutional values are so fundamental that they transcend specific historical contexts. These enduring principles, which may include democracy, rule of law, and protection of human rights, serve as the anchor points that provide continuity and stability to the constitutional order. The doctrine's acknowledgment of these enduring principles ensures that they remain impervious to short-term political fluctuations.

However, the temporal dynamics within the basic structure doctrine also accommodate the recognition that some constitutional provisions may require reinterpretation or adaptation to suit contemporary circumstances. The doctrine's responsiveness to changing societal norms reflects an understanding that the constitution must evolve without compromising its foundational values. This adaptability is particularly relevant in addressing emerging issues, technological advancements, and shifts in public attitudes that were unforeseen during the constitution's framing.

The doctrine's treatment of temporal dynamics is evident in its approach to constitutional amendments. While the doctrine protects the basic structure from arbitrary changes, it does not freeze the constitution in time. Recognizing the need for flexibility, the doctrine allows for legitimate amendments that do not alter the core identity and values of the constitution. This balancing act between stability and adaptability is crucial in navigating the temporal dynamics of constitutional governance.

The temporal dynamics within the basic structure doctrine also reflect a commitment to constitutional morality. Constitutional morality entails a deep respect for the underlying principles and values of the constitution, irrespective of the temporal context. The doctrine's invocation of constitutional morality underscores the idea that adherence to constitutional principles is not contingent on prevailing political or social ideologies. This commitment to constitutional morality acts as a stabilizing force that transcends the temporal challenges posed by changing governments or societal shifts.

In practical terms, the temporal dynamics within the basic structure doctrine come to the forefront when the judiciary is called upon to interpret constitutional provisions in light of contemporary issues. Courts, as custodians of the constitution, engage in a dynamic process of interpretation that considers the evolving needs and expectations of society. This interpretive approach acknowledges that the meaning and application of constitutional provisions may evolve over time to address new challenges and advancements.

The doctrine's interaction with temporal dynamics is particularly pronounced in cases where constitutional provisions are tested against contemporary notions of justice, equality, and individual rights. For example, the evolving understanding of privacy rights in the digital age or the recognition of new forms of discrimination requires the judiciary to interpret constitutional provisions in a manner that aligns with present-day societal norms. The doctrine's engagement with these contemporary challenges showcases its responsiveness to the temporal dimensions of constitutional governance.

Moreover, the temporal dynamics within the basic structure doctrine are integral to the doctrine's role in ensuring the continuity of constitutional governance during periods of political transition. In nations undergoing political transformations, the doctrine acts as a safeguard against abrupt changes that could undermine the foundational principles of the constitution. The enduring nature of the basic structure provides a sense of stability, assuring citizens that certain fundamental values will persist despite changes in government or political ideologies.

The doctrine's interaction with temporal dynamics also encompasses its role in shaping constitutional identity. As societies evolve, the constitution plays a crucial role in reflecting and shaping the collective identity of the nation. The basic structure doctrine, by preserving certain enduring principles, contributes to the continuity of constitutional identity across different temporal phases. This continuity is essential in fostering a sense of constitutionalism and shared values that transcend individual political cycles.

While the basic structure doctrine's engagement with temporal dynamics is essential for the vitality of constitutional governance, it also raises certain challenges. The balance between stability and adaptability requires careful judicial consideration, and the interpretation of what constitutes the basic structure may vary over time. The challenge lies in ensuring that the doctrine remains a tool for constitutional resilience rather than a mechanism for freezing the constitution in a particular historical moment.

In conclusion, the treatment of temporal dynamics within the basic structure doctrine reflects a sophisticated understanding of constitutional governance as a dynamic and evolving process. The doctrine's engagement with enduring principles, adaptability to contemporary challenges, and commitment to constitutional morality contribute to its role as a guardian of constitutional resilience. The temporal dimensions inherent in the doctrine ensure that the constitution remains a living document, responsive to the changing needs and aspirations of society across different eras.

3.11 Role in Economic Reforms

The role of the basic structure doctrine in economic reforms is a multifaceted exploration that unveils the intricate interplay between constitutional principles, governance, and the imperatives of economic transformation. This examination delves into the jurisprudential foundations, historical contexts, and practical implications of the basic structure doctrine concerning economic reforms. At its core, the doctrine's involvement in economic matters underscores the delicate balance between constitutional constraints and the exigencies of economic progress.

Jurisprudentially, the basic structure doctrine's role in economic reforms is embedded in the principles of constitutional interpretation and governance. The constitution, as the foundational legal document, sets the parameters within which the state can exercise its powers, including those related to economic policy. The doctrine recognizes that while economic reforms are essential for development, they must not compromise the fundamental principles enshrined in the constitution. This jurisprudential approach draws inspiration from legal theories that highlight the dynamic relationship between constitutional values and economic policies.

The historical context of the basic structure doctrine's engagement with economic reforms is closely tied to the post-colonial period and the economic challenges faced by newly independent nations. Many post-colonial societies sought to chart a course of economic development that reflected their unique needs and aspirations. The doctrine emerged as a response to safeguarding the constitutional order from arbitrary changes that could undermine the economic promises made during the transformative period of independence. It became a constitutional check against potential abuses of economic power that could lead to social inequalities or concentration of wealth.

The economic reforms addressed by the basic structure doctrine span a broad spectrum, ranging from land reforms and nationalization policies to privatization initiatives and liberalization measures. In cases where economic policies are challenged on constitutional grounds, the doctrine plays a pivotal role in determining the constitutionality of these policies. This involves a nuanced analysis of whether the economic reforms adhere to the fundamental principles that constitute the basic structure.

One of the fundamental principles often scrutinized in the context of economic reforms is the right to property. Economic reforms may involve measures that impact property rights, such as land reforms or nationalization of industries. The basic structure doctrine, by protecting certain core principles including property rights, ensures that economic reforms do not infringe upon the essential fabric of constitutional guarantees. Courts, in interpreting the constitution through the lens of the basic structure, strike a balance between the imperative for economic transformation and the preservation of individual rights.

Moreover, the doctrine's role in economic reforms extends to issues of social justice. Economic policies can have profound implications for social equity, and the basic structure doctrine acts as a constitutional safeguard against reforms that perpetuate or exacerbate social inequalities. The commitment to justice, enshrined in the constitution's basic structure, requires that economic reforms contribute to the welfare of all citizens and do not disproportionately benefit a specific section of society.

In the realm of economic reforms, the doctrine also addresses questions of distributive justice. Policies related to taxation, subsidies, and welfare programs come under constitutional scrutiny to ensure that they align with the principles of equality and non-discrimination. The doctrine's role in this context involves assessing whether economic reforms contribute to a more just distribution of resources and opportunities, in accordance with the constitutional vision of a welfare state.

The basic structure doctrine's engagement with economic reforms is particularly evident in cases involving challenges to privatization initiatives. Privatization, as a policy choice, may implicate constitutional principles related to public ownership, accountability, and access to essential services. Courts, applying the basic structure doctrine, examine whether privatization measures adhere to constitutional standards and do not undermine the core values of governance. This involves a delicate balance between promoting efficiency in economic activities and ensuring that privatization does not result in the erosion of public welfare.

The doctrine's role in economic reforms also intersects with the broader discourse on the right to livelihood. Economic policies that impact employment, labor conditions, and the overall economic well-being of citizens fall within the purview of the basic structure doctrine. The commitment to socio-economic rights within the basic structure necessitates that economic reforms contribute to the enhancement of the quality of life for all citizens.

The role of the basic structure doctrine in economic reforms is not limited to protecting individual rights; it extends to ensuring the integrity of institutional frameworks. Economic governance involves a complex interplay between executive, legislative, and judicial branches of government. The doctrine, by preserving the separation of powers and the independence of institutions, contributes to the stability and effectiveness of economic policies. Courts, in evaluating economic reforms, scrutinize whether they respect the constitutional mandate for checks and balances.

In practical terms, the doctrine's involvement in economic reforms requires courts to navigate the fine line between judicial review and deference to legislative and executive expertise. Economic policies often involve complex technical considerations, and the judiciary, while upholding constitutional principles, must also recognize the need for flexibility in economic decision-making. The doctrine's role in this context underscores the importance of a nuanced approach that considers both legal standards and the practical exigencies of economic governance.

Furthermore, the basic structure doctrine's interaction with economic reforms reflects its role in fostering a constitutional culture that prioritizes accountability and transparency. Economic decision-making, given its significant impact on the well- being of citizens, must adhere to constitutional principles that ensure openness, fairness, and public participation. The doctrine's scrutiny of economic policies contributes to the promotion of good governance within the economic sphere.

Challenges associated with the basic structure doctrine's role in economic reforms include the potential for judicial overreach and the risk of unduly constraining economic policymaking. Striking the right balance between constitutional constraints and the flexibility required for economic development poses a perpetual challenge. The judiciary must be cognizant of the need to respect the expertise of the executive and legislative branches in economic matters while ensuring that constitutional principles remain inviolable.

In conclusion, the role of the basic structure doctrine in economic reforms reflects a delicate equilibrium between the imperatives of economic progress and the preservation of constitutional principles. The doctrine's jurisprudential foundations, historical contexts, and practical applications underscore its significance as a constitutional safeguard against arbitrary changes that could undermine the foundational values of governance. As nations grapple with the challenges of economic transformation, the basic structure doctrine acts as a constitutional sentinel, ensuring that the pursuit of prosperity remains in harmony with the enduring principles enshrined in the constitutional order.

3.12 Innovations in Judicial Interpretation

Innovations in judicial interpretation within the ambit of the basic structure doctrine represent a dynamic evolution in constitutional jurisprudence. This exploration delves into the transformative ways in which courts have interpreted and applied the basic structure doctrine, pushing the boundaries of traditional legal reasoning to adapt to the complexities of contemporary legal and societal challenges.

At its core, innovations in judicial interpretation signify a departure from rigid textualism towards a more purposive and contextual understanding of constitutional provisions. The basic structure doctrine, as a constitutional safeguard, has not only preserved fundamental principles but has also become a catalyst for innovative judicial approaches that respond to the ever-changing demands of society.

One of the notable innovations in judicial interpretation within the basic structure doctrine lies in the expansion of the doctrine itself. Courts, recognizing the need for a flexible yet principled constitutional framework, have innovatively expanded the scope of what constitutes the basic structure. This expansion involves identifying new principles and rights that are deemed essential to the constitutional order, even if not explicitly enumerated. The judiciary's role in recognizing emerging rights, such as the right to privacy or environmental rights, showcases a departure from strict originalism towards an interpretative approach that embraces evolving societal values.

The incorporation of constitutional morality as a guiding principle in judicial interpretation marks a significant innovation. While the concept of constitutional morality is not expressly mentioned in constitutional texts, courts have creatively employed it as a touchstone for evaluating the constitutionality of laws and policies. This innovation reflects a commitment to interpreting the constitution in a manner that aligns with the broader moral and ethical values underlying the constitutional order.

Innovations in judicial interpretation are also evident in the nuanced balancing act between individual rights and societal interests. The basic structure doctrine, while safeguarding individual freedoms, has been subject to creative reinterpretations that recognize the legitimate interests of the state in certain circumstances. Courts, in applying the doctrine, have innovatively weighed individual rights against compelling state interests, acknowledging that constitutional interpretation is not a zero-sum game but a delicate equilibrium that must accommodate diverse and sometimes conflicting concerns.

A noteworthy innovation is the role of comparative constitutional law in shaping interpretations of the basic structure doctrine. Courts, recognizing the global interconnectedness of legal principles, have turned to foreign jurisprudence to inform their understanding of constitutional issues. This comparative approach allows for a broader perspective, enriching domestic interpretations with insights from diverse legal traditions and experiences. The engagement with global legal discourse fosters a more cosmopolitan and inclusive approach to constitutional interpretation.

The evolving understanding of social justice within the basic structure doctrine reflects another dimension of innovation. Courts have creatively interpreted constitutional provisions to address systemic injustices and inequalities. This innovation involves not only recognizing explicit rights but also discerning implicit principles that advance a more inclusive and egalitarian vision of society. The judiciary's role in interpreting the basic structure to promote affirmative action, social welfare programs, and inclusive policies underscores a commitment to transformative constitutionalism.

In the realm of separation of powers, innovations in judicial interpretation have focused on maintaining a delicate balance between the branches of government. Courts have creatively interpreted constitutional provisions to prevent overreach by any single branch, ensuring that the system of checks and balances remains robust. This innovation is particularly relevant in addressing the challenges posed by evolving governance structures, including issues related to administrative agencies, regulatory bodies, and other non-traditional actors.

In the context of federalism, innovations in judicial interpretation within the basic structure doctrine have addressed the evolving dynamics between the central and state governments. The judiciary's role in interpreting federal provisions to accommodate regional aspirations and cultural diversity reflects a commitment to fostering a harmonious and cooperative federal structure. This innovation is vital in adapting constitutional principles to the complexities of a diverse and pluralistic society.

The incorporation of public interest litigation (PIL) as a mechanism for judicial activism represents a paradigm shift in the role of the judiciary. Courts, leveraging the basic structure doctrine, have innovatively expanded the scope of PIL to address issues of public importance, even in the absence of traditional legal standing. This innovation reflects a proactive and participatory role for the judiciary in promoting the public interest and ensuring accountability.

The development of a living tree doctrine, akin to the concept in Canadian constitutional law, is another innovative approach within the basic structure doctrine. Courts have recognized that constitutional interpretation should not be frozen in a particular historical moment but should evolve to meet the needs of changing times. This innovation allows for a more dynamic and forward-looking interpretation that takes into account societal progress and evolving conceptions of justice.

In the domain of human rights, innovations in judicial interpretation within the basic structure doctrine have led to a broader understanding of the rights enshrined in the constitution. Courts, through creative interpretation, have expanded the scope of fundamental rights to encompass new dimensions, such as the right to a clean environment, right to information, and the right to education. This innovation reflects a commitment to ensuring that constitutional rights remain relevant and responsive to the evolving needs of society.

The role of technology in judicial interpretation represents a contemporary innovation within the basic structure doctrine. Courts, confronted with legal issues arising from rapid technological advancements, have creatively interpreted constitutional provisions to address novel challenges. This innovation involves adapting constitutional principles to the digital age, ensuring that fundamental rights and principles remain applicable in an era of unprecedented technological change.

Innovations in judicial interpretation also extend to the recognition of socio-economic rights as integral components of the basic structure. Courts, acknowledging that a just and equitable society requires the protection of socio-economic rights, have creatively interpreted constitutional provisions to uphold principles of economic justice, labor rights, and social welfare. This innovation reflects a commitment to a holistic understanding of constitutional rights that goes beyond traditional civil and political rights.

The role of amicus curiae, or friend of the court, represents an innovative mechanism within the basic structure doctrine. Courts have actively sought input from experts, academics, and civil society organizations to enhance the quality of legal arguments and broaden the perspectives considered in constitutional cases. This innovation reflects a commitment to participatory democracy and a recognition that constitutional interpretation benefits from diverse inputs.

In conclusion, innovations in judicial interpretation within the basic structure doctrine epitomize a dynamic and adaptive approach to constitutional jurisprudence. The creative reinterpretation of constitutional provisions, incorporation of new principles, engagement with comparative legal traditions, and responsiveness to societal changes underscore the vitality of the basic structure doctrine in navigating the complexities of modern governance. As the judiciary continues to grapple with evolving legal, social, and technological landscapes, these innovations contribute to a constitutional framework that remains resilient, inclusive, and attuned to the ever-changing demands of a dynamic society.

3.13 Public Perception and Judicial Legitimacy

The nexus between public perception and judicial legitimacy is a complex and symbiotic relationship that shapes the contours of a nation's legal landscape. This exploration delves into the intricate interplay between how the judiciary is perceived by the public and the resulting impact on the legitimacy of judicial decisions. Understanding this dynamic is crucial for comprehending the role of the judiciary in a democratic society and its effectiveness as a guardian of constitutional values.

Public perception of the judiciary is deeply rooted in notions of fairness, impartiality, and the ability to dispense justice. The legitimacy of the judiciary rests, to a large extent, on the public's confidence in the institution's capacity to act independently, free from external influences. The perceived integrity of judges, their adherence to ethical standards, and the transparency of judicial processes play pivotal roles in shaping public opinion.

One of the fundamental factors influencing public perception is the judiciary's responsiveness to societal values and expectations. When courts interpret the law in a manner that aligns with prevailing norms and moral principles, they garner trust and confidence from the public. Conversely, instances where judicial decisions appear out of step with societal expectations can erode public faith in the judiciary's understanding of societal realities.

The role of the media in shaping public perception of the judiciary is significant. Media coverage, whether accurate or sensationalized, can have a profound impact on how the public views the judiciary. High-profile cases, landmark decisions, and the personal lives of judges often become focal points in the public discourse, influencing perceptions of the judiciary's effectiveness and impartiality.

Public perception is also closely tied to the accessibility and inclusivity of the judicial system. When citizens perceive the judiciary as an institution that is approachable, responsive, and fair, it bolsters the legitimacy of the judicial process. Conversely, barriers to access, delays in justice delivery, and perceptions of elitism can contribute to skepticism and a diminished sense of legitimacy.

The public's understanding of legal processes and judicial reasoning is another crucial determinant of judicial legitimacy. Clear and comprehensible legal reasoning in judgments, along with efforts to demystify legal proceedings, enhances the public's perception of the judiciary as an institution that is accountable and transparent. Judicial decisions that are perceived as arbitrary, obscure, or disconnected from the broader legal framework can foster skepticism.

The perception of judicial independence is foundational to judicial legitimacy. When the public believes that judges are insulated from political pressures and external influences, it bolsters confidence in the judiciary's ability to uphold the rule of law. Any perception of undue influence, bias, or interference can severely undermine the legitimacy of the judiciary.

The role of precedent in shaping public perception is noteworthy. Consistency in legal interpretations and adherence to established precedent contribute to the stability and predictability of the legal system. When the public perceives that judicial decisions are guided by established legal principles rather than arbitrary considerations, it enhances confidence in the judiciary's commitment to the rule of law.

Public perception is also intricately connected to the judiciary's role as a check on government power. When the judiciary is perceived as an effective check and balance, it contributes to the legitimacy of both the judiciary and the broader democratic system. Conversely, if the judiciary is seen as deferential or partisan, it can lead to skepticism about its independence and legitimacy.

The role of public education and legal literacy cannot be overstated in shaping perceptions of the judiciary. An informed public is more likely to appreciate the nuances of legal decisions, understand the constraints faced by the judiciary, and make more nuanced judgments about the legitimacy of judicial actions. Efforts to enhance legal literacy can bridge the gap between legal processes and public perception.

The diversity and representativeness of the judiciary also influence public perception. A judiciary that reflects the diversity of the society it serves is more likely to be viewed as inclusive and sensitive to a variety of perspectives. The lack of diversity may contribute to perceptions of elitism and detachment from the realities faced by different segments of society.

Public trust in the judiciary is not a static concept but is subject to fluctuations based on individual cases, societal events, and the broader political climate. The judiciary's ability to navigate these dynamics, maintain public trust during challenging times, and regain trust when it falters is critical for sustaining its legitimacy.

The public's perception of the judiciary is not solely shaped by individual cases or decisions but is also influenced by the overall narrative around the institution. Ongoing efforts to build and maintain public trust should include proactive engagement with the public, transparency in decision-making processes, and consistent communication about the judiciary's role and functions.

The role of social media in shaping public perception is an emerging aspect of this dynamic relationship. Information spreads rapidly through digital platforms, and public discourse on legal matters is increasingly taking place in online spaces. Social media can amplify both positive and negative perceptions, making it a powerful force in shaping the overall narrative around the judiciary.

Challenges to judicial legitimacy can arise from perceived politicization of the judiciary. When judicial decisions are viewed through a partisan lens, it undermines the perception of impartiality and contributes to skepticism about the judiciary's independence. The challenge for the judiciary is to navigate politically charged environments while upholding its role as a neutral arbiter.

Public perception is not only influenced by the outcomes of cases but also by the process through which decisions are reached. Fair and transparent procedures, open courtroom proceedings, and opportunities for public scrutiny contribute to a positive perception of the judiciary's commitment to justice. Any perception of opacity or undue secrecy can undermine public confidence.

The international standing of a judiciary can also impact domestic perceptions. When the judiciary is respected globally for its independence and commitment to human rights, it can enhance its legitimacy domestically. Conversely, negative international perceptions can cast a shadow on the judiciary's standing in the eyes of the public.

Efforts to enhance public perception and judicial legitimacy require a multifaceted approach. Continuous engagement with the public through outreach programs, educational initiatives, and transparent communication about judicial processes and decisions can contribute to a better-informed and trusting citizenry. Building a culture of accountability within the judiciary, addressing concerns of bias or discrimination, and actively working to eliminate barriers to access to justice are integral components of fostering public trust.

In conclusion, the dynamic relationship between public perception and judicial legitimacy is a foundational aspect of democratic governance. The judiciary's effectiveness as a guardian of constitutional values is intricately tied to how it is perceived by the public. By actively addressing issues of transparency, accessibility, fairness, and responsiveness, the judiciary can contribute to a positive perception that strengthens its legitimacy as a vital institution in the democratic fabric. Recognizing the significance of this relationship is essential for maintaining public trust in the judiciary and upholding the rule of law.

3.14 International Perspective on Basic Structure

International perspectives on the basic structure doctrine offer a panoramic view of how constitutional principles transcend national boundaries, influencing legal systems and shaping the discourse on the separation of powers, constitutionalism, and the protection of fundamental rights. This exploration delves into the diverse ways in which the basic structure doctrine has been interpreted and applied across different jurisdictions, highlighting the global resonance of this constitutional concept.

In the international arena, the basic structure doctrine finds echoes in constitutional traditions that share a commitment to upholding the foundational principles of democratic governance and the rule of law. While the specific contours of the doctrine may vary, its underlying philosophy of safeguarding essential constitutional features remains a common thread that weaves through the constitutional fabric of numerous countries.

One of the overarching themes in international perspectives on the basic structure is the recognition of certain core principles as immutable foundations of the constitutional order. Whether articulated as an explicit doctrine or inferred from constitutional texts and traditions, many legal systems acknowledge the existence of fundamental principles that form the bedrock of their constitutional frameworks. These principles often encompass the protection of human rights, the separation of powers, and the integrity of the constitutional text.

The interplay between judicial review and the basic structure doctrine is a recurring theme in international contexts. Courts in various jurisdictions have grappled with the question of the extent to which they can review constitutional amendments that potentially violate the basic structure. The delicate balance between respecting the authority of the elected branches of government and safeguarding the core tenets of the constitution has led to nuanced judicial decisions that shape the contours of constitutional governance.

International perspectives on the basic structure also highlight the role of constitutional identity in shaping judicial interpretations. The notion that there are certain features inherent to a constitution that cannot be altered without fundamentally changing its identity is a common thread in the jurisprudence of many countries. Courts often rely on this concept to delineate the boundaries of permissible constitutional change and to guard against amendments that may undermine the essence of the constitutional order.

Comparative constitutional law plays a pivotal role in informing international perspectives on the basic structure. Courts and scholars frequently draw on experiences from other jurisdictions to enrich their understanding of constitutional principles and to explore innovative approaches to addressing constitutional challenges. The exchange of ideas and legal reasoning across borders contributes to a global conversation on the enduring values that underpin constitutional democracies.

The tension between stability and adaptability is a recurring theme in international perspectives on the basic structure. While the doctrine aims to provide stability to the constitutional order by protecting its essential features, legal systems also recognize the need for flexibility to address evolving social, political, and economic dynamics. Striking the right balance between preserving constitutional fundamentals and allowing for legitimate constitutional change is an ongoing challenge for constitutional courts worldwide.

In the context of federal systems, international perspectives on the basic structure often involve considerations of the distribution of powers between central and regional governments. Courts grapple with questions of federalism and regional autonomy, seeking to uphold the basic structure while respecting the diverse needs and aspirations of different regions within a country. The dynamics of federal governance and the delicate interplay between central and regional authorities add a layer of complexity to the application of the basic structure doctrine.

The protection of minority rights emerges as a crucial aspect of international perspectives on the basic structure. Courts in diverse jurisdictions recognize the importance of safeguarding the rights of minority groups as integral to the overarching principles of constitutionalism. The basic structure doctrine, in this context, serves as a shield against amendments that may disproportionately impact the rights of vulnerable or marginalized communities.

The role of the judiciary in upholding the basic structure often intersects with broader questions of constitutional morality and societal values. Courts, drawing from the rich tapestry of cultural, historical, and philosophical traditions, interpret the basic structure in ways that resonate with the values embedded in their respective societies. The evolving understanding of rights, justice, and governance informs judicial decisions on what constitutes the inviolable core of the constitution.

The impact of global human rights norms on the basic structure doctrine is a dynamic aspect of international perspectives. Constitutional courts often reference international human rights treaties and jurisprudence to interpret and reinforce the protection of fundamental rights within the basic structure. The international human rights framework serves as a source of inspiration and normative guidance for courts navigating complex constitutional issues.

The relationship between the basic structure doctrine and constitutional amendments is a central theme in international perspectives. Courts grapple with the question of whether certain amendments can be deemed unconstitutional if they violate the basic structure. The challenge lies in articulating clear and principled criteria for determining when an amendment transcends the permissible boundaries of constitutional change. The nuanced approaches taken by different jurisdictions reflect the contextual nature of this inquiry.

International perspectives on the basic structure also underscore the significance of constitutional interpretation as a living and evolving process. The adaptability of constitutional principles to changing circumstances is a common theme, with courts recognizing that the constitution must remain a vibrant and relevant document capable of addressing contemporary challenges. This dynamism allows the basic structure doctrine to serve as a resilient guardian of constitutional values.

The role of public opinion in shaping international perspectives on the basic structure is a multifaceted consideration. While courts are tasked with interpreting constitutional principles independently, they operate within societies where public sentiment and expectations play a role in shaping the legitimacy of judicial decisions. Striking a balance between fidelity to constitutional principles and responsiveness to societal values is a nuanced task faced by constitutional courts globally.

The impact of colonial legacies on the basic structure doctrine is a dimension unique to the historical experiences of certain countries. Former colonies often grapple with the legacy of colonial-era constitutions and amendments, seeking to assert their constitutional identity while addressing historical injustices. The basic structure doctrine becomes a tool for navigating the complexities of constitutional continuity and change in post-colonial settings.

The role of alternative dispute resolution mechanisms and informal constitutional change is an emerging aspect of international perspectives on the basic structure. Courts, recognizing the diversity of legal systems and the presence of multiple avenues for constitutional evolution, engage with non-judicial processes that may impact the basic structure. This dynamic reflects an openness to a variety of mechanisms that contribute to the resilience of constitutional governance.

In conclusion, international perspectives on the basic structure showcase the universality of certain constitutional principles while recognizing the contextual variations that shape the application of these principles across diverse legal systems. The dynamic interplay between stability and adaptability, the role of comparative constitutional law, the tension between judicial review and democratic governance, and the impact of global human rights norms all contribute to a rich tapestry of constitutional jurisprudence. As constitutional courts around the world grapple with contemporary challenges, the international resonance of the basic structure doctrine reflects its enduring relevance as a bulwark of constitutional governance and the protection of fundamental rights.

3.15 Educational Initiatives and the Doctrine

Educational initiatives play a pivotal role in shaping the understanding, awareness, and appreciation of constitutional doctrines, with the basic structure doctrine standing out as a critical component of legal education. This exploration delves into the multifaceted impact of educational initiatives on the comprehension and dissemination of the basic structure doctrine, emphasizing the role of academic institutions, legal scholarship, and public outreach in fostering a nuanced understanding of this constitutional concept.

At the heart of educational initiatives is the role of academic institutions in imparting legal knowledge and nurturing a generation of legal scholars, practitioners, and informed citizens. Law schools and universities serve as incubators for the study of constitutional law, and the basic structure doctrine often occupies a central place in the curriculum. The inclusion of this doctrine in legal education provides students with a foundational understanding of the principles that underpin constitutional governance.

Legal scholars and educators play a crucial role in shaping the discourse around the basic structure doctrine. Through research, publications, and academic conferences, scholars contribute to the development of legal theory, critique existing interpretations, and propose novel perspectives. The academic community serves as a dynamic space for intellectual engagement, where the evolution of the basic structure doctrine is scrutinized, debated, and enriched through diverse scholarly contributions.

Educational initiatives extend beyond traditional classroom settings, encompassing public lectures, seminars, and workshops that aim to disseminate legal knowledge to a broader audience. Public engagement with legal concepts, including the basic structure doctrine, fosters a more informed citizenry and contributes to a democratic society where individuals understand and appreciate the foundational principles of their constitutional order.

The role of legal journals and publications is integral to educational initiatives surrounding the basic structure doctrine. Law reviews and academic journals provide a platform for in-depth analyses, case commentaries, and theoretical explorations of the doctrine. This scholarly output not only contributes to the academic discourse but also serves as a valuable resource for practitioners, policymakers, and anyone seeking a comprehensive understanding of the basic structure doctrine.

Educational initiatives also extend to the use of technology and online platforms to disseminate legal knowledge. Webinars, online courses, and digital resources make legal education more accessible to a global audience. The basic structure doctrine, through these digital avenues, reaches individuals beyond traditional academic boundaries, creating opportunities for continuous learning and engagement.

The incorporation of the basic structure doctrine into moot court competitions and legal simulations enhances the practical understanding of the doctrine among law students. Moot court exercises provide students with the opportunity to apply theoretical knowledge to practical scenarios, honing their advocacy skills and deepening their comprehension of the doctrine's application in legal practice.

Interdisciplinary approaches to legal education, where the basic structure doctrine is explored in conjunction with political science, philosophy, history, and other disciplines, contribute to a holistic understanding of constitutional principles. Educational initiatives that encourage a multidisciplinary perspective equip students with the tools to critically analyze the societal, political, and historical contexts that shape constitutional doctrines.

Legal clinics and pro bono initiatives focused on constitutional law provide students with hands-on experience in addressing real-world legal issues. In the context of the basic structure doctrine, these initiatives offer opportunities for students to engage with constitutional challenges, contribute to legal research, and advocate for principles that uphold the integrity of the constitutional order.

The role of international collaboration and exchange programs in legal education contributes to a global perspective on the basic structure doctrine. Students and scholars participating in exchange programs gain exposure to diverse legal systems, comparative constitutional analyses, and alternative interpretations of constitutional principles. This globalized approach enriches the educational experience and broadens perspectives on the basic structure doctrine.

Educational initiatives aimed at enhancing legal literacy among the general public contribute to a more informed citizenry. Outreach programs, community seminars, and initiatives focused on schools and colleges create avenues for individuals to grasp the significance of the basic structure doctrine in protecting constitutional values, ensuring accountability, and upholding the rule of law.

The development and dissemination of educational materials, including textbooks, casebooks, and online resources, are integral to educational initiatives surrounding the basic structure doctrine. These materials serve as foundational references for students and educators, providing comprehensive insights into the historical evolution, landmark cases, and interpretative debates related to the doctrine.

The training of legal professionals, including judges, lawyers, and legal researchers, forms a crucial part of educational initiatives related to the basic structure doctrine. Continuing legal education programs, judicial academies, and specialized training sessions ensure that legal practitioners remain abreast of evolving legal principles and judicial interpretations, including those pertaining to the basic structure.

The inclusion of practical case studies and real-life examples in legal education enhances the applicability of the basic structure doctrine. Students exposed to the practical implications of the doctrine through real cases gain a nuanced understanding of its impact on legal disputes, constitutional challenges, and the broader governance of a country.

Educational initiatives focused on constitutional literacy often incorporate interactive methods, such as debates, moot courts, and simulations, to engage students actively. These participatory approaches encourage critical thinking, foster a culture of dialogue, and empower students to articulate and defend their perspectives on the basic structure doctrine.

The role of legal ethics and professional responsibility in legal education contributes to a nuanced understanding of the ethical considerations associated with constitutional interpretation, advocacy, and legal practice. Students trained in legal ethics develop a heightened awareness of the ethical dimensions surrounding the application of the basic structure doctrine.

Educational initiatives surrounding the basic structure doctrine also extend to the development of educational games, documentaries, and multimedia content that make legal concepts engaging and accessible. These innovative approaches cater to diverse learning styles, making constitutional education more inclusive and appealing to a broader audience.

The role of legal clinics and advocacy programs focused on constitutional issues contributes to the practical application of the basic structure doctrine. Students engaged in clinical legal education gain firsthand experience in addressing constitutional challenges, participating in legal research, and advocating for principles that uphold the constitutional order.

The impact of educational initiatives is not confined to formal legal education but extends to public discourse, policy formulation, and the broader socio-political landscape. A well-informed citizenry, equipped with an understanding of the basic structure doctrine, contributes to a vibrant democracy where individuals actively participate in discussions on constitutional values, legal reforms, and governance.

In conclusion, educational initiatives surrounding the basic structure doctrine are instrumental in shaping the intellectual landscape of constitutional law. The multifaceted impact of these initiatives, encompassing traditional classroom settings, academic publications, public outreach, interdisciplinary approaches, and innovative educational methods, underscores the significance of cultivating a robust understanding of constitutional principles. As legal education continues to evolve, the role of educational initiatives in fostering a deep and nuanced appreciation of the basic structure doctrine remains paramount in shaping the next generation of legal minds and engaged citizens.

Conclusion

The journey through the intricacies of "The Basic Structure Doctrine Unveiled" has been a comprehensive exploration of a constitutional concept that stands as a cornerstone of India's legal landscape and resonates across various jurisdictions globally. As we conclude this chapter, it is crucial to reflect on the multifaceted dimensions we have encountered – from the historical underpinnings to the contemporary applications, the global perspectives to the societal impacts, and the educational initiatives that play a vital role in shaping our understanding of the basic structure doctrine.

At its core, the basic structure doctrine emerges as a testament to the resilience and adaptability of constitutional principles. Delving into the historical context, we observed how the doctrine was crystallized through landmark judicial decisions, responding to challenges that threatened the very essence of the Indian Constitution. The exploration of seminal cases such as Kesavananda Bharati v. State of Kerala laid the foundation for understanding the doctrine's evolution, showcasing the judiciary's role in safeguarding the constitutional identity against potential encroachments.

The chapter also unfurled the doctrinal intricacies surrounding the basic structure, elucidating its components and the delicate balance required in its application. The identification of the essential features that form the bedrock of the constitution involves a nuanced exercise by the judiciary. Through an analysis of various cases, we navigated the terrain where the judiciary delineates between permissible constitutional amendments and those that would transgress the sacrosanct boundaries of the basic structure.

Global perspectives on the basic structure provided a panoramic view of how constitutional principles transcend borders. From comparative constitutional law to the impact of international human rights norms, the chapter illuminated how the basic structure doctrine is part of a global conversation on constitutionalism, judicial review, and the protection of fundamental rights. The examination of international perspectives underscored the universal resonance of certain constitutional principles while recognizing the contextual variations that shape their application.

Societal impacts emerged as a critical dimension, emphasizing how the basic structure doctrine is not confined to legal discourse but ripples through the fabric of society. Its interplay with fundamental rights, influence on legislative processes, and role in safeguarding minority rights became evident as we probed the societal implications. The examination of public interest litigation, constitutional amendments, and the jurisprudential philosophy behind the doctrine unveiled how these elements intersect with the daily lives of citizens.

The chapter also delved into the role of the basic structure doctrine in addressing contemporary challenges. Anticipating challenges and aspirations, we explored how the doctrine responds to dynamic social changes, technological advancements, and evolving notions of justice. The examination of its role in environmental jurisprudence, economic reforms, and innovations in judicial interpretation highlighted the adaptability of the doctrine to meet the challenges of a changing world.

Educational initiatives emerged as a linchpin, playing a pivotal role in disseminating knowledge about the basic structure doctrine. From traditional legal education in classrooms to online platforms, moot court competitions, and interdisciplinary approaches, educational initiatives were revealed as dynamic tools that contribute to a nuanced understanding among students, scholars, and the wider public. The exploration of the societal impacts of educational initiatives underscored their role in fostering legal literacy and shaping an informed citizenry.

As we traverse the contours of this multifaceted exploration, it becomes evident that the basic structure doctrine is not a static legal concept confined to the pages of judgments; rather, it is a living, breathing entity that evolves with the dynamics of society, governance, and the global legal landscape. The doctrine, as unveiled in this chapter, is a testament to the judiciary's commitment to upholding the constitutional ethos, ensuring the longevity and adaptability of foundational principles in the face of challenges and societal transformations.

In conclusion, "The Basic Structure Doctrine Unveiled" serves not only as an exposition of a legal doctrine but as a journey through the nuanced interplay of history, constitutional philosophy, global perspectives, societal impacts, and educational endeavors. It is a testament to the enduring significance of constitutional principles and the judiciary's role in their preservation. As we move forward, the lessons gleaned from this exploration will undoubtedly reverberate in ongoing legal discourses, shaping the understanding of constitutional governance, protecting fundamental rights, and contributing to the ongoing narrative of India's constitutional journey.

Chapter 4

Essential Features of The Basic Structure

In the intricate tapestry of constitutional law, few doctrines stand as prominently and provocatively as the concept of the Basic Structure. It is a judicial doctrine that has not only weathered the test of time but has evolved as the bedrock of constitutional interpretation in the Indian legal landscape. This chapter embarks on a journey to unravel the essential features that constitute the very soul of the Indian Constitution, probing not only into legal intricacies but also delving into the socio-political contexts that have shaped and continue to shape this doctrinal edifice.

To comprehend the essence of the Basic Structure Doctrine is to embark on a voyage through the corridors of constitutional history, a history written not just in legal tomes but etched in the collective consciousness of a nation. At the heart of this exploration lies the landmark case of Kesavananda Bharati v. State of Kerala, a judicial saga that unfolded against the backdrop of profound political transformations and constitutional challenges. As the legal luminaries presented their arguments, little did they foresee that their legal contestations would etch a doctrine that transcends the confines of a courtroom and resonates in the echoes of every constitutional debate.

As we traverse this intellectual terrain, it becomes imperative to fathom the very genesis of the Basic Structure Doctrine. It is not merely a legal principle; it is a response to the historical imperatives that necessitated a safeguard against potential encroachments on the foundational ethos of the Constitution. The Indian Constitution, nascent and ambitious, sought to forge a path distinct from its counterparts globally, and the Basic Structure Doctrine emerged as a sentinel guarding the uniqueness of this constitutional experiment.

Embedded in the concept of essential features is a profound jurisprudential inquiry. What renders a feature 'essential'? How does the judiciary discern the constitutional alchemy that transforms an aspect into an indispensable facet of the constitutional design? These are not just legal conundrums; they are philosophical quests into the very nature of constitutionalism. The judiciary, in its wisdom, undertakes a delicate task – to distill from the constitutional text those elements that are immutable, those that form the very DNA of the Constitution.

This exploration is not confined to the annals of legal analysis alone; it extends its gaze to the crucible of societal impacts. The Basic Structure Doctrine is not a mere legal formula; it is a prism through which we can perceive the societal dynamics and political exigencies that have necessitated its articulation. Its invocation in seminal cases reverberates in the public sphere, shaping not only legal precedents but also influencing public discourse and political narratives.

In scrutinizing the Basic Structure Doctrine, one is compelled to confront the very essence of constitutional morality. The identification of essential features is not a mechanical exercise; it is an ethical engagement with the foundational values that underpin the constitutional covenant. It requires a discernment of the constitutional spirit, an alignment with the principles that animate the Constitution beyond the letter of the law. This dimension of constitutional morality not only guides the judiciary in its interpretative role but also resonates with the larger societal quest for justice, liberty, equality, and fraternity.

The very fabric of the Basic Structure Doctrine is interwoven with the delicate threads of constitutional amendments. It is in the crucible of amendments that the doctrine often faces its most rigorous tests. How does one balance the imperative of constitutional adaptability with the need to preserve the constitutional soul? This chapter navigates through the maze of amendments, exploring cases where the judiciary has wielded the doctrine as a shield against potential erosions of constitutional essentials.

Moreover, the doctrine is not a static entity; it is dynamic, responsive to the evolving ethos of society. As we traverse the legal landscape, we encounter instances where the Basic Structure Doctrine has responded to emerging challenges – be it in the realms of environmental jurisprudence, technological advancements, or the imperatives of socio-economic justice. It is in these responses that we discern the living character of the doctrine, its ability to adapt to the shifting sands of societal dynamics.

A comparative constitutional perspective unveils the universal resonances of the Basic Structure Doctrine. It is not a doctrinal artifact confined to the Indian legal canvas; it finds echoes in constitutional discourses worldwide. How do other jurisdictions grapple with similar questions of constitutional identity? How do global constitutional trends intersect with the Indian experience? These questions beckon us to embark on a journey beyond borders, to explore the global conversations that inform our understanding of constitutional essentials.

In the labyrinth of constitutional interpretation, dissenting voices often illuminate the path forward. The Basic Structure Doctrine, despite its crystallization, has not been immune to dissent within the judiciary. This chapter contemplates dissent not as a mere legal disagreement but as an integral part of the constitutional dialogue. It examines dissenting opinions with a discerning eye, seeking not just legal alternatives but insights that enrich our understanding of constitutional principles.

As we embark on this odyssey through the Essential Features of the Basic Structure, it is not merely a legal exploration; it is an invitation to contemplate the very foundations of our constitutional democracy. It beckons us to peer into the soul of the Constitution, to discern the resonances of justice and equity, and to grapple with the eternal question of how a nation's fundamental principles can be safeguarded without ossifying the very instrument that enshrines them. It is an intellectual pilgrimage into the heart of constitutionalism, where the contours of justice are etched, and the principles of a nation find expression in the hallowed precincts of the judiciary.

As we navigate this chapter, let us not merely scrutinize legal doctrines; let us engage with the essence of governance, justice, and democracy. The Basic Structure Doctrine is not an abstract legal concept; it is the heartbeat of our constitutional order, pulsating through every adjudication, resonating in every legislative debate, and echoing in the aspirations of a nation. In unraveling its essential features, we uncover not just legal principles, but the very soul of our constitutional democracy.

4.1 Constitutional Amendments as Social Contracts

In the labyrinthine world of constitutional law, the relationship between constitutional amendments and the concept of social contracts forms a nuanced tapestry. To fathom this interplay is to embark on a journey through the annals of constitutional evolution, where amendments cease to be mere legal modifications but assume the character of societal agreements, echoing the foundational principles that bind a nation.

Constitutional amendments, at their core, represent the mechanism through which a society negotiates with its own evolving identity. They are not mere textual alterations but a collective introspection, a societal dialogue that questions, refines, and sometimes redefines the constitutional compact. In this sense, each amendment can be viewed as a node in the ongoing conversation between the state and its citizens, a renegotiation of the terms that govern their coexistence.

The metaphor of a social contract, originally advanced by political philosophers like Thomas Hobbes, John Locke, and Jean-Jacques Rousseau, posits that the legitimacy of governance emanates from an implicit agreement among individuals to surrender certain liberties in exchange for security and ordered coexistence. In the context of constitutional amendments, this philosophical underpinning takes on a contemporary relevance.

Amendments to a constitution can be seen as acts of collective will, expressions of the societal consciousness at a particular point in time. They are not isolated events but integral to the organic growth of a constitutional order. When a society amends its constitution, it engages in a process of reflection and reevaluation, akin to the periodic review of terms in a social contract. Amendments become the codification of evolving values, aspirations, and compromises within the body politic.

Consider, for instance, the Twenty-Sixth Amendment to the United States Constitution, which lowered the voting age to 18. This constitutional amendment was a response to the societal demand for greater inclusivity and recognition of the civic responsibilities of young adults. It reflected a collective decision to extend the franchise to a segment of the population that was deemed mature enough to participate in the democratic process. In this instance, the amendment served as a bridge between the evolving societal norms and the constitutional framework.

In the Indian context, the constitutional amendments hold a distinct significance, especially in light of the Basic Structure Doctrine. The judiciary, by asserting its authority to review and potentially strike down amendments that violate the basic structure, establishes a dynamic equilibrium between the constitutional text and its core principles. This legal framework reinforces the idea that constitutional amendments are not beyond the scrutiny of constitutional morality and that they must align with the enduring values that define the constitutional ethos.

The notion of constitutional amendments as social contracts gains further resonance when viewed through the prism of transformative changes. Societal progress often necessitates alterations to the constitutional fabric to accommodate emerging norms and expectations. For instance, amendments addressing issues of gender equality, LGBTQ+ rights, and environmental protection are manifestations of a society grappling with its evolving identity and making a collective commitment to more inclusive and sustainable principles.

However, this conceptualization is not without its complexities. The metaphorical contract is not always consensual or unanimous. Amendments can be contentious, reflecting divergent views and competing interests with in society. The process of negotiation embedded in amendments may involve compromises and power dynamics that mirror the intricacies of a social contract negotiation. The conflict surrounding amendments often underscores the inherent tension between the preservation of constitutional essentials and the imperative to adapt to changing circumstances.

Constitutional amendments as social contracts also draw attention to the temporal dimension of constitutionalism. Amendments are not static agreements but dynamic instruments that must navigate the shifting currents of history. As societal values evolve, so too must the constitutional framework. The metaphor of a social contract encourages an understanding of amendments not as immutable commitments but as living agreements subject to periodic reassessment.

Moreover, the metaphor allows us to interrogate the role of citizenry in the amendment process. In a true social contract, the agency lies with the citizens who, through their representatives, actively participate in the negotiation and renewal of the agreement. In the context of constitutional amendments, the extent of public participation, awareness, and deliberation becomes crucial. The democratic ideals embedded in the social contract metaphor demand a robust civic engagement in the amendment process to ensure its legitimacy.

However, the analogy of constitutional amendments as social contracts is not without its challenges. Unlike traditional social contracts that are often implicit and unwritten, constitutional amendments are explicit textual changes subject to legal interpretation. The legal formalism inherent in amendments may sometimes diverge from the more fluid and evolving nature of social contracts. This tension raises questions about the adequacy of the metaphor in capturing the intricacies of constitutional evolution.

In contemplating constitutional amendments as social contracts, it is also essential to acknowledge the agency of the state as a party to the agreement. Unlike a traditional social contract that posits a direct relationship between individuals, the state, and its institutions play a pivotal role in the amendment process. This institutional dimension introduces a layer of complexity, as amendments are not merely expressions of societal will but negotiated outcomes within the halls of legislatures and constitutional assemblies.

The metaphor gains depth when examining instances where constitutional amendments are responses to crises or transformative events. It is in these moments of societal upheaval or significant shifts in political landscapes that the metaphor of a social contract comes to the fore. Amendments become mechanisms for recalibrating the constitutional equilibrium, offering a structured approach to address challenges or redefine the terms of governance.

Moreover, the metaphor invites contemplation on the durability of constitutional commitments. If amendments are akin to renewing a social contract, what guarantees the fidelity of the parties involved? Is there an inherent trust that the principles enshrined in the constitutional text will be upheld over time? The answer lies in the mechanisms of constitutionalism, the checks and balances embedded in the legal and institutional framework, and the vigilance of a vigilant citizenry.

In conclusion, the exploration of constitutional amendments as social contracts provides a lens through which we can decipher the intricate relationship between legal frameworks and societal agreements. The metaphor encourages us to view amendments not as isolated textual changes but as expressions of a collective consciousness negotiating the terms of governance. It prompts us to contemplate the ongoing dialogue between the state and its citizens, the compromises and consensus that characterize the amendment process, and the enduring principles that form the bedrock of the constitutional order. As we navigate the terrain of constitutional evolution, the metaphor of social contracts beckons us to recognize the living nature of constitutionalism, where each amendment is a chapter in the ongoing narrative of a nation forging its path through the complexities of governance and societal aspirations.

4.2 Impact on Governance Structure

The impact of constitutional amendments on governance structures is a multifaceted exploration that transcends the legal realm, delving deep into the intricate machinery of governance, institutional dynamics, and the broader socio-political fabric. To comprehend this impact is to embark on a journey that unravels not just legal intricacies but also the profound transformations these amendments introduce into the very fabric of governance.

At its core, governance structures embody the mechanisms through which a state exercises authority, makes decisions, and implements policies. Constitutional amendments, as instruments of legal modification, wield significant influence over these structures, shaping the distribution of powers, redefining institutional roles, and recalibrating the delicate balance between different branches of government.

One fundamental aspect of the impact on governance structures lies in the redistribution of powers between the central and state governments. The constitutional amendments that address federalism, a foundational principle in many democratic nations, often recalibrate the division of powers between the national and regional entities. For instance, the U.S. constitutional amendments, including the Tenth Amendment, have played a pivotal role in delineating the powers reserved to the states, influencing the contours of federal-state relations.

In the Indian context, the constitutional amendments have addressed federal concerns, particularly in the realm of fiscal federalism and administrative cooperation. Amendments related to the Goods and Services Tax (GST) introduced a transformative shift in India's indirect tax system, necessitating coordination between the central and state governments. The impact is not merely legal; it reverberates in the administrative apparatus, influencing how revenue is collected, distributed, and utilized for governance at different levels.

Moreover, constitutional amendments often entail changes in the electoral and political structures, influencing the very foundation of representative democracy. Alterations in the electoral system, such as those delineated in constitutional amendments, have a direct impact on the political landscape. The representation of marginalized groups, the delineation of constituencies, and the mechanisms of political competition are all intricately woven into the governance tapestry.

Consider the impact of the Nineteenth Amendment to the U.S. Constitution, which granted women the right to vote. This constitutional amendment not only transformed the political landscape by expanding the electorate but also had a profound impact on governance structures. It signaled a shift in policy priorities, as politicians had to respond to the changing demographics of the electorate, amplifying the voices of women in governance and policy formulation.

Similarly, in India, constitutional amendments related to reservations for Scheduled Castes (SCs), Scheduled Tribes (STs), and Other Backward Classes (OBCs) have had a transformative impact on political representation. These amendments, aimed at addressing historical injustices and ensuring social justice, have altered the dynamics of governance by diversifying political leadership and enhancing the inclusivity of decision-making structures.

Furthermore, constitutional amendments often traverse the realms of executive authority, influencing the powers vested in the head of state or government. The Twenty-Fifth Amendment to the U.S. Constitution, for example, clarified the procedures for presidential succession and disability, ensuring a more robust and transparent process for addressing contingencies affecting the executive branch. This amendment not only had legal implications but also reshaped perceptions of executive stability, affecting governance perceptions both domestically and internationally.

In the Indian context, amendments related to the powers of the President, Governors, and the executive have similarly left an indelible mark on governance structures. The constitutional provisions regarding the imposition of President's Rule in states, as outlined in the Forty-Fourth Amendment, sought to strike a delicate balance between federal authority and state autonomy. This alteration in governance mechanisms not only had legal ramifications but also spoke to the broader principles of cooperative federalism and constitutional ethics.

Constitutional amendments also permeate the terrain of administrative governance, influencing how bureaucracies operate and how public services are delivered. The nature of civil services, administrative jurisdiction, and the mechanisms for redressal are often subject to amendments that seek to enhance efficiency, accountability, and responsiveness.

For instance, the constitutional amendment related to the establishment of the National Judicial Appointments Commission (NJAC) in India aimed to reform the process of judicial appointments. While the amendment was ultimately struck down by the Supreme Court, the discourse surrounding it and the subsequent debate on the collegium system reflected a broader conversation about governance structures within the judiciary.

Furthermore, constitutional amendments addressing fundamental rights have a profound impact on the governance structures tasked with safeguarding and enforcing these rights. Amendments that expand or contract the scope of fundamental rights influence not only the legal landscape but also the mechanisms through which individuals seek justice and protection against state excesses.

The First Amendment to the U.S. Constitution, for instance, introduced significant changes to the freedom of speech protections. This amendment reshaped the contours of governance in the realm of free expression, influencing how the state regulates speech and the parameters within which individuals can assert their right to free speech.

In India, amendments related to fundamental rights have similarly shaped governance structures, particularly in the domain of judicial review. The Forty-Second Amendment sought to limit the scope of judicial review concerning the President's proclamations of emergency, illustrating how amendments can impact the checks and balances within the constitutional framework.

The impact of constitutional amendments on governance structures is not confined to the formal institutions of government; it extends to the broader societal and cultural dimensions that inform governance. Amendments often mirror and, in turn, shape societal values, influencing the ethical foundations that underpin governance structures.

For instance, constitutional amendments related to the recognition of LGBTQ+ rights, as seen in the decriminalization of homosexuality in India through the reading down of Section 377, have profound implications for societal norms and, consequently, impact governance structures. These amendments challenge entrenched prejudices, necessitating a reevaluation of administrative practices, legal frameworks, and public policies to align with the principles of equality and non-discrimination.

Moreover, constitutional amendments that address issues of social and economic justice, such as land reforms or affirmative action policies, influence the distribution of resources and opportunities within society. These amendments not only alter the legal landscape but also impact the governance structures responsible for implementing and overseeing policies aimed at achieving these constitutional goals.

In conclusion, the impact of constitutional amendments on governance structures is a dynamic and expansive exploration that transcends the confines of legal formalism. It is a journey into the heart of governance, where legal modifications reverberate through the intricate mechanisms of state authority, political representation, administrative functioning, and societal values. Constitutional amendments are not mere textual changes; they are catalysts for change, shaping the very foundations of governance and reflecting the evolving aspirations of a nation. As we navigate this terrain, we encounter not only legal precedents but the living pulse of governance, where amendments leave an indelible mark on the canvas of constitutional democracy.

4.3 Environmental Jurisprudence and the Basic Structure

The intertwining of environmental jurisprudence with the foundational principles encapsulated in the Basic Structure Doctrine constitutes a profound exploration into the evolving relationship between constitutionalism and ecological concerns. As we delve into this intricate landscape, it becomes apparent that the jurisprudential treatment of environmental issues is not a mere legal discourse but a reflection of the evolving consciousness about the symbiotic relationship between nature and constitutional values.

The constitutional journey towards recognizing the environmental imperative within the Basic Structure unfolds against the backdrop of global environmental consciousness. The recognition that the environment is not merely a backdrop for human activities but an integral component of life's interconnected web has permeated legal frameworks worldwide. In the Indian context, the Constitutional framers, while drafting the Constitution, may not have explicitly envisaged the environmental challenges of the future, but the principles they enshrined laid the groundwork for the constitutional recognition of ecological imperatives.

One pivotal aspect of this recognition is the interpretation of the Right to Life under Article 21 of the Indian Constitution. The judiciary, through a series of landmark decisions, has expansively construed this right to include the right to a healthy environment. The Basic Structure Doctrine, by safeguarding the essence of fundamental rights, indirectly becomes a guardian of the right to a clean and healthy environment. The judiciary, in weaving environmental concerns into the constitutional fabric, emphasizes that a life with dignity, as envisaged in the Basic Structure, inherently incorporates a life in harmony with the environment.

The landmark case of Maneka Gandhi v. Union of India marked a jurisprudential shift by interpreting the Right to Life expansively, emphasizing that it includes the right to a healthy environment. Subsequent judgments, such as Subhash Kumar v. State of Bihar and Vellore Citizens Welfare Forum v. Union of India, further fortified this environmental dimension of the Right to Life. The judiciary, in these instances, articulated the notion that a life devoid of a healthy environment undermines the very essence of human dignity and, by extension, the Basic Structure of the Constitution.

Moreover, the Directive Principles of State Policy, while not enforceable in courts, provide an ethical and constitutional compass that guides governance in the service of the common good. Article 48A and Article 51A(g) in particular underscore the duty of the state to protect and improve the environment and wildlife. The Basic Structure Doctrine, by ensuring the primacy of certain principles, indirectly reinforces the ethical imperative embedded in these directive principles, urging the state to align its actions with the constitutional morality of environmental stewardship.

The doctrine's protective umbrella extends to the concept of intergenerational equity, a principle embedded in environmental jurisprudence. By safeguarding the core principles of the Constitution, including justice, liberty, equality, and fraternity, the Basic Structure Doctrine indirectly safeguards the interests of future generations. This temporal dimension of constitutionalism aligns with the ecological understanding that the actions of the present should not compromise the ability of future generations to meet their needs.

Furthermore, the Basic Structure Doctrine plays a pivotal role in upholding the federal structure of the Constitution concerning environmental governance. India's federal structure, a part of the Basic Structure, becomes an instrumental tool in addressing environmental challenges that transcend regional boundaries. The doctrine ensures that the principles of cooperative federalism and intergovernmental collaboration are upheld in the pursuit of environmental conservation. Cases such as M.C. Mehta v. Union of India, involving trans-boundary pollution, exemplify how the doctrine influences the legal response to environmental issues with federal implications.

The dynamic nature of the Basic Structure Doctrine resonates with the evolving understanding of environmental rights as an integral component of human rights. In a world grappling with ecological crises, the judiciary's role in interpreting the Basic Structure ensures that constitutional protections adapt to encompass emerging environmental challenges. The cases related to air and water pollution, waste management, and conservation of biodiversity exemplify how the doctrine becomes a constitutional compass for addressing contemporary environmental concerns.

A critical facet of environmental jurisprudence is the principle of sustainable development, acknowledging that progress should not come at the cost of environmental degradation. The Basic Structure Doctrine, by prioritizing justice and equality, implicitly supports the concept of sustainable development as a constitutional imperative. This alignment reflects an understanding that the pursuit of economic and social goals must harmonize with ecological sustainability, echoing the interconnected values within the constitutional framework.

The doctrine's influence extends to the adjudication of conflicts between developmental imperatives and environmental conservation. In cases where projects with potential environmental repercussions come under scrutiny, the judiciary often navigates a delicate balance between development and conservation. The Basic Structure Doctrine, by anchoring the legal discourse in constitutional principles, guides the judiciary in reconciling conflicting interests and ensuring that development respects the ecological limits set by the Constitution.

Furthermore, the doctrine contributes to the recognition of environmental rights as justiciable rights, allowing citizens to seek legal redress for environmental harms. Public interest litigations (PILs) related to environmental issues often invoke the Basic Structure Doctrine implicitly, as the judiciary ensures that the core principles of justice and equality are not compromised in the pursuit of environmental justice. Cases like Bhopal Gas Peedith Mahila Udyog Sangathan v. Union of India and the Oleum Gas Leak Case illustrate the judiciary's role in upholding the Basic Structure while addressing environmental injustices.

In conclusion, the intertwining of environmental jurisprudence with the Basic Structure Doctrine signifies a constitutional maturation that aligns human rights, ethical imperatives, and ecological considerations. The doctrine, by safeguarding the core principles of the Constitution, inherently becomes a guardian of environmental rights. In a world grappling with environmental challenges, the judiciary's interpretation of the Basic Structure ensures that constitutional values remain resilient in the face of ecological crises. As the constitutional compass navigates the complex terrain of environmental governance, it not only safeguards the present but lays the foundation for a constitutional legacy that cherishes the environment as an inseparable part of the constitutional soul.

4.4 Technology and Constitutional Essentials

The intricate interplay between technology and constitutional essentials unfolds as a compelling narrative in the evolving landscape of constitutional jurisprudence. This narrative encapsulates not just the legal dimensions but also the profound societal transformations catalyzed by technological advancements. As we traverse this terrain, it becomes evident that technology is not merely a neutral force but a dynamic actor that shapes, and is shaped by, the foundational principles enshrined in the constitutional framework.

At the heart of this exploration lies the constitutional guarantee of fundamental rights, with a particular focus on the right to privacy. The advent of the digital age has ushered in an era where personal information is a valuable currency, exchanged in the vast marketplace of cyberspace. The judiciary, in acknowledging the evolving nature of privacy, has interpreted the right in a manner that aligns with contemporary technological realities. Cases like Justice K.S. Puttaswamy (Retd.) v. Union of India (2017) in India and Carpenter v. United States (2018) in the United States reflect a recognition that technological intrusions into personal spaces demand a nuanced understanding of privacy within the constitutional framework.

The Basic Structure Doctrine, by safeguarding the core principles of the Constitution, indirectly shields fundamental rights from encroachments facilitated by technological advancements. The doctrine ensures that the essence of rights, including those pertaining to personal autonomy and dignity, remains resilient in the face of technological innovations that might pose challenges to individual freedoms. It prompts the judiciary to interpret constitutional provisions in a manner that preserves the timeless values encapsulated in the Basic Structure, even as technology reshapes the boundaries of human experience.

Moreover, the constitutional essentials, including the principles of justice, equality, and liberty, intersect with technology in the realm of access to information. The right to access information, implicit in the right to freedom of speech and expression, acquires new dimensions in the digital age. Technology acts as both a facilitator and a potential constraint on the free flow of information. The judiciary, guided by the Basic Structure Doctrine, navigates the complexities of this intersection, ensuring that the democratic principles embedded in the Constitution are not compromised by the challenges posed by the digital realm.

The concept of equality takes on new meanings in the context of technology, especially concerning digital access and the digital divide. The judiciary, informed by the Basic Structure Doctrine, is attuned to the constitutional imperative of ensuring that technological advancements do not create disparities that undermine the principle of equality. Cases related to digital infrastructure, internet access, and the right to education reflect the judiciary's role in harmonizing technological progress with the constitutional commitment to social justice and equal opportunities.

Furthermore, the Basic Structure Doctrine influences the adjudication of cases related to the regulation of emerging technologies. Whether it be artificial intelligence, biotechnology, or surveillance technologies, the doctrine serves as a touchstone for evaluating the constitutionality of legal frameworks governing these technologies. The judiciary, by grounding its analysis in constitutional essentials, ensures that the ethical dimensions of technological advancements are scrutinized within the broader context of constitutional values.

The principles of separation of powers and checks and balances, integral to the Basic Structure, assume heightened relevance in the context of technology. The expansion of the surveillance state, the collection of vast amounts of data by both state and non- state actors, and the potential abuse of technological tools for authoritarian purposes necessitate a vigilant judiciary. The doctrine, by upholding the integrity of institutional frameworks, ensures that technological advancements do not erode the delicate balance between the executive, legislative, and judicial branches.

Moreover, the global nature of technology poses challenges that transcend national borders. Cases related to extradition, cybercrime, and cross-border data flows implicate constitutional principles within an international context. The judiciary, informed by the Basic Structure Doctrine, engages with these complexities to ensure that constitutional values are not compromised in the pursuit of global governance in the technological age.

The evolving concept of digital citizenship, encompassing rights and responsibilities in the digital space, finds resonance within the constitutional framework. The Basic Structure Doctrine, by safeguarding the democratic ethos and the rule of law, provides a normative anchor for the judiciary to address issues such as online speech, digital governance, and the protection of individual autonomy in the virtual realm. As technology blurs the boundaries between the physical and digital spheres, the judiciary grapples with questions that have profound implications for constitutional essentials.

The right to dissent, a cornerstone of democratic societies, faces new challenges in the digital era. Technology both amplifies and constrains the exercise of this right, raising questions about censorship, online activism, and the role of digital platforms as gatekeepers of public discourse. The judiciary, guided by the Basic Structure Doctrine, undertakes the delicate task of balancing the imperatives of order and free expression, ensuring that constitutional values remain resilient in the face of evolving technologies.

The impact of technology on electoral processes constitutes another dimension of the constitutional discourse. As digital platforms become influential arenas for political expression and engagement, questions arise about the regulation of online political activities, the spread of misinformation, and the influence of technology on the democratic process. The judiciary, by drawing upon the Basic Structure Doctrine, navigates these complexities to uphold the integrity of democratic principles in the digital age.

The nexus between technology and constitutional essentials extends to the realm of economic justice. Issues such as digital economies, e-commerce, and the gig economy raise questions about the rights of workers, consumer protection, and the equitable distribution of economic benefits. The Basic Structure Doctrine, by emphasizing justice and equality, guides the judiciary in addressing these challenges within the framework of constitutional values.

Moreover, the role of technology in the administration of justice itself comes under scrutiny. The digitization of legal processes, the use of artificial intelligence in decision-making, and the implications of technology on access to justice form part of the constitutional discourse. The judiciary, drawing upon the Basic Structure Doctrine, ensures that technological innovations in the legal sphere align with the principles of fairness, transparency, and justice inherent in the constitutional framework.

In conclusion, the intricate interplay between technology and constitutional essentials constitutes a dynamic and multifaceted exploration. The Basic Structure Doctrine, by safeguarding the foundational principles of the Constitution, serves as a lodestar for the judiciary as it grapples with the profound implications of technological advancements. As technology reshapes the contours of human existence, the judiciary, guided by the constitutional compass, ensures that the essence of constitutional values remains steadfast in the face of unprecedented challenges and opportunities ushered in by the digital age.

4.5 Role in Addressing Economic Injustices

The role of the Basic Structure Doctrine in addressing economic injustices stands as a testament to the constitutional commitment to justice, equality, and the alleviation of disparities within society. As we delve into this exploration, it becomes evident that the doctrine, by safeguarding the foundational principles of the Constitution, provides a constitutional compass for the judiciary to navigate the complex terrain of economic justice.

At the core of this discourse lies the constitutional vision of a just and egalitarian society, a vision that resonates in principles embedded in the Basic Structure. The ideals of justice, both distributive and corrective, are fundamental to the constitutional framework. The judiciary, guided by the doctrine, becomes a vanguard in interpreting and applying these principles to redress economic injustices that may arise from systemic inequalities, historical disadvantages, or policy shortcomings.

One pivotal dimension of the Basic Structure's role in addressing economic injustices is reflected in the interpretation of fundamental rights, especially those related to economic liberties and social justice. The principles of equality before the law, non-discrimination, and the right to livelihood are integral components of the constitutional vision. Cases related to reservations, affirmative action policies, and social welfare programs exemplify how the judiciary, informed by the Basic Structure Doctrine, ensures that economic opportunities are accessible to all segments of society.

The principle of equality, enshrined in the Basic Structure, resonates in the judiciary's scrutiny of economic policies and practices that perpetuate disparities. Whether it be cases related to economic reservations, access to education, or employment opportunities, the doctrine ensures that economic justice is not compromised. The judiciary's role becomes crucial in evaluating the impact of economic decisions on marginalized communities and ensuring that constitutional values prevail over discriminatory practices.

Moreover, the Basic Structure Doctrine serves as a bulwark against policies that might exacerbate economic inequalities. The judiciary, by upholding the principles of justice and equality, scrutinizes economic measures that disproportionately burden vulnerable populations or perpetuate systemic disadvantages. Cases related to taxation, social welfare schemes, and economic policies are subject to constitutional scrutiny to ensure that they align with the overarching principles of the Basic Structure.

The constitutional commitment to social justice, embedded in the Basic Structure, finds expression in cases related to land reforms, agrarian policies, and rural development. Economic injustices in the agrarian sector, such as unequal land distribution or exploitation of agricultural labor, fall within the purview of the judiciary's scrutiny. The doctrine ensures that economic policies are consonant with the constitutional goals of reducing economic disparities and fostering inclusive growth.

Furthermore, the Basic Structure Doctrine intersects with the concept of economic democracy, emphasizing the need for a just and participatory economic order. The judiciary, by safeguarding the principles of justice and liberty, evaluates economic policies to ensure that they align with the democratic ethos of participation and accountability. Cases related to corporate governance, economic regulation, and consumer protection exemplify how the doctrine contributes to shaping an economic order that is not just efficient but also equitable.

The principles of distributive justice, inherent in the Basic Structure, guide the judiciary's approach to economic issues. The doctrine prompts the judiciary to scrutinize policies that might concentrate wealth and resources in the hands of a few, perpetuating economic injustices. Cases related to anti-monopoly laws, economic concentration, and fair competition exemplify how the judiciary, informed by the Basic Structure, ensures that economic power is not wielded in a manner that undermines constitutional values.

The role of the Basic Structure Doctrine in addressing economic injustices also extends to the protection of labor rights. The principles of justice, equality, and dignity inform the judiciary's approach to cases related to workers' rights, fair wages, and workplace conditions. The doctrine ensures that economic activities do not exploit labor or compromise the dignity of workers, aligning economic practices with constitutional imperatives.

Moreover, the Basic Structure's role in economic justice is manifested in cases related to environmental regulations. The doctrine recognizes the interconnectedness of economic activities and environmental well-being. Cases related to industrial pollution, natural resource exploitation, and sustainable development exemplify how the judiciary, guided by the Basic Structure, ensures that economic pursuits do not compromise environmental integrity or infringe on the rights of future generations.

The concept of economic justice also extends to access to essential services such as healthcare, education, and housing. The judiciary, informed by the Basic Structure, evaluates policies and practices that impact these economic dimensions of individuals' lives. Cases related to healthcare infrastructure, educational opportunities, and housing policies exemplify how the doctrine contributes to shaping an economic order that prioritizes the well-being and dignity of all citizens.

The Basic Structure Doctrine's role in addressing economic injustices is intricately linked to the concept of inclusive growth. The judiciary, by upholding the principles of justice and equality, ensures that economic policies are not exclusionary but foster an environment where all segments of society can participate in and benefit from economic activities. Cases related to economic reservations, affirmative action, and social welfare programs illustrate how the doctrine contributes to creating an inclusive economic order.

Furthermore, the Basic Structure's role in economic justice intersects with issues of economic globalization and trade policies. The judiciary, guided by principles of justice and national interest, evaluates the impact of economic agreements and trade policies on the domestic economy. Cases related to trade regulations, foreign investment, and economic treaties exemplify how the doctrine contributes to ensuring that economic interactions align with constitutional values.

In conclusion, the Basic Structure Doctrine's role in addressing economic injustices is a dynamic and multifaceted engagement with constitutional principles. The judiciary, as the guardian of the Basic Structure, ensures that economic policies and practices align with the overarching goals of justice, equality, and the well-being of all citizens. As economic issues evolve in complexity and scope, the Basic Structure Doctrine remains a resilient and adaptive framework that guides the judiciary in fostering an economic order that is not only efficient but also just and inclusive.

4.6 Basic Structure as a Shield Against Populism

The Basic Structure Doctrine, a cornerstone of constitutional interpretation, assumes a pivotal role as a shield against the onslaught of populism within democratic systems. As we navigate the contours of this exploration, it becomes evident that the doctrine, by safeguarding the foundational principles of the Constitution, stands as a bulwark against populist impulses that may pose threats to the rule of law, democratic institutions, and individual rights.

At the heart of this discourse lies an understanding of populism as a political ideology that seeks to appeal to the interests and grievances of the general populace, often by presenting a simplistic and charismatic leader as the champion of the people against an alleged corrupt elite. While populism may find expression in various forms and contexts, the Basic Structure Doctrine, rooted in the principles of justice, liberty, equality, and the rule of law, emerges as a counterforce that restrains the potential excesses of populist movements.

One fundamental dimension of the Basic Structure's role in countering populism lies in its commitment to the rule of law. Populist leaders, buoyed by popular support, may be tempted to bypass established legal norms and constitutional safeguards in pursuit of their political agendas. The judiciary, guided by the Basic Structure, acts as the guardian of the rule of law, ensuring that constitutional principles are upheld even in the face of populist pressures. Cases related to executive overreach, abuse of emergency powers, and attempts to curtail individual rights illustrate how the doctrine acts as a check against the erosion of the rule of law.

Moreover, the Basic Structure serves as a bulwark against the erosion of democratic institutions, which is a common feature of populist movements. Populist leaders may seek to concentrate power in the executive, undermine the independence of the judiciary, or weaken other democratic checks and balances. The doctrine, by emphasizing the separation of powers and the independence of institutions, prompts the judiciary to scrutinize actions that threaten the democratic fabric. Cases related to attacks on the independence of the judiciary, interference with electoral processes, and attempts to stifle dissent showcase how the Basic Structure acts as a guardian of democratic principles.

The principles of justice and equality embedded in the Basic Structure provide a counterpoint to the often exclusionary and divisive nature of populist rhetoric. Populist leaders may exploit societal fault lines, pitting one group against another for political gain. The doctrine, by upholding the ideals of justice and equality, ensures that policies and actions that exacerbate social divisions are subject to constitutional scrutiny. Cases related to discrimination, minority rights, and affirmative action exemplify how the Basic Structure guards against the divisive tendencies of populism.

Furthermore, the Basic Structure serves as a protector of individual rights in the face of populist majoritarianism. Populist leaders, claiming to represent the will of the majority, may seek to curtail the rights of individuals or minority groups. The doctrine, by safeguarding the principles of liberty and individual dignity, ensures that the rights enshrined in the Constitution remain inviolable. Cases related to freedom of speech, religious freedom, and the protection of minority rights illustrate how the Basic Structure acts as a shield for individual liberties.

The commitment to constitutional morality, inherent in the Basic Structure, provides a normative anchor against the erosion of ethical considerations in governance. Populist movements, driven by immediate popular sentiments, may eschew long-term ethical considerations in policy-making. The doctrine prompts the judiciary to evaluate the ethical dimensions of policies and actions, ensuring that constitutional values are not sacrificed at the altar of short-term populism. Cases related to corruption, ethical governance, and adherence to constitutional norms showcase how the Basic Structure upholds the ethical foundations of governance.

Moreover, the Basic Structure's role as a shield against populism extends to economic policies that may prioritize short-term gains over long-term sustainability. Populist leaders, aiming to garner immediate popular support, may adopt economic measures that are politically expedient but economically unsustainable. The doctrine, by emphasizing principles of economic justice and sustainability, ensures that economic policies align with constitutional imperatives. Cases related to economic reservations, environmental regulations, and social welfare programs exemplify how the Basic Structure guards against the economic populism that may undermine long-term stability.

The judiciary's role as the interpreter of the Basic Structure becomes particularly crucial during times of heightened populist fervor. Populist leaders may attempt to undermine the judiciary's independence or challenge its authority in the name of representing the will of the people. The doctrine empowers the judiciary to withstand such challenges and ensures that constitutional principles are not subjugated to populist whims. Cases related to judicial independence, contempt of court, and challenges to constitutional amendments illustrate how the Basic Structure acts as a safeguard for the judiciary in the face of populist pressures.

The Basic Structure's resilience against populism is further evident in its role in protecting the federal structure of the Constitution. Populist movements may seek to centralize power at the national level, diminishing the autonomy of states or regions. The doctrine, by upholding the federal principles embedded in the Constitution, ensures that the distribution of powers between the center and the states remains in consonance with constitutional values. Cases related to federalism, state autonomy, and disputes between center and states showcase how the Basic Structure acts as a check against the centralizing tendencies of populism.

In conclusion, the Basic Structure Doctrine emerges as a formidable shield against the challenges posed by populism to constitutional principles and democratic governance. By upholding the rule of law, democratic institutions, individual rights, ethical considerations, and the federal structure, the doctrine ensures that the populist tide does not erode the foundational principles enshrined in the Constitution. As a beacon of constitutional values, the Basic Structure stands resilient, guiding the judiciary in its role as the guardian of the constitutional order in the face of populist pressures.

4.7 Global Constitutional Trends and Basic Structure

The Basic Structure Doctrine, while rooted in the specific constitutional context of India, resonates within the broader tapestry of global constitutional trends. As we embark on an exploration of the intersection between the Basic Structure and global constitutional developments, it becomes evident that the doctrine transcends its national origins to engage with universal principles that shape constitutionalism across diverse jurisdictions.

At the heart of this discourse lies the universality of constitutional ideals that underpin the Basic Structure. The principles of justice, liberty, equality, and the rule of law, which form the bedrock of the Basic Structure, are not unique to the Indian Constitution. These principles resonate in constitutions worldwide, reflecting a shared commitment to creating governance structures that safeguard human dignity, individual rights, and democratic governance. As global constitutionalism evolves, the Basic Structure becomes a touchstone for engaging with these shared values in diverse constitutional landscapes.

One prominent dimension of the Basic Structure's relevance in a global context lies in its role as a guardian of constitutional democracy. Across different jurisdictions, the challenges to democratic governance manifest in various forms, including executive overreach, erosion of democratic institutions, and populist pressures. The Basic Structure's emphasis on the separation of powers, checks and balances, and democratic principles offers insights for global constitutional trends grappling with similar challenges. The doctrine prompts constitutional scholars and jurists worldwide to reflect on the centrality of preserving democratic values in the face of evolving political landscapes.

Furthermore, the Basic Structure's resonance with global constitutionalism is evident in its approach to protecting fundamental rights. Constitutional frameworks worldwide grapple with ensuring the protection of individual liberties, preventing executive abuses, and fostering inclusivity. The Basic Structure, by prioritizing the safeguarding of fundamental rights, serves as a source of inspiration for constitutional developments beyond India. Comparative constitutional analyses often draw upon the Basic Structure to evaluate how different jurisdictions navigate the delicate balance between individual freedoms and the necessities of governance.

The Basic Structure's engagement with principles of justice aligns with global constitutional trends addressing issues of social justice and equality. As constitutions evolve to respond to contemporary challenges, the quest for creating inclusive societies, addressing historical injustices, and promoting socio-economic rights gains prominence. The Basic Structure, with its emphasis on justice as a foundational principle, offers insights into how constitutional frameworks can grapple with the imperative of ensuring equitable outcomes for all citizens.

Moreover, the Basic Structure's role in constitutional interpretation finds echoes in global constitutional jurisprudence. The interpretive approaches that prioritize the essence of constitutional provisions, protect constitutional values, and ensure the resilience of constitutional principles resonate with judiciaries facing similar interpretive dilemmas worldwide. Comparative constitutional scholars often engage with the Basic Structure to explore how constitutional interpretation can evolve to meet the needs of contemporary constitutional challenges.

The global discourse on constitutional identity and its role in shaping constitutional developments finds resonance with the Basic Structure. As different countries navigate the complexities of multiculturalism, pluralism, and diverse identities, the Basic Structure's emphasis on preserving the core identity of the Constitution becomes a point of reference. Comparative constitutional analyses often explore how constitutional identity, as safeguarded by the Basic Structure, can serve as a guiding principle for harmonizing diverse cultural, religious, and social identities within a constitutional framework.

The Basic Structure's responsiveness to technological advancements aligns with global constitutional trends addressing the challenges posed by the digital age. As technology reshapes the nature of governance, privacy, and individual autonomy, the Basic Structure's principles of justice, liberty, and equality offer insights into how constitutional frameworks can adapt to the demands of the digital era. Comparative constitutional scholars often examine the Basic Structure to draw lessons on how constitutional principles can guide legal responses to the complex issues raised by technological advancements.

Furthermore, the Basic Structure's engagement with environmental concerns aligns with global constitutional trends addressing the imperative of environmental protection. As climate change and ecological sustainability become central issues, constitutions worldwide grapple with incorporating environmental principles into their frameworks. The Basic Structure, by emphasizing the interconnection between constitutional values and environmental well-being, provides a model for how constitutional frameworks can integrate environmental considerations into their core principles.

In the realm of constitutional amendments and transformative constitutionalism, the Basic Structure's role as a check against constitutional overreach finds resonance in global constitutional developments. As countries revisit their constitutional foundations to address historical injustices, promote social justice, and respond to changing societal norms, the Basic Structure offers insights into how transformative constitutional processes can be guided by a commitment to core constitutional values.

The Basic Structure's engagement with federalism aligns with global constitutional trends grappling with questions of decentralization, regional autonomy, and subnational governance. As constitutional frameworks adapt to accommodate diverse regional aspirations, the Basic Structure serves as a reference point for understanding how federal principles can be preserved while addressing the needs of regional diversity.

In conclusion, the Basic Structure Doctrine transcends its national boundaries to engage with and contribute to global constitutional discourse. Its principles of justice, liberty, equality, and the rule of law resonate with constitutional developments worldwide, offering insights and inspiration for jurists, scholars, and policymakers grappling with similar constitutional challenges. As constitutionalism evolves in response to the complexities of the contemporary world, the Basic Structure stands as a beacon, guiding constitutional thinkers in their quest to create governance structures that uphold universal principles and values.

4.8 Essential Features in Plural Societies

In the intricate tapestry of plural societies, the recognition and protection of essential features within constitutional frameworks become imperative to fostering social cohesion, preserving individual freedoms, and upholding the principles of justice and equality. Pluralistic societies, characterized by diverse cultural, religious, linguistic, and ethnic identities, pose unique challenges and opportunities for constitutional designers. As we navigate the nuances of this exploration, it becomes apparent that the identification and safeguarding of essential features within the constitutional fabric are instrumental in ensuring the harmonious coexistence of diverse communities.

One fundamental aspect of constitutional design in plural societies lies in the acknowledgment of cultural and linguistic diversity. The Basic Structure Doctrine, with its emphasis on preserving the core identity of the Constitution, offers insights into how constitutional frameworks can navigate the complexities of multiculturalism. In pluralistic societies, the recognition of diverse cultural identities as essential features becomes a constitutional imperative. The judiciary, guided by the Basic Structure, plays a crucial role in interpreting and applying constitutional provisions to ensure that cultural diversity is not only acknowledged but also celebrated within the constitutional framework.

Moreover, the protection of religious freedom emerges as a paramount essential feature in plural societies. The Basic Structure's commitment to liberty and equality underscores the importance of safeguarding individuals' rights to practice their religions freely. Pluralistic constitutional frameworks often grapple with the challenge of balancing religious freedoms with other constitutional principles. The Basic Structure provides a normative anchor for the judiciary to navigate these complexities, ensuring that the right to religious freedom remains inviolable while also respecting the overarching constitutional values.

The Basic Structure's engagement with the protection of linguistic diversity aligns with the imperatives of constitutional design in plural societies. Recognizing multiple languages as essential features within the constitutional framework becomes crucial to fostering inclusivity and equal representation. The doctrine prompts constitutional scholars and jurists to reflect on how linguistic diversity can be accommodated within the constitutional order, ensuring that linguistic minorities are not marginalized and that linguistic rights are protected as integral components of the constitutional identity.

Furthermore, the Basic Structure's role in protecting minority rights resonates profoundly in pluralistic constitutional contexts. Plural societies are often characterized by numerical majorities and minorities, and the protection of minority rights becomes an essential feature to prevent the tyranny of the majority. The Basic Structure's commitment to justice and equality provides a guiding framework for the judiciary to evaluate policies and practices that may impact minority communities adversely. Cases related to affirmative action, representation of minorities, and protection against discrimination illustrate how the Basic Structure ensures that minority rights are not subjugated to majoritarian pressures.

In the realm of constitutional federalism, the Basic Structure offers insights into how plural societies can accommodate regional aspirations and diverse governance structures. Recognizing the autonomy of subnational units as an essential feature becomes integral to preserving the federal character of the constitution. The doctrine guides the judiciary in adjudicating disputes between center and states, ensuring that federal principles are not compromised in the pursuit of national unity. Cases related to federalism, regional autonomy, and decentralization illustrate how the Basic Structure contributes to creating a constitutional framework that accommodates diverse regional identities.

The protection of individual freedoms, irrespective of cultural or religious affiliations, emerges as a foundational aspect of constitutional design in plural societies. The Basic Structure's commitment to liberty ensures that constitutional rights are not contingent upon adherence to a particular cultural or religious identity. The judiciary, guided by the doctrine, safeguards individual freedoms from encroachments based on cultural or religious considerations. Cases related to freedom of speech, expression, and personal autonomy illustrate how the Basic Structure acts as a bulwark against attempts to curtail individual liberties in the name of preserving cultural or religious norms.

Furthermore, the Basic Structure's role in ensuring social justice aligns with the imperatives of constitutional design in plural societies. Pluralistic contexts often witness historical injustices and social inequalities that need redress. The doctrine's commitment to justice prompts the judiciary to scrutinize policies and practices that perpetuate social disparities. Cases related to reservations, affirmative action, and access to educational and economic opportunities exemplify how the Basic Structure contributes to creating a constitutional framework that addresses historical injustices and fosters social equity.

The Basic Structure's responsiveness to the principles of constitutional morality becomes crucial in plural societies where diverse moral and ethical perspectives coexist. Recognizing constitutional morality as an essential feature ensures that constitutional values prevail over individual or community-specific moral standards. The judiciary, guided by the doctrine, becomes a guardian of constitutional morality, evaluating policies and practices that may infringe upon these shared values. Cases related to ethical governance, moral policing, and the protection of individual choices illustrate how the Basic Structure upholds constitutional morality in the face of diverse ethical considerations.

Moreover, the Basic Structure's role in protecting the rights of indigenous communities aligns with the imperatives of constitutional design in plural societies with distinct indigenous populations. Recognizing the rights of indigenous communities as essential features within the constitutional framework becomes integral to preserving their distinct cultural identities, land rights, and self- governance. The doctrine guides the judiciary in adjudicating disputes related to indigenous rights, ensuring that constitutional protections are extended to these communities.

In conclusion, the recognition and protection of essential features within constitutional frameworks are pivotal to navigating the complexities of plural societies. The Basic Structure Doctrine, with its emphasis on justice, liberty, equality, and the preservation of constitutional identity, provides a resilient framework for constitutional designers and judiciaries in pluralistic contexts. By safeguarding cultural diversity, religious freedom, minority rights, linguistic plurality, and individual liberties, the Basic Structure ensures that constitutional principles resonate with the diverse identities that constitute plural societies. In doing so, the doctrine contributes to the creation of constitutional frameworks that foster social harmony, protect individual freedoms, and uphold the principles of justice and equality within the rich tapestry of diverse communities.

4.9 Citizen Activism and the Basic Structure

Citizen activism, as a potent force in democratic societies, intersects with the foundational principles encapsulated in the Basic Structure Doctrine, serving as a dynamic catalyst for the preservation and enhancement of constitutional values. In our exploration of the symbiotic relationship between citizen activism and the Basic Structure, it becomes apparent that engaged and informed citizenry constitutes a bulwark against potential erosions of democratic norms, the rule of law, and fundamental rights.

At the heart of this discourse lies the recognition that citizen activism acts as a vital check and balance in democratic governance, a concept deeply intertwined with the Basic Structure's emphasis on the separation of powers and the accountability of governmental institutions. In democratic systems, citizens, as active participants and vigilant watchdogs, play a crucial role in holding the government accountable for its actions. The Basic Structure, by upholding democratic principles, aligns with the idea that an informed and active citizenry is essential for the functioning of a robust democracy.

Moreover, citizen activism contributes significantly to upholding the principles of justice within the Basic Structure. Activism often emerges as a response to perceived injustices, inequalities, or violations of rights. The Basic Structure, with its commitment to justice, provides a normative framework through which citizen activism can advocate for legal, policy, or institutional changes that rectify these perceived injustices. Cases related to social justice, human rights, and equal protection exemplify how citizen activism aligns with the Basic Structure's commitment to justice.

Fundamental to the Basic Structure is the protection of individual liberties, and citizen activism becomes a formidable force in defending these liberties from potential encroachments. Activists, by raising awareness, advocating for civil liberties, and challenging government actions that infringe upon individual rights, contribute to the preservation of the Basic Structure's commitment to liberty. Cases related to freedom of speech, privacy, and due process illustrate how citizen activism serves as a guardian against attempts to curtail individual liberties.

Additionally, citizen activism plays a pivotal role in the defense of democracy itself. The Basic Structure Doctrine recognizes democracy as an essential feature, and activism becomes a crucial instrument in safeguarding democratic institutions and processes. Activists often mobilize to protect the integrity of elections, advocate for electoral reforms, and resist attempts to undermine democratic norms. The Basic Structure, by emphasizing democratic principles, aligns with citizen activism's role in preserving the core tenets of democratic governance.

Citizen activism serves as a counterforce against potential executive overreach, a concern central to the Basic Structure's emphasis on the separation of powers and checks and balances. Activists, through legal challenges, public awareness campaigns, and grassroots movements, act as a check on the exercise of arbitrary or excessive executive powers. The judiciary, guided by the Basic Structure, plays a role in adjudicating cases that involve challenges to executive actions, ensuring that the principles of the Constitution are not compromised by unchecked executive authority.

Furthermore, the Basic Structure's commitment to ethical governance finds resonance in the role of citizen activism in exposing and challenging corruption and unethical practices within government institutions. Activists often play a crucial role in uncovering instances of corruption, advocating for transparency, and holding public officials accountable for ethical lapses. The Basic Structure, by emphasizing the importance of constitutional morality, aligns with citizen activism's efforts to promote ethical governance.

Citizen activism also intersects with the Basic Structure in the realm of social and environmental justice. Activists, driven by a commitment to justice and equality, often advocate for policies and practices that address social disparities and environmental concerns. The Basic Structure's principles of justice and its recognition of environmental protection align with the goals of citizen activists striving for a more just and sustainable society. Cases related to environmental conservation, climate justice, and social welfare illustrate how citizen activism contributes to the realization of the Basic Structure's ideals.

Moreover, citizen activism plays a crucial role in influencing legislative processes, contributing to the Basic Structure's commitment to democratic governance. Activists engage in advocacy, lobbying, and public campaigns to shape legislative agendas, influence the passage of laws, and advocate for constitutional reforms. The Basic Structure, by emphasizing democratic participation, aligns with the idea that citizen input is integral to the legislative processes that shape the legal and constitutional landscape.

In the context of constitutional amendments, citizen activism becomes a significant force in influencing public opinion and mobilizing resistance or support for proposed changes. The Basic Structure's role in ensuring that constitutional amendments do not violate the core principles of the Constitution aligns with citizen activism's potential to scrutinize and challenge amendments that may threaten the constitutional order. Cases related to constitutional amendments, particularly those that involve challenges based on the Basic Structure, illustrate how citizen activism contributes to the constitutional discourse surrounding amendments.

Furthermore, the Basic Structure's commitment to federal principles finds resonance in citizen activism's role in advocating for regional autonomy and addressing regional grievances. In diverse and federal societies, activists often mobilize to protect the rights and interests of specific regions, ensuring that federal principles are respected. The Basic Structure, by recognizing the importance of federalism, aligns with citizen activism's efforts to preserve the constitutional balance between the center and the states.

Citizen activism also contributes to the evolution of constitutional jurisprudence, a dimension aligned with the Basic Structure's emphasis on the rule of law and constitutional interpretation. Activists, through strategic litigation and legal advocacy, shape the legal landscape and contribute to the development of constitutional principles. The judiciary, guided by the Basic Structure, plays a role in interpreting constitutional provisions in light of evolving societal values and the legal arguments put forth by activists.

In conclusion, citizen activism emerges as a vibrant force that resonates with and contributes to the principles embedded in the Basic Structure Doctrine. As a dynamic expression of democratic participation, activism becomes an essential component in the realization and preservation of justice, liberty, equality, and the rule of law. In its various forms, citizen activism aligns with the constitutional ideals upheld by the Basic Structure, serving as a vital link between the aspirations of a vigilant citizenry and the foundational principles that shape democratic governance. In this symbiotic relationship, citizen activism and the Basic Structure together form a resilient framework for the protection and advancement of constitutional values in the complex and dynamic landscape of democratic societies.

4.10 Basic Structure and Intergenerational Equity

The nexus between the Basic Structure Doctrine and intergenerational equity unfolds as a critical exploration into the constitutional fabric's responsiveness to the needs and rights of present and future generations. At the heart of this discourse lies the recognition that the Basic Structure, with its commitment to justice, equality, and the rule of law, provides a normative framework for addressing intergenerational concerns, environmental stewardship, and the sustainable allocation of resources. In delving into this intricate relationship, it becomes apparent that the Basic Structure serves as a constitutional anchor for principles that promote the well-being of current and future generations.

One foundational aspect of this connection lies in the Basic Structure's acknowledgment of environmental justice and its role in safeguarding the ecological balance for the benefit of present and future generations. As societies grapple with the impacts of climate change, resource depletion, and environmental degradation, the Basic Structure's principles of justice find resonance in cases and legal arguments that seek to ensure intergenerational equity in the use and conservation of natural resources. The judiciary, guided by the Basic Structure, plays a pivotal role in adjudicating cases related to environmental protection, climate change mitigation, and sustainable development, thereby contributing to the broader framework of intergenerational equity.

Furthermore, the Basic Structure's engagement with social justice aligns with the imperative of addressing intergenerational disparities. The doctrine's commitment to equality prompts constitutional scholars and jurists to reflect on how policies and practices impact different generations, particularly in areas such as education, healthcare, and economic opportunities. Cases related to intergenerational poverty, access to education, and social welfare illustrate how the Basic Structure's principles of justice and equality contribute to shaping constitutional responses that seek to bridge gaps between present and future generations.

The protection of fundamental rights within the Basic Structure becomes a crucial dimension of ensuring intergenerational equity. As technological advancements, scientific progress, and societal changes redefine the scope of individual liberties, the Basic Structure offers a resilient framework for interpreting and expanding constitutional rights in a manner that remains relevant across generations. Cases related to privacy, freedom of expression, and technological innovations illustrate how the judiciary, guided by the Basic Structure, navigates the evolving landscape of rights to ensure their protection for present and future citizens.

Moreover, the Basic Structure's commitment to democratic governance finds resonance in its role in shaping policies and institutions that consider the long-term interests of future generations. The doctrine emphasizes the importance of accountable and transparent governance, which becomes essential in making decisions that impact the well-being of citizens over extended periods. Cases related to democratic processes, institutional reforms, and participatory decision-making exemplify how the Basic Structure contributes to the creation of governance structures that prioritize the interests of both current and future generations.

In the realm of economic justice, the Basic Structure's principles find application in addressing intergenerational concerns related to resource allocation, economic development, and social welfare. The doctrine prompts constitutional scholars and jurists to examine economic policies through the lens of justice and equality, ensuring that economic benefits and opportunities are distributed equitably across generations. Cases related to intergenerational economic disparities, access to economic resources, and equitable development illustrate how the Basic Structure's commitment to economic justice contributes to constitutional responses that transcend temporal boundaries.

Additionally, the Basic Structure's responsiveness to the principles of constitutional morality becomes crucial in navigating ethical considerations that extend beyond the immediate timeframe. As societal norms and ethical standards evolve, the doctrine provides a guiding framework for evaluating policies and practices that have intergenerational implications. Cases related to ethical governance, technological ethics, and bioethical considerations illustrate how the Basic Structure contributes to constitutional responses that uphold moral and ethical standards for the benefit of future generations.

The protection of cultural and educational rights within the Basic Structure aligns with the imperative of preserving and transmitting cultural heritage and knowledge to subsequent generations. The doctrine recognizes the importance of cultural diversity and the role of education in shaping the values and perspectives of future citizens. Cases related to cultural rights, language preservation, and educational access illustrate how the Basic Structure's commitment to these fundamental aspects contributes to intergenerational equity by safeguarding cultural legacies and promoting knowledge dissemination.

Furthermore, the Basic Structure's role in constitutional interpretation becomes pivotal in ensuring that legal principles adapt to the changing needs and challenges faced by future generations. The judiciary, guided by the doctrine, engages in dynamic interpretation that considers the evolving context of constitutional provisions. Cases related to constitutional amendments, evolving technologies, and emerging legal issues illustrate how the Basic Structure facilitates an interpretive framework that accommodates the diverse and complex challenges that future generations may encounter.

In conclusion, the Basic Structure Doctrine emerges as a constitutional lodestar that navigates the intricate landscape of intergenerational equity. Its principles of justice, equality, and the rule of law resonate with the imperatives of addressing the needs and rights of present and future generations. As the doctrine guides constitutional responses to environmental concerns, social justice issues, economic disparities, cultural preservation, and ethical considerations, it becomes evident that the Basic Structure provides a resilient framework for promoting a just and equitable society across temporal boundaries. In this symbiotic relationship, the Basic Structure serves as a constitutional guardian, ensuring that the rights and interests of future generations are accorded due consideration within the evolving tapestry of democratic governance.

4.11 Alternative Dispute Resolution and Constitutional Essentials

The intersection of alternative dispute resolution (ADR) and constitutional essentials unfolds as a multifaceted exploration into the dynamics of justice, fairness, and the rule of law within the constitutional framework. As we delve into this intricate relationship, it becomes apparent that ADR mechanisms, while operating outside traditional courtroom settings, are deeply embedded within the constitutional fabric. The Basic Structure Doctrine, with its commitment to justice, equality, and the rule of law, provides a normative anchor for assessing the role of

ADR in ensuring constitutional principles permeate the resolution of disputes.

One fundamental dimension of this relationship lies in the alignment of ADR with constitutional values of justice and fairness. The Basic Structure underscores the importance of justice as a guiding principle, and ADR mechanisms, by promoting alternative avenues for dispute resolution, seek to provide accessible, timely, and fair outcomes. The judiciary, guided by the Basic Structure, plays a role in validating and upholding ADR processes that adhere to the principles of procedural and substantive justice.

Moreover, the constitutional protection of individual liberties finds resonance in the context of ADR, particularly in cases where privacy and autonomy are central to dispute resolution. The Basic Structure's commitment to liberty ensures that individuals have the freedom to choose ADR processes voluntarily and without coercion. Cases related to confidentiality, privacy, and the voluntariness of arbitration agreements illustrate how the Basic Structure safeguards individual liberties within the realm of alternative dispute resolution.

The Basic Structure's emphasis on equality aligns with the role of ADR in providing a level playing field for disputing parties, irrespective of their socio-economic status or legal acumen. ADR mechanisms, such as mediation and arbitration, strive to create an environment where parties have an equal opportunity to present their cases and negotiate mutually acceptable resolutions. The judiciary, guided by the Basic Structure, assesses the fairness and equality of ADR processes to ensure they do not perpetuate systemic inequalities.

Additionally, the role of ADR in relieving the burden on the formal judicial system aligns with the Basic Structure's commitment to efficient and accessible justice. The doctrine recognizes the importance of expeditious dispute resolution, and ADR mechanisms contribute to the alleviation of court congestion and delays. Cases related to the enforceability of arbitration awards, the efficiency of mediation, and the constitutionality of ADR processes illustrate how the Basic Structure guides the judiciary in promoting timely and effective alternatives to traditional litigation.

The Basic Structure's engagement with the separation of powers finds application in the constitutional assessment of ADR mechanisms, particularly in cases where arbitral tribunals or mediators exercise quasi-judicial functions. The doctrine emphasizes the importance of checks and balances to prevent the concentration of power, and the judiciary, guided by the Basic Structure, evaluates the constitutional validity of delegating dispute resolution functions to non-judicial entities. Cases related to the independence and impartiality of arbitrators exemplify how the Basic Structure contributes to maintaining a constitutional equilibrium in the ADR landscape.

Furthermore, the constitutional recognition of diversity and pluralism aligns with the role of ADR in providing culturally sensitive and context-specific approaches to dispute resolution. ADR mechanisms, such as culturally tailored mediation or conciliation processes, accommodate diverse perspectives and cultural nuances. The Basic Structure, by emphasizing the importance of respecting and preserving diverse identities, contributes to the assessment of ADR processes that recognize and value cultural diversity.

The protection of procedural due process within the Basic Structure becomes integral to evaluating the constitutional validity of ADR mechanisms. The doctrine ensures that individuals have a fair and meaningful opportunity to be heard, and the judiciary, guided by the Basic Structure, scrutinizes ADR processes to ascertain their adherence to due process principles. Cases related to the procedural fairness of arbitration proceedings and mediation confidentiality highlight how the Basic Structure safeguards the constitutional right to a fair hearing.

Moreover, the Basic Structure's commitment to constitutional morality becomes pertinent in evaluating the ethical dimensions of ADR processes. ADR mechanisms, such as ethics codes for mediators or arbitrators, align with the constitutional imperative of maintaining ethical standards in dispute resolution. The judiciary, guided by the Basic Structure, assesses the constitutionality of ethical guidelines within the ADR landscape. Cases related to mediator misconduct, conflicts of interest, and ethical breaches illustrate how the Basic Structure contributes to the ethical integrity of alternative dispute resolution.

The Basic Structure's role in constitutional interpretation finds resonance in cases where ADR agreements contain choice of law clauses or involve issues of constitutional interpretation. The doctrine guides the judiciary in interpreting constitutional provisions or resolving disputes that involve constitutional questions arising from ADR processes. Cases related to the constitutional validity of arbitration agreements, the enforcement of ADR decisions, and conflicts between ADR outcomes and constitutional provisions illustrate how the Basic Structure shapes constitutional jurisprudence in the realm of alternative dispute resolution.

In conclusion, the relationship between alternative dispute resolution and constitutional essentials underscores the nuanced interplay between mechanisms aimed at resolving conflicts outside the traditional courtroom setting and the foundational principles enshrined in the Basic Structure Doctrine. As ADR processes continue to evolve and diversify, the Basic Structure provides a constitutional compass that ensures justice, equality, individual liberties, and procedural fairness are upheld within the alternative dispute resolution landscape. In this symbiotic relationship, ADR mechanisms become integral components in the constitutional pursuit of a fair, efficient, and accessible justice system that adheres to the principles ingrained in the constitutional fabric.

4.12 Role of Legal Education in Understanding Essential Features

The role of legal education in comprehending the essential features of constitutional frameworks marks a pivotal exploration into the nexus between academic pursuits and the foundational principles that underpin the legal landscape. As we delve into this intricate relationship, it becomes apparent that legal education serves as the crucible through which future jurists, advocates, and legal scholars develop an understanding of the constitutional essentials. The Basic Structure Doctrine, with its commitment to justice, liberty, equality, and the rule of law, emerges as a touchstone guiding legal education in unraveling the complexities of constitutional frameworks.

One fundamental aspect of this relationship lies in legal education's role in instilling a deep appreciation for the principles of justice embedded within the Basic Structure. As aspiring legal professionals engage with constitutional texts, landmark judgments, and jurisprudential debates, they are exposed to the imperative of interpreting and applying legal principles in a manner that upholds justice. Legal education, guided by the Basic Structure, becomes a transformative experience that equips students with the tools to critically analyze legal issues through the lens of justice.

Moreover, the commitment to individual liberties within the Basic Structure finds resonance in legal education's emphasis on cultivating an understanding of fundamental rights and freedoms. As students navigate through constitutional provisions, case law, and legal scholarship, they encounter the evolving contours of individual liberties and the nuanced ways in which these rights intersect with societal values. Legal education becomes a conduit for imparting the importance of safeguarding personal freedoms within the constitutional tapestry.

The Basic Structure's commitment to equality becomes a focal point in legal education's endeavor to foster a nuanced understanding of anti-discrimination principles and the pursuit of equal justice under the law. Through the study of constitutional provisions related to equality, landmark judgments addressing discrimination, and critical discussions on social justice, legal education becomes a catalyst for nurturing a commitment to egalitarian ideals. Students learn to analyze legal issues with a sensitivity to the diverse impacts of legal doctrines on different segments of society.

Additionally, legal education plays a pivotal role in shaping future legal practitioners' comprehension of the rule of law within the constitutional context. The Basic Structure, by emphasizing the supremacy of the Constitution and the need for a transparent and accountable legal system, becomes a foundational concept in legal education. As students engage with constitutional interpretation, administrative law, and legal ethics, they develop an appreciation for the rule of law as an essential pillar of democratic governance.

The Basic Structure's engagement with federal principles becomes integral to legal education's exploration of the distribution of powers between the central and state governments. Through the study of federalism, constitutional provisions related to the division of powers, and landmark federalism-related cases, legal education provides students with the analytical tools to navigate the complex interplay between different tiers of government. The Basic Structure serves as a guide in understanding the constitutional balance between federal and state authority.

Furthermore, legal education's role in shaping constitutional interpretation aligns with the Basic Structure's emphasis on evolving jurisprudential philosophies. As students grapple with diverse schools of legal thought, engage with seminal judgments, and participate in legal research, they contribute to the ongoing discourse on constitutional interpretation. Legal education, guided by the Basic Structure, becomes a forum for critical examination and dialogue on the ever-evolving nature of constitutional principles.

The protection of minority rights within the Basic Structure becomes a critical dimension of legal education's commitment to instilling a sense of justice and fairness. As students delve into constitutional provisions related to minority rights, landmark cases addressing the rights of marginalized communities, and discussions on inclusivity, they develop a sensitivity to the need for protecting the rights of all individuals within a diverse society. Legal education becomes a platform for cultivating an awareness of the unique challenges faced by minority groups and the legal mechanisms available to address these challenges.

Moreover, legal education contributes to the ethical foundation of future legal professionals, aligning with the Basic Structure's commitment to constitutional morality. As students engage with legal ethics, professional responsibility, and discussions on the ethical dimensions of legal practice, they internalize the importance of upholding ethical standards within the legal profession. The Basic Structure serves as a guide in navigating ethical dilemmas and promoting a commitment to constitutional values in legal practice.

In the context of constitutional amendments, legal education becomes a crucial arena for examining the implications of changes to the constitutional order. As students study the amendment process, analyze constitutional amendments, and engage in debates on constitutional reform, they contribute to the ongoing dialogue on the constitutional evolution guided by the Basic Structure. Legal education serves as a platform for critically evaluating proposed amendments in light of constitutional principles and ensuring that any changes align with the foundational values enshrined in the Basic Structure.

Furthermore, legal education's role in fostering public interest litigation (PIL) aligns with the Basic Structure's commitment to justice and the protection of constitutional values. As students learn about the history of PIL, engage in clinical legal education programs, and explore avenues for public interest advocacy, they become active participants in the constitutional discourse. Legal education becomes a transformative experience that empowers students to use the law as a tool for social justice, guided by the principles of the Basic Structure.

The Basic Structure's recognition of the dynamic nature of constitutional principles aligns with legal education's emphasis on staying abreast of legal developments and contributing to the ongoing evolution of the law. Through continuous legal research, engagement with contemporary legal issues, and participation in academic and professional forums, legal education becomes a dynamic force in shaping the discourse on constitutional essentials. The Basic Structure serves as a compass guiding legal education in navigating the ever-changing legal landscape.

In conclusion, the role of legal education in understanding essential features reflects a symbiotic relationship between academic pursuits and the foundational principles embedded within the Basic Structure Doctrine. As students engage with constitutional principles, legal doctrines, and the evolving jurisprudential landscape, legal education becomes a transformative journey that equips future legal professionals with the knowledge and ethical grounding necessary to navigate the complexities of constitutional frameworks. The Basic Structure serves as a guiding framework that infuses legal education with a commitment to justice, liberty, equality, and the rule of law, ensuring that the next generation of legal professionals contributes to the preservation and advancement of constitutional values.

Chapter 5

Landmark Cases Shaping The Doctrine

5.1 Introduction to the Landmark Cases

The journey through constitutional jurisprudence in India is an odyssey marked by landmark cases that have indelibly shaped the contours of the Basic Structure Doctrine. These legal sagas, unfolding in the hallowed halls of the judiciary, have not merely interpreted the Constitution but have sculpted its foundational principles, laying the groundwork for a dynamic and resilient constitutional framework. In this chapter, we embark on a narrative exploration of these seminal cases, each a distinct brushstroke on the canvas of Indian constitutionalism.

As we delve into this tapestry of judicial decisions, our compass is Kesavananda Bharati v. State of Kerala (1973), a landmark case often hailed as the "Constitution's Epitome." Here, the judiciary ventured into uncharted waters, enunciating a doctrine that would become the constitutional lodestar-the Basic Structure Doctrine. This monumental decision was a constitutional watershed, setting the stage for a nuanced interplay between the powers of the state and the inviolable core of constitutional principles.

From the crucible of Kesavananda Bharati, we navigate to the turbulent political landscape of the mid-1970s in the case of Indira Gandhi v. Raj Narain (1975). Here, the judiciary grappled with the delicate balance between the authority of the executive and the sacrosanct principles embedded in the Basic Structure. The case not only tested the resilience of the doctrine but also underscored its indispensable role in preserving the democratic ethos of the nation.

Our journey continues to the labyrinthine corridors of constitutional amendments in Minerva Mills Ltd. v. Union of India (1980). In this legal saga, the court confronted the challenge of ensuring that the constitutional framework remained impervious to transitory political whims. The verdict stands as a testament to the judiciary's commitment to upholding the sanctity of the Basic Structure even in the face of legislative endeavors to alter the constitutional landscape.

Waman Rao v. Union of India (1981) beckons us next, offering a nuanced examination of the delicate dance between the judiciary and the political establishment. Here, the judiciary asserted its role as the sentinel of the Basic Structure, emphasizing the need for an independent and assertive judiciary to safeguard constitutional principles from encroachments.

The canvas widens to encompass the federal dimensions of the Indian polity in SR Bommai v. Union of India (1994). This case, a constitutional landmark in federalism, scrutinized the delicate balance between the powers of the center and the states. The Basic Structure, once again, emerged as the touchstone for ensuring a harmonious federal structure, emphasizing the decentralized yet interwoven nature of Indian governance.

Our journey through the annals of constitutional jurisprudence encounters L. Chandra Kumar v. Union of India (1997), a case that resonates with the echoes of judicial independence. In this legal odyssey, the judiciary affirmed its constitutional stature as a co-equal branch of government. The Basic Structure, as elucidated in Kesavananda Bharati, stood sentinel over the judiciary, ensuring an unassailable bastion against attempts to compromise its independence.

The narrative thread now leads us to I.R. Coelho v. State of Tamil Nadu (2007), a case that grappled with the intricate dance between parliamentary sovereignty and the immutable principles of the Basic Structure. Here, the court rendered a verdict that echoed the constitutional symphony, harmonizing the need for legislative authority with the imperative of preserving the foundational principles of the Constitution.

The judicial expedition takes a leap into the 21st century with the pivotal case of Justice K.S. Puttaswamy (Retd.) v. Union of India (2017). This case, etched in the constitutional saga, addressed the contours of privacy as a fundamental right-a dimension hitherto unexplored. The court's recognition of the right to privacy as an integral part of the Basic Structure underscores the adaptability of constitutional principles to the evolving societal ethos.

The canvas is not static; it pulsates with the rhythm of contemporary legal challenges and developments. The legal voyages post-2017 have seen the Basic Structure Doctrine navigating the uncharted waters of technological advancements, social dynamics, and evolving conceptions of justice. These recent cases serve as testament to the enduring relevance and adaptability of the Basic Structure Doctrine in the face of the ever-changing tapestry of constitutional challenges.

As we traverse this jurisprudential landscape, we engage in a comparative analysis, drawing parallels with global perspectives on constitutional principles. The interplay of constitutional doctrines across jurisdictions enriches our understanding of the Basic Structure, transcending the confines of national boundaries.

The journey would be incomplete without navigating the intricate currents of scholarly critiques and debates surrounding the Basic Structure Doctrine. The intellectual discourse, sometimes a tempest of conflicting viewpoints, adds layers of complexity to our understanding. We delve into these debates with a discerning eye, exploring alternative perspectives and challenges that have shaped-and continue to shape-the trajectory of the doctrine.

In this narrative, there are no subheadings, for the chapters of constitutional jurisprudence are not isolated islands but interconnected threads weaving a rich tapestry. The Basic Structure Doctrine, the guiding constellation, illuminates our path through these legal narratives, anchoring us in the foundational principles of justice, liberty, equality, and the rule of law.

This chapter is not a mere chronicle of legal decisions; it is an exploration of the constitutional soul of India, imprinted with the jurisprudential footprints of judges who, through their verdicts, have become custodians of the constitutional flame. It is an odyssey that invites contemplation on the interplay between the written text of the Constitution and the living, breathing principles it enshrines—an exploration of the constitutional spirit that transcends the parchment barriers of legal texts.

5.2 Kesavananda Bharati v. State of Kerala (1973)

Kesavananda Bharati v. State of Kerala (1973) unfolded as a constitutional epic, but its impact radiated far beyond the courtroom, shaping the very fabric of India's constitutional journey. As we delve deeper into the layers of this landmark case, we find ourselves not merely traversing legal nuances but exploring the profound implications that reverberate through the corridors of history, politics, and societal transformation.

To comprehend the full spectrum of Kesavananda Bharati's influence, we must contextualize the case within the sociopolitical milieu of its time. The early 1970s marked a period of political ferment, with the government of the day contemplating transformative constitutional amendments. Against this backdrop, Kesavananda Bharati emerged as a sentinel, challenging the constitutional validity of these amendments and, in doing so, invoking a constitutional debate that would define an era.

Nani Palkhivala's advocacy during the proceedings was not merely legal rhetoric; it was a clarion call for the protection of constitutional principles that transcend transient political considerations. Palkhivala's argumentation, steeped in constitutional philosophy, underscored the notion that while Parliament possessed the authority to amend the Constitution, this authority was circumscribed by an uncodified but inherent set of principles-the Basic Structure Doctrine.

Chief Justice Sikri and the bench, in their seminal judgment, embarked on a delicate balancing act. The recognition of the Basic Structure Doctrine represented a paradigm shift in constitutional interpretation-a departure from earlier jurisprudence and a watershed moment in affirming the supremacy of constitutional principles. This recognition, however, was not without its complexities, as the court grappled with the challenge of defining the contours of the Basic Structure without unduly restricting parliamentary sovereignty.

The Basic Structure Doctrine, as articulated in Kesavananda Bharati, became the constitutional bedrock upon which subsequent legal challenges would be adjudicated. It was an acknowledgment that while constitutional flexibility was imperative, there existed an immutable core that safeguarded the essence of the Constitution. This judicial assertion ushered in an era where the judiciary assumed the role of a constitutional guardian, entrusted with the task of ensuring that the spirit of the Constitution remained inviolate.

Kesavananda Bharati, beyond its legal pronouncements, resonated as a philosophical inquiry into the nature of the Indian Constitution. The case explored the delicate interplay between the written text of the Constitution and the unwritten principles that underpin its foundation. This exploration, in turn, prompted a broader societal reflection on the ideals that animate the nation's supreme law.

The judgment's transformative impact on Indian democracy cannot be overstated. It marked a pivot from a purely positivist understanding of constitutional law to a more holistic approach that recognized the Constitution as a living document, capable of evolving without losing its core identity. The Basic Structure Doctrine, emerging from this case, instilled a sense of permanence and continuity in the constitutional order, even as the nation underwent political, social, and economic transformations.

The legacy of Kesavananda Bharati extends to the role of the judiciary as a check on the excesses of the executive and legislative branches. By asserting the authority to review constitutional amendments, the judiciary positioned itself as a constitutional bulwark, ensuring that the principles embedded in the Basic Structure were not subverted for momentary political gains. This role, while crucial for maintaining the delicate balance of powers, also raised questions about the appropriate scope of judicial intervention in matters of constitutional amendments.

As we delve into the societal impact of Kesavananda Bharati, we witness its profound influence on the collective consciousness. The case sparked a constitutional awakening, prompting citizens to engage with the foundational principles of their governance. The notion that the Constitution encapsulated enduring values that could withstand the transient dynamics of politics became ingrained in public discourse, fostering a sense of constitutionalism that transcended partisan affiliations.

Moreover, the judgment sparked a renewed interest in constitutional education and awareness. The public discourse around Kesavananda Bharati facilitated a broader understanding of constitutional principles among the citizenry. It became a touchstone for civic engagement, encouraging individuals to actively participate in discussions about the direction of their constitutional democracy.

The case's impact also reverberated through the corridors of political power. Kesavananda Bharati acted as a constraint on arbitrary and unilateral exercises of power by the legislative and executive branches. Political actors, cognizant of the judiciary's role as the guardian of the Basic Structure, were compelled to navigate the constitutional landscape with a heightened awareness of its enduring principles.

Kesavananda Bharati, in its aftermath, became a reference point for future constitutional challenges. Subsequent judgments, while affirming the Basic Structure Doctrine, also grappled with its scope and limitations. The case, therefore, set in motion a continual process of judicial interpretation and refinement-a process that remains ongoing as the nation confronts new constitutional challenges.

The societal impact of Kesavananda Bharati also intersects with questions of democratic governance and political legitimacy. The case raised fundamental questions about the relationship between the judiciary and elected representatives. While the judgment affirmed the judiciary's authority to review constitutional amendments, it also prompted debates about the appropriate boundaries of judicial review in a democratic polity.

In the context of federalism, Kesavananda Bharati assumed a pivotal role in defining the delicate balance between the powers of the center and the states. The recognition of federal principles as part of the Basic Structure underscored the importance of a harmonious federal structure in the Indian constitutional order. The case, therefore, became a touchstone for adjudicating disputes between different tiers of government.

The enduring impact of Kesavananda Bharati is not confined to its immediate aftermath; it continues to shape the nation's constitutional discourse in the 21st century. The case, often cited and debated, remains a lodestar for understanding the delicate interplay between constitutional principles and political exigencies. Its legacy is not static; it evolves with each judicial pronouncement and constitutional development, influencing the trajectory of Indian democracy.

In conclusion, Kesavananda Bharati v. State of Kerala (1973) is a constitutional saga that transcends its legal dimensions. It is a narrative that intertwines with the evolving dynamics of Indian democracy, leaving an indelible mark on the nation's constitutional consciousness. The case is not a frozen moment in time; it is a living testament to the resilience of constitutional principles in the face of political challenges. As we navigate the intricate tapestry woven by Kesavananda Bharati, we find ourselves in a continual dialogue with the constitutional spirit-a dialogue that shapes the destiny of a democratic republic.

5.3 Indira Gandhi v. Raj Narain (1975)

In the political landscape of 1971, India witnessed a defining moment in the form of the general elections. Prime Minister Indira Gandhi's resounding victory initially seemed to consolidate her political dominance. However, beneath the surface of this electoral triumph, a legal and constitutional drama unfolded, fundamentally altering the dimensions of executive accountability, judicial review, and the core tenets of democratic governance.

The genesis of what would become the Indira Gandhi v. Raj Narain case lay in the electoral contest between Prime Minister Indira Gandhi and her opponent Raj Narain in the Rae Bareli constituency. What began as a routine electoral process swiftly transformed into a legal odyssey as

Narain filed an election petition alleging electoral malpractices. The ensuing legal battle went beyond the scope of an ordinary electoral dispute, evolving into a constitutional conundrum that would scrutinize the bedrock of India's democratic framework.

At its heart, this case posed profound questions about the rule of law and equality before it. Led by Chief Justice A.N. Ray, the judiciary found itself at the intricate crossroads of legal principles and the practicalities of political reality. The case necessitated a nuanced exploration of the boundaries of executive privilege and the extent of judicial review, especially in matters of heightened political significance.

One of the pivotal aspects of the judgment was the reaffirmation of the principle that no individual, regardless of their position, stands above the law. The court's ruling underscored the sacrosanct nature of equality before the law, emphasizing that even the Prime Minister could not evade legal scrutiny when facing allegations of electoral malpractices. This pronouncement resonated as a resolute assertion of democratic ideals, challenging any notion of executive immunity from legal accountability.

As the legal saga unfolded, it became evident that the case was not merely about electoral malpractices. It represented a constitutional moment that would define the trajectory of India's democratic governance. The judgment set a precedent for the sanctity of the electoral process, laying the groundwork for evolving jurisprudence on elections and political accountability.

The aftermath of the judgment witnessed an unprecedented chapter in India's democratic history-the declaration of a state of emergency by Indira Gandhi in 1975. This period of heightened executive authority posed severe challenges to constitutional governance, leading to curtailed civil liberties. Subsequent legal challenges during the emergency further tested the judiciary's commitment to upholding constitutional principles, with the courts eventually reiterating the supremacy of the Constitution even during times of crisis.

The enduring impact of Indira Gandhi v. Raj Narain goes beyond its legal pronouncements. It is a narrative that intertwines with the evolving dynamics of Indian democracy, leaving an indelible mark on the nation's constitutional consciousness. The case is not a frozen moment in time; it is a living testament to the resilience of constitutional principles in the face of political challenges.

The case also delved into the delicate interplay between the three branches of government, particularly the limits of executive privilege and the scope of judicial review. While recognizing the importance of executive authority, the court asserted that such authority was not absolute and subject to legal scrutiny. This nuanced exploration of the separation of powers defined the parameters within which the judiciary could intervene in matters of high political significance.

As the legal saga unfolded, it became clear that the case was not merely about electoral malpractices; it was a constitutional moment that would define the trajectory of India's democratic governance. The judgment set a precedent for the sanctity of the electoral process, laying the groundwork for evolving jurisprudence on elections and political accountability.

The aftermath of the judgment witnessed an unprecedented chapter in India's democratic history-the declaration of a state of emergency by Indira Gandhi in 1975. This period of heightened executive authority posed severe challenges to constitutional governance, leading to curtailed civil liberties. Subsequent legal challenges during the emergency further tested the judiciary's commitment to upholding constitutional principles, with the courts eventually reiterating the supremacy of the Constitution even during times of crisis.

The enduring impact of Indira Gandhi v. Raj Narain goes beyond its legal pronouncements. It is a narrative that intertwines with the evolving dynamics of Indian democracy, leaving an indelible mark on the nation's constitutional consciousness. The case is not a frozen moment in time; it is a living testament to the resilience of constitutional principles in the face of political challenges.

In conclusion, Indira Gandhi v. Raj Narain (1975) is a constitutional saga that transcends its legal dimensions. It is a narrative that intertwines with the evolving dynamics of Indian democracy, leaving an indelible mark on the nation's constitutional consciousness. The case is not a frozen moment in time; it is a living testament to the resilience of constitutional principles in the face of political challenges. As we navigate the intricate tapestry woven by Indira Gandhi v. Raj Narain, we find ourselves in a continual dialogue with the constitutional spirit-a dialogue that shapes the destiny of a democratic republic.

5.4 Minerva Mills Ltd. v. Union of India (1980)

In the annals of Indian constitutional jurisprudence, Minerva Mills Ltd. v. Union of India (1980) stands as a landmark case that traversed the intricate terrain of fundamental rights, judicial review, and the delicate balance between the legislature and the judiciary. This legal saga unfolded against the backdrop of constitutional amendments and power struggles, ultimately leaving an indelible mark on the constitutional fabric of the country.

The genesis of the Minerva Mills case lies in the socio-political climate of the late 1970s. India was navigating a period marked by political turbulence and constitutional challenges. The case emanated from the aftermath of the notorious 42nd Amendment to the Constitution, a sweeping legislative act that sought to alter the constitutional landscape significantly. Among its many provisions, the amendment aimed to nullify the impact of certain judicial decisions that had interpreted the scope of the legislative power to amend the Constitution.

At the heart of the legal dispute was the interpretation of Article 31C, which had been introduced through the 42nd Amendment. This article sought to immunize certain laws from judicial review on the ground that they were enacted to give effect to the Directive Principles of State Policy contained in Article 39(b) and (c). Minerva Mills Ltd., a private company, challenged the constitutional validity of Article 31C, contending that it violated the basic structure of the Constitution, a concept propounded by the judiciary itself.

The case reached the Supreme Court, and a Constitution Bench was constituted to deliberate on the constitutional validity of Article 31C. This legal battle involved not only intricate questions of constitutional law but also delved into the foundational principles that underpin the Indian Constitution.

The Supreme Court, in its landmark judgment, struck down significant parts of the 42nd Amendment, including the controversial Article 31C. The court, through a meticulous analysis, held that Article 31C violated the basic structure of the Constitution. The judgment affirmed the judiciary's role as the guardian of the Constitution's basic features and reinforced the principle that no constitutional amendment could transgress those features.

The Minerva Mills case holds particular significance in shaping the contours of judicial review in India. It underscored the judiciary's authority to review and strike down constitutional amendments that threaten the basic structure. This assertion marked a crucial check on the powers of the legislature and reinforced the idea that no organ of the state is beyond the purview of constitutional scrutiny.

Beyond its legal implications, the Minerva Mills case had far-reaching consequences for the separation of powers and the delicate equilibrium between the legislative and judicial branches. It reaffirmed the principle that the judiciary has the authority to determine the constitutional validity of legislative actions, even those involving amendments to the Constitution. This aspect of the judgment has resonated in subsequent cases, shaping the jurisprudence on the limits of constitutional amendments.

Furthermore, the Minerva Mills judgment had an impact on the trajectory of the Directive Principles of State Policy (DPSP) in Indian constitutional law. By striking down the overreaching provisions of Article 31C, the court reiterated the significance of a harmonious interpretation between fundamental rights and directive principles. It emphasized that the DPSP cannot be used as a carte blanche to undermine fundamental rights and that any attempt to do so would be subject to judicial scrutiny.

The case also contributed to the evolution of the basic structure doctrine, which had been articulated in the famous Kesavananda Bharati case (1973). The Minerva Mills judgment reinforced the idea that the basic structure is not a static concept but a dynamic and evolving one. The judiciary, through this case, demonstrated its commitment to adapting constitutional principles to the changing needs of society while ensuring the preservation of the core values enshrined in the Constitution.

Moreover, the Minerva Mills case is emblematic of the Indian judiciary's commitment to upholding constitutional values even in challenging times. The period during which the case was decided was marked by political events that tested the resilience of democratic institutions. The judgment showcased the judiciary's independence and its willingness to act as a bulwark against potential erosions of constitutional principles.

In conclusion, Minerva Mills Ltd. v. Union of India (1980) is not just a legal pronouncement; it is a constitutional narrative that echoes through the corridors of Indian democracy. The case, with its profound implications for judicial review, the basic structure doctrine, and the separation of powers, has left an enduring imprint on the constitutional jurisprudence of the nation. It serves as a reminder that, in the constitutional framework, each branch of government has a defined role, and no constitutional amendment can transgress the inviolable limits set by the basic structure. The Minerva Mills judgment is a testament to the judiciary's role as the guardian of the Constitution, ensuring that its principles endure, evolve, and thrive in the service of justice and democratic governance.

5.5 Waman Rao v. Union of India (1981)

In the vast expanse of India's constitutional jurisprudence, Waman Rao v. Union of India (1981) occupies a pivotal position, resonating with constitutional principles and legal doctrines that have enduring implications. The case unfolded against the backdrop of a complex interplay between legislative powers, judicial review, and the delicate balance between federal and state authority. As the legal saga of Waman Rao unfolded, it traversed the intricacies of the Tenth Schedule, commonly known as the "Anti-Defection Law," and left an indelible mark on the constitutional landscape.

The genesis of the Waman Rao case can be traced to the political dynamics of the early 1980s. The Tenth Schedule had been introduced through the 52nd Amendment to the Constitution in 1985, seeking to curb the malaise of political defections that plagued the Indian political system. This amendment was a response to the perceived instability caused by elected representatives switching allegiances for personal or political gain. While the intent behind the Anti-Defection Law was to fortify the democratic process, its implementation and interpretation posed intricate constitutional challenges.

Waman Rao, a Member of the Legislative Assembly (MLA) from the state of Maharashtra, found himself entangled in the legal intricacies of the Anti-Defection Law. He had been disqualified under the Tenth Schedule by the Speaker of the Maharashtra Legislative Assembly for his alleged act of defection. Dissatisfied with this decision, Waman Rao approached the judiciary, challenging the constitutional validity of the Anti-Defection Law and the Speaker's authority to adjudicate on disqualification matters.

The case reached the Supreme Court of India, which constituted a larger bench to deliberate on the constitutional questions raised by Waman Rao. At its core, the case required the court to navigate the fine line between upholding the integrity of the democratic process and safeguarding the rights of elected representatives.

The Supreme Court, in its considered judgment, embarked on a comprehensive analysis of the constitutional dimensions of the Anti-Defection Law. The court recognized the importance of curbing defections to ensure stable governance but also emphasized the need to balance this objective with the constitutional rights of elected representatives.

One of the central issues addressed by the court was the role of the Speaker in adjudicating on disqualification matters. The judgment underscored the quasi-judicial nature of the Speaker's functions under the Tenth Schedule and emphasized the importance of ensuring a fair and impartial process. The court held that decisions of the Speaker could be subject to judicial review, providing a crucial check on potential misuse or arbitrary exercise of power.

Furthermore, the Waman Rao judgment delved into the scope and application of the Anti-Defection Law. The court clarified that the law applied not only to individual members but also to political parties, preventing wholesale defections that could undermine the stability of elected governments. The court's interpretation sought to strike a balance between preserving the individual's right to dissent and preventing actions that could subvert the democratic mandate.

The case also addressed the constitutional validity of certain provisions of the Anti- Defection Law. The court upheld the law's general constitutionality while striking down specific provisions that were deemed excessive or arbitrary. This nuanced approach reflected the judiciary's commitment to preserving the constitutional balance and ensuring that legislative measures align with the fundamental principles enshrined in the Constitution.

The Waman Rao judgment, while affirming the constitutionality of the Anti-Defection Law, established crucial precedents for the interpretation and application of the Tenth Schedule. The court's emphasis on the quasi-judicial nature of the Speaker's role and the availability of judicial review ensured that the law's implementation would be subject to checks and balances, safeguarding the rights of elected representatives.

Beyond its immediate implications, the Waman Rao case contributed to the broader discourse on constitutionalism and the separation of powers. The court's meticulous analysis underscored the judiciary's role as the guardian of constitutional values, ensuring that legislative measures, even those aimed at preserving the democratic process, adhere to the overarching principles of justice, fairness, and individual rights.

Moreover, the Waman Rao case reflected the judiciary's commitment to evolving constitutional principles in response to the dynamic challenges faced by the Indian polity. The court's interpretation of the Anti-Defection Law acknowledged the need for flexibility in governance while reinforcing the constitutional ethos that underlies India's democratic framework.

In conclusion, Waman Rao v. Union of India (1981) is not merely a legal precedent; it is a constitutional narrative that unfolds within the tapestry of India's democratic journey. The case, through its nuanced examination of the Anti-Defection Law, reaffirms the judiciary's role as a sentinel of constitutional values. It stands as a testament to the delicate equilibrium that must be maintained between legislative powers, individual rights, and the imperative of stable governance. As the echoes of Waman Rao reverberate through the corridors of constitutional law, they serve as a reminder of the enduring commitment to justice, fairness, and the foundational principles that shape India's constitutional identity.

5.6 SR Bommai v. Union of India (1994)

The case of S.R. Bommai v. Union of India (1994) stands as a watershed moment in the constitutional history of India, marked by its profound impact on the principles of federalism, secularism, and the powers vested in the political executive. This legal saga unfolded against the backdrop of political turmoil, with the dismissal of state governments and the imposition of President's Rule becoming a recurring phenomenon. The judgment not only clarified the contours of the powers vested in the President and the Governor but also reinforced the principles that safeguard the federal structure of the Indian Constitution.

The genesis of the S.R. Bommai case can be traced to the political landscape of the late 1980s and early 1990s. This period was characterized by coalition politics and shifting alliances, leading to frequent changes in state governments. Amidst this political flux, questions arose about the constitutional validity of the dismissal of state governments by the Union government and the subsequent imposition of President's Rule under Article 356 of the Constitution.

S.R. Bommai, the then Chief Minister of Karnataka, found himself at the center of this constitutional conundrum when his government was dismissed in 1989, leading to the imposition of President's Rule in the state. Dissatisfied with the manner in which his government was ousted, Bommai challenged the dismissal, triggering a legal battle that would resonate far beyond the political contours of Karnataka.

The case reached the Supreme Court, and a Constitution Bench was constituted to address the constitutional questions at hand. The central issue before the court was the extent of the President's powers under Article 356 and the justiciability of the Proclamation of President's Rule. The court was tasked with determining whether the President's satisfaction, as mentioned in Article 356, was immune from judicial review.

In its landmark judgment, the Supreme Court articulated a set of principles that would guide the application of Article 356 and delineate the boundaries of executive action in the realm of state governments. The court, through a comprehensive analysis, clarified that the President's satisfaction, as mentioned in Article 356, was not beyond judicial review. It held that the court could scrutinize whether the material relied upon by the President was relevant and whether it objectively justified the imposition of President's Rule.

Furthermore, the court laid down the doctrine of "floor test" as a constitutional safeguard against arbitrary dismissals of state governments. It held that if a Chief Minister lost the majority in the legislative assembly, the proper course of action was to prove the majority on the floor of the house rather than resorting to the drastic measure of imposing President's Rule.

The judgment also addressed the role of the Governor in recommending the imposition of President's Rule. The court emphasized that the Governor's report was not immune from judicial review and that the court could examine whether the material relied upon by the Governor was relevant and whether it justified the imposition of central rule.

One of the significant contributions of the S.R. Bommai case was its elucidation on the concept of secularism in the Indian context. The court held that a government could not be dismissed solely on the grounds of a party or parties espousing a particular ideology. It reinforced the constitutional mandate of secularism and underscored that the dismissal of a state government must be based on valid grounds related to its failure to adhere to the constitutional framework.

Beyond its immediate implications for the powers of the President and the Governor, the S.R. Bommai judgment had far-reaching consequences for the federal structure of the Indian Constitution. The court's delineation of principles sought to prevent the arbitrary use of Article 356, ensuring that the constitutional fabric of federalism remained intact. The judgment served as a crucial check on potential misuse of executive authority, reinforcing the delicate balance between the Union and the states.

The S.R. Bommai case also contributed to the evolution of constitutional principles surrounding the dismissal of state governments. It set a precedent for a more nuanced and judicious approach, emphasizing the importance of preserving the democratic mandate and ensuring that constitutional norms were adhered to in matters related to the dismissal of elected governments.

Moreover, the judgment underscored the pivotal role of the judiciary in upholding constitutional values. It established that the court could act as a bulwark against executive excesses, ensuring that the principles of federalism, secularism, and democratic governance were not undermined.

In conclusion, S.R. Bommai v. Union of India (1994) is not merely a legal decision; it is a constitutional pronouncement that echoes through the corridors of India's federal structure. The case, with its profound impact on the principles of federalism, secularism, and executive authority, remains a beacon in the constitutional jurisprudence of the nation. As the echoes of S.R. Bommai reverberate in discussions on federal relations, the judgment stands as a testament to the resilience of constitutional values and the enduring commitment to preserving the delicate balance between the Union and the states.

5.7 L. Chandra Kumar v. Union of India (1997)

L. Chandra Kumar v. Union of India (1997) represents a significant chapter in the constitutional history of India, delving into the complex interplay between the judiciary and the executive, particularly in the realm of administrative tribunals. The case unfolded against the backdrop of a changing administrative landscape, with the establishment of tribunals tasked with adjudicating disputes across various sectors. The judgment not only addressed the constitutional validity of these tribunals but also delved into the broader principles of separation of powers and the independence of the judiciary.

The genesis of the L. Chandra Kumar case can be traced to the increasing reliance on administrative tribunals as specialized forums for the resolution of disputes. The Administrative Tribunals Act, 1985, was enacted to provide for the establishment of tribunals for the adjudication of disputes related to the recruitment and conditions of service of persons appointed to public services. However, concerns were raised regarding the constitutional validity of certain provisions of the Act, particularly those impinging on the jurisdiction of the High Courts under Article 226 of the Constitution.

L. Chandra Kumar, a judicial officer, challenged the constitutional validity of the provisions that ousted the jurisdiction of High Courts in matters falling under the jurisdiction of administrative tribunals. The case reached the Supreme Court, and the constitutional questions it raised necessitated a nuanced examination of the delicate balance between administrative expediency and constitutional imperatives.

In its seminal judgment, the Supreme Court undertook a comprehensive analysis of the constitutional scheme, focusing on the principles of separation of powers and the independence of the judiciary. The central issue revolved around whether Parliament had the authority to exclude the jurisdiction of High Courts in matters falling within the purview of administrative tribunals.

The court, in its wisdom, recognized the importance of administrative tribunals as specialized forums equipped to deal with technical and complex issues. However, it also underscored the significance of preserving the constitutional role of the High Courts as the ultimate guardians of fundamental rights. The judgment struck a delicate balance, holding that while Parliament had the authority to create administrative tribunals, it could not completely exclude the jurisdiction of High Courts.

Crucially, the court affirmed that the power of judicial review, including the power of the High Courts under Article 226, was an integral and essential part of the basic structure of the Constitution. Any attempt to curtail or exclude this power would be subject to constitutional scrutiny. The judgment reinforced the principle that the right to constitutional remedies, including the writ jurisdiction of the High Courts, was a sacrosanct aspect of the constitutional framework.

Furthermore, the L. Chandra Kumar case delved into the question of the independence of administrative tribunals. The court emphasized that for tribunals to be effective and credible, they must be insulated from executive interference. The judgment held that the appointment process of members to tribunals, particularly those with a judicial background, must ensure their independence and security of tenure.

The court's reasoning in L. Chandra Kumar marked a departure from earlier decisions that upheld the absolute exclusion of the jurisdiction of the High Courts in matters within the domain of administrative tribunals. The judgment represented a nuanced understanding of the constitutional principles at stake, recognizing the need for specialized forums while affirming the supremacy of the High Courts in the constitutional framework.

Beyond its immediate implications for administrative tribunals, the L. Chandra Kumar case contributed to the broader discourse on constitutional law. It underscored the judiciary's role as the guardian of the Constitution, ensuring that attempts to alter or dilute its jurisdiction were subject to constitutional scrutiny. The judgment reinforced the foundational principles of the Constitution and asserted that no legislative measure could undermine the basic structure or the essential features of the legal and constitutional framework.

Moreover, L. Chandra Kumar set a precedent for the jurisprudence on administrative law and the functioning of tribunals in India. The court's insistence on the independence of tribunals and the preservation of the writ jurisdiction of the High Courts had a lasting impact on the evolution of the administrative justice system in the country.

In conclusion, L. Chandra Kumar v. Union of India (1997) is more than a legal decision; it is a constitutional pronouncement that delineates the contours of judicial authority, administrative justice, and the delicate balance between the branches of government. The judgment, with its meticulous analysis and principled reasoning, stands as a testament to the resilience of constitutional values and the unwavering commitment to upholding the rule of law in India.

5.8 I.R. Coelho v. State of Tamil Nadu (2007)

I.R. Coelho v. State of Tamil Nadu (2007) is a landmark judgment that etches itself into the constitutional canvas of India, unraveling the intricacies of the Ninth Schedule and its impact on the judicial review of laws. The case unfolded against the backdrop of legal challenges to land reform laws and sought to scrutinize the extent to which laws placed in the Ninth Schedule could be shielded from judicial review. The judgment not only redefined the contours of the basic structure doctrine but also reaffirmed the supremacy of the Constitution as the ultimate touchstone for evaluating the validity of laws.

The genesis of the I.R. Coelho case can be traced to the agrarian reforms initiated by the State of Tamil Nadu through the Tamil Nadu Backward Classes, Scheduled Castes, and Scheduled Tribes (Reservation of Seats in Educational Institutions and of Appointments or Posts in the Services under the State) Act, 1993. The legislation aimed at providing reservation benefits to backward classes and certain other categories in educational institutions and public services. Challenging the constitutionality of this law, I.R. Coelho contended that it violated the principles laid down by the Supreme Court in earlier decisions.

The pivotal issue before the court was the validity of laws placed in the Ninth Schedule of the Constitution. The Ninth Schedule had been introduced by the First Amendment in 1951 to protect land reform laws and other social welfare legislations from judicial review. Over the years, the scope of the Ninth Schedule expanded, encompassing a wide array of laws.

The I.R. Coelho case was heard by a nine-judge bench of the Supreme Court, reflecting the magnitude of the constitutional questions at stake. The central question revolved around whether laws placed in the Ninth Schedule were immune from judicial review and whether the doctrine of basic structure could be applied to test their constitutionality.

In its comprehensive judgment, the Supreme Court engaged in a thorough analysis of the constitutional framework and the evolution of the basic structure doctrine. The court, in a historic pronouncement, held that laws placed in the Ninth Schedule were not immune from judicial review if they violated or destroyed the basic structure of the Constitution. This marked a significant departure from earlier decisions that afforded absolute protection to laws in the Ninth Schedule.

The court outlined that the basic structure doctrine, articulated in the landmark Kesavananda Bharati case, was an essential feature of the Constitution. The basic structure comprised the core values and principles that formed the bedrock of India's constitutional identity. Any law, irrespective of its inclusion in the Ninth Schedule, would be subject to judicial review if it transgressed these foundational principles.

The judgment recognized that while Parliament had the power to amend the Constitution, this power was not absolute. The court asserted its authority to review constitutional amendments and struck down the notion that laws placed in the Ninth Schedule could be shielded from scrutiny. The ruling reiterated the supremacy of the Constitution and affirmed the judiciary's role as the guardian of its essential features.

Furthermore, I.R. Coelho clarified that the scope of the basic structure was not static but dynamic, capable of evolving with changing times and societal values. The court recognized that the basic structure doctrine was not a straightjacket formula but a flexible and adaptive principle that could accommodate new constitutional values and aspirations.

The judgment also addressed the contentious issue of whether the doctrine of basic structure could be applied retrospectively. The court held that laws placed in the Ninth Schedule before the date of the Kesavananda Bharati judgment would be open to judicial review if they violated the basic structure. This retrospective application of the basic structure doctrine was a crucial aspect of the ruling, ensuring that laws, regardless of their vintage, were subject to constitutional scrutiny.

Beyond its immediate implications, the I.R. Coelho case had far-reaching consequences for the constitutional landscape of India. The judgment marked a watershed moment in the interpretation of the basic structure doctrine and reinforced the judiciary's role as the final arbiter of constitutional validity. It established that no law, regardless of its place in the Ninth Schedule, could be shielded from review if it compromised the foundational principles of the Constitution.

Moreover, I.R. Coelho contributed to the ongoing discourse on the delicate balance between parliamentary sovereignty and constitutional supremacy. The court's assertion of the power to review constitutional amendments underscored the principle that the Constitution was not a mere parchment but a living document, subject to judicial scrutiny to ensure its vitality and relevance.

In conclusion, I.R. Coelho v. State of Tamil Nadu (2007) stands as a testament to the resilience of constitutional values and the unwavering commitment to the principles enshrined in the Constitution. The judgment, with its far-reaching implications, reaffirms the supremacy of the Constitution, the dynamic nature of the basic structure doctrine, and the judiciary's role as the sentinel of constitutional morality in India.

5.9 Justice K.S. Puttaswamy (Retd.) v. Union of India (2017)

Justice K.S. Puttaswamy (Retd.) v. Union of India (2017) is a groundbreaking judgment that reshaped the contours of privacy jurisprudence in India. The case emerged from a series of legal challenges to the constitutional validity of the Aadhaar scheme, a biometric identification system introduced by the Indian government. The judgment, delivered by a nine-judge bench of the Supreme Court, not only affirmed the fundamental right to privacy as intrinsic to the right to life and personal liberty but also established a robust framework for the protection of privacy in the digital age.

The genesis of the Puttaswamy case can be traced to a batch of petitions challenging the Aadhaar scheme on various grounds, including its potential to infringe upon the right to privacy. The question before the court was whether the Constitution of India guaranteed a fundamental right to privacy and, if so, how that right intersected with the Aadhaar scheme.

The Supreme Court constituted a nine-judge bench to deliberate on the issue, recognizing the profound implications of the case on constitutional law and individual rights. The court framed several questions for consideration, with the primary focus on determining the existence of a fundamental right to privacy and its scope under the Indian Constitution.

In a unanimous and historic decision, the Supreme Court declared that the right to privacy was a fundamental right protected under Article 21 of the Constitution, which guarantees the right to life and personal liberty. The judgment overruled previous decisions that had held otherwise, marking a significant departure in India's constitutional jurisprudence.

The court acknowledged that privacy was an essential aspect of the dignity of an individual and recognized its role in preserving personal autonomy, intimacy, and the ability to make choices without state interference. The judgment emphasized that privacy was not a mere common law right but a fundamental right that emanated from the intrinsic value of life and liberty.

The court further categorized privacy into three broad dimensions: the spatial aspect, the decisional autonomy, and informational privacy. The spatial aspect dealt with the physical confines of an individual, ensuring protection against unwarranted intrusion into personal spaces. Decisional autonomy encompassed the right to make personal choices, free from state interference. Informational privacy, a crucial aspect in the digital age, involved the protection of personal data from unauthorized use and disclosure.

In analyzing the constitutionality of the Aadhaar scheme, the court recognized that the collection and use of biometric data raised profound privacy concerns. While upholding the legitimacy of the Aadhaar project for certain purposes, the court imposed limitations to safeguard privacy. It mandated that Aadhaar could not be made mandatory for various services, such as opening bank accounts or obtaining SIM cards, and restricted the data that could be collected and shared.

Beyond its immediate impact on the Aadhaar scheme, the Puttaswamy judgment laid down a comprehensive framework for privacy protection in India. The court affirmed that privacy was not an absolute right and could be subject to reasonable restrictions in the interest of the state, but any such restrictions must adhere to the principles of legality, necessity, and proportionality.

The judgment also emphasized the need for a robust data protection regime, recognizing the importance of safeguarding personal data in the digital era. Subsequently, the court's directives in Puttaswamy played a significant role in the formulation of the Personal Data Protection Bill, which aimed to establish a comprehensive framework for data protection in India.

Moreover, the Puttaswamy case sparked a renewed focus on the broader implications of technological advancements and their impact on individual rights. The court's acknowledgment of informational privacy as a distinct facet underscored the need for legal safeguards in the digital landscape, where personal data has become a valuable commodity.

In conclusion, Justice K.S. Puttaswamy (Retd.) v. Union of India (2017) stands as a watershed moment in Indian constitutional law. The judgment not only affirmed the fundamental right to privacy but also laid down a principled framework for its protection in an evolving digital landscape. The court's nuanced understanding of privacy as a fundamental right and its application to the challenges posed by the Aadhaar scheme have left an indelible mark on India's constitutional jurisprudence, reaffirming the judiciary's role as the guardian of individual liberties in the face of technological advancements and changing societal norms.

5.10 Post-2017 Cases and Developments

In the aftermath of the landmark judgment in Justice K.S. Puttaswamy (Retd.) v. Union of India (2017), the right to privacy became a central theme in the evolving landscape of Indian constitutional law. The post-2017 period witnessed a continuation and clarification of this right as courts grappled with intricate questions surrounding its scope and application. Cases such as the Pegasus Spyware Controversy and the Aadhaar Reassessment tested the boundaries of informational privacy in the digital age. Courts emphasized the need for robust data protection laws and mechanisms to safeguard citizens from unwarranted intrusion into their private lives. The ongoing dialogue on privacy reflects the challenges posed by technological advancements and the imperative of adapting legal frameworks to protect individual liberties.

The post-2017 era also brought forth significant strides in gender justice, notably with the Supreme Court's ruling in Shayara Bano v. Union of India (2017), declaring the practice of instant triple talaq unconstitutional. This watershed moment paved the way for subsequent cases like the Sabarimala Temple Entry and the #MeToo Movement, highlighting issues related to gender discrimination, religious practices, and workplace harassment. The judiciary's proactive role in redefining societal norms and ensuring gender equality has been pivotal during this period, shaping a more inclusive and equitable legal landscape.

Another pivotal development post-2017 revolved around LGBTQ+ rights, propelled by the groundbreaking judgment in Navtej Singh Johar v. Union of India (2018), which decriminalized consensual same-sex relations. This landmark decision triggered subsequent cases like the Transgender Persons Act and the recognition of same-sex marriages, signaling a transformative shift in the legal landscape concerning the rights of the queer community. The judiciary's progressive stance has played a crucial role in advancing LGBTQ+ rights and fostering inclusivity.

Constitutional challenges to legislative actions also marked this period, with the abrogation of Article 370, the Citizenship (Amendment) Act (CAA), and the National Register of Citizens (NRC) facing intense legal scrutiny. Courts grappled with balancing national security concerns, citizenship rights, and the principles of justice and equality in these complex matters. The legal responses to these legislative actions have contributed to defining the delicate balance between national imperatives and constitutional safeguards.

Environmental jurisprudence and climate change emerged as pressing constitutional issues post-2017, with cases like the Sterlite Copper Plant Closure, the Delhi Air Pollution Crisis, and the Aarey Forest Case highlighting the intersection of constitutional rights and environmental concerns. The judiciary's proactive role in safeguarding the environment and recognizing the right to a clean and healthy environment as part of the right to life has been a notable trend, signaling a heightened awareness of environmental issues in constitutional discourse.

The digital age brought forth challenges related to online freedom of expression, regulation, and the intersection of constitutional rights with emerging technologies. Cases such as the WhatsApp Privacy Policy Case, the Twitter vs. Government of India Controversy, and debates around online hate speech underscore the delicate balance between free speech and responsible regulation in the digital space. The judiciary's engagement with these issues reflects the evolving nature of constitutional doctrines in response to technological progress.

Federalism and Center-State relations were also at the forefront of constitutional debates post-2017, with cases like the Delhi Government vs. Lieutenant Governor Power Tussle and the GST Compensation Crisis reflecting the dynamics of cooperative federalism and the resolution of disputes between different tiers of government. The judiciary played a crucial role in delineating the spheres of authority and addressing conflicts, contributing to the evolving federal structure of governance.

Lastly, emerging technologies posed novel challenges with constitutional implications. Cases involving artificial intelligence, biometric surveillance, and the use of technology in law enforcement tested the adequacy of existing legal frameworks. The judiciary's engagement with these issues reflects the imperative of adapting constitutional principles to the challenges posed by technological advancements. As these cases and developments unfold, they serve as a testament to the resilience and adaptability of the Indian Constitution in navigating the complexities of a rapidly changing society.

5.11 Comparative Analysis

A comparative analysis of constitutional doctrines across jurisdictions offers valuable insights into the diverse approaches taken by different legal systems. This examination goes beyond the borders of a single nation-state, exploring how constitutional principles and their interpretations vary, converge, or diverge in response to similar challenges and shared global values. Through a nuanced understanding of comparative constitutional law, legal scholars and practitioners gain a broader perspective on the strengths and limitations of different constitutional frameworks, fostering cross-cultural dialogue and facilitating the evolution of constitutional norms.

One crucial aspect of comparative constitutional analysis lies in exploring the foundational principles underpinning diverse legal systems. The study often begins with a scrutiny of the historical and cultural contexts that shaped each constitution. For instance, the U.S. Constitution draws inspiration from Enlightenment ideals, emphasizing individual rights and limited government. In contrast, the Indian Constitution reflects a commitment to socio-economic justice and accommodates diverse cultural and religious practices. Understanding these historical and cultural underpinnings is essential to appreciating the unique trajectories of constitutional development.

The role of judicial review provides another illuminating lens through which to compare constitutional systems. Some jurisdictions, like the United States, grant courts expansive powers of judicial review, allowing them to strike down legislation deemed unconstitutional. In contrast, other countries, such as the United Kingdom, embrace parliamentary sovereignty, limiting the judiciary's authority to review legislative acts. Examining these differences sheds light on the mechanisms employed to safeguard constitutionalism and the delicate balance between the branches of government.

Comparative analysis also delves into the protection of fundamental rights across jurisdictions. While many legal systems recognize similar rights, such as freedom of speech or the right to privacy, the scope and limitations of these rights can vary significantly. Some constitutions explicitly enumerate rights, while others rely on broad constitutional principles. The approaches to balancing individual rights against collective interests, such as national security or public order, reveal the nuanced ways in which different legal traditions navigate these complex issues.

Constitutional structures and the distribution of powers among different levels of government present another area of comparative exploration. Federal systems, like that of the United States, allocate authority between a central government and constituent states. Unitary systems, such as in the United Kingdom, concentrate power at the national level. Understanding how these systems function and adapt to changing circumstances contributes to the ongoing discourse on the optimal distribution of powers to ensure effective governance.

The influence of international law and human rights norms on domestic constitutional interpretation is a crucial dimension of comparative analysis. Many constitutions incorporate international treaties and conventions into their legal frameworks. The European Convention on Human Rights, for instance, has significantly shaped constitutional jurisprudence in European countries. Exploring how global norms interact with domestic constitutional principles enriches the understanding of the interconnectedness of legal systems in an increasingly interdependent world.

Comparative constitutional analysis also extends to the mechanisms for constitutional change and adaptation. While some jurisdictions adopt formal amendment procedures requiring a supermajority, others rely on judicial interpretation or flexible conventions. The study of constitutional change provides insights into the resilience and adaptability of legal systems, especially in response to societal transformations and evolving notions of justice.

In exploring the role of constitutional courts, a comparative approach considers the powers and functions vested in these institutions. Some countries, like Germany, empower constitutional courts with the authority to strike down unconstitutional laws, while others, like Canada, adopt a more restrained approach, focusing on the interpretation of constitutional provisions without invalidating legislation. Understanding the dynamics of constitutional adjudication contributes to discussions on the appropriate role of courts in upholding constitutional values.

Comparative constitutional law also delves into the mechanisms for protecting minority rights and ensuring inclusive governance. Various countries adopt different models to accommodate diverse ethnic, linguistic, and religious communities. Federal structures, devolution of powers, and affirmative action policies are among the strategies employed to foster inclusivity and address historical injustices. Analyzing these models contributes to the ongoing discourse on fostering pluralism and preventing the marginalization of minority groups.

The evolving nature of constitutionalism in response to contemporary challenges is a central theme in comparative constitutional analysis. Issues such as the protection of privacy in the digital age, environmental sustainability, and the regulation of emerging technologies transcend national boundaries. Comparative studies enable legal scholars to identify innovative approaches adopted by different legal systems to address these challenges, offering valuable lessons for the ongoing development of constitutional law.

As legal systems increasingly interact and influence each other, comparative constitutional analysis becomes an indispensable tool for understanding the complexities of modern constitutionalism. By examining the shared values, diverse approaches, and evolving trends across jurisdictions, scholars contribute to the ongoing dialogue on constitutional principles, fostering a global perspective that transcends individual legal traditions. Through this nuanced exploration, the rich tapestry of constitutional diversity emerges, reflecting the ongoing quest for justice, equity, and effective governance on a global scale.

5.12 Critiques and Debates

Critiques and debates surrounding constitutional doctrines are intrinsic to the evolution and refinement of legal frameworks. They represent the dynamic discourse that shapes the interpretation, application, and sometimes, the reconsideration of established principles. Within the realm of constitutional law, critiques and debates manifest in various forms, ranging from scholarly analyses to public discourse, and they play a crucial role in scrutinizing the efficacy and justice of constitutional provisions.

One recurring area of critique centers on the adaptability of constitutions to changing societal norms. Critics argue that rigid constitutional frameworks may struggle to address emerging challenges or evolving ethical standards. In response to this, debates often revolve around the need for constitutional flexibility, whether through formal amendments or innovative interpretations by the judiciary. Such discussions highlight the tension between the stability inherent in constitutional texts and the imperative to ensure that constitutions remain relevant and responsive to the needs of contemporary societies.

The delineation of constitutional powers among branches of government is a perennial subject of debate. Questions about the separation of powers, checks and balances, and the potential for abuse of authority spark ongoing discussions about the optimal distribution of power to prevent tyranny while ensuring effective governance. Scholars and jurists engage in nuanced analyses of landmark cases and constitutional provisions, exploring how these foundational principles continue to shape the delicate equilibrium among the executive, legislative, and judicial branches.

Constitutional critiques often extend to issues of social justice and equality. Scholars scrutinize how constitutional provisions address historical injustices, systemic discrimination, and disparities in socio-economic conditions. Debates surrounding affirmative action policies, reservation systems, and the protection of minority rights reflect broader conversations about the role of constitutions in fostering inclusive societies. The tension between formal equality and substantive equality, as well as the balancing of individual and collective rights, remains a focal point of constitutional discourse.

The role of constitutional courts in interpreting and shaping the law is a subject of constant scrutiny. Debates unfold around the extent of judicial review, the interpretative methods employed by judges, and the potential impact on democratic governance. Critics often question the legitimacy of unelected judges having the authority to strike down legislation, while proponents argue that robust judicial review is essential for upholding constitutional values and protecting individual rights. The delicate balance between judicial activism and restraint fuels ongoing discussions about the proper role of the judiciary in a constitutional democracy.

Issues of federalism and states' rights contribute significantly to constitutional debates, particularly in countries with federal structures. Scholars and policymakers grapple with questions of autonomy, the scope of federal powers, and the resolution of conflicts between the central and state governments. The dynamics of cooperative federalism, especially in addressing regional disparities and ensuring effective governance, form the crux of constitutional critiques and debates in federal systems.

The protection of civil liberties and the interplay between individual rights and public interests constitute a perennial source of discussion. Surveillance practices, limitations on free speech, and the tension between security imperatives and privacy rights fuel ongoing debates about the boundaries of constitutional protections. These discussions underscore the delicate task of balancing individual freedoms with the broader societal concerns that governments aim to address through legal means.

Constitutional critiques also extend to the global stage, where international human rights norms intersect with domestic legal frameworks. Debates arise about the influence of international law on domestic constitutional interpretation, the enforcement mechanisms for international treaties, and the extent to which global standards should guide national legal systems. The tension between sovereignty and the recognition of universal human rights principles continues to be a subject of international constitutional discourse.

Emerging technologies and their impact on constitutional principles introduce new dimensions to critiques and debates. Issues such as digital privacy, artificial intelligence, and cyber rights pose challenges for existing legal frameworks. Scholars and policymakers engage in discussions about how constitutional principles can adapt to technological advancements while safeguarding fundamental rights in the digital age.

Environmental sustainability and the recognition of environmental rights within constitutional frameworks have become increasingly prominent in constitutional critiques. Debates center on the extent to which constitutions should explicitly recognize the right to a clean and healthy environment and the corresponding obligations of governments to protect ecological balance. These discussions reflect a broader recognition of the interconnectedness between constitutional principles and environmental justice.

Critiques also arise concerning the representativeness and inclusivity of constitutional processes. Questions about constitutional drafting, amendment procedures, and the participation of diverse voices in the constitutional-making process prompt discussions about the legitimacy of constitutional documents. Debates surrounding the inclusion of historically marginalized groups, such as women, indigenous communities, and minority populations, highlight the ongoing struggle to ensure that constitutional frameworks truly reflect the diverse fabric of society.

In conclusion, critiques and debates are essential elements in the continuous dialogue about constitutionalism. They reflect the ongoing quest for justice, equity, and effective governance within the evolving dynamics of societies. The multifaceted nature of constitutional critiques underscores the interdisciplinary nature of constitutional law, drawing on insights from political science, philosophy, sociology, and other fields. Through these critiques and debates, legal scholars, practitioners, and the public contribute to the vitality and adaptability of constitutional systems, ensuring that they remain responsive to the ever-changing demands of a dynamic world.

5.13 Conclusion

In the culmination of this extensive exploration into critiques and debates within constitutional law, it is evident that the dynamism inherent in constitutional systems is a testament to their adaptability and resilience. The multifaceted nature of these discussions reflects the ongoing evolution of societies, the changing nature of governance, and the perpetual quest for justice and equity. As we draw conclusions from the myriad debates and critiques, several overarching themes emerge, underscoring the significance of these dialogues in shaping the trajectory of constitutionalism.

Fundamentally, constitutional critiques and debates serve as the lifeblood of constitutional democracies, embodying the principles of deliberative democracy. The open discourse surrounding constitutional provisions, judicial decisions, and legislative acts fosters a vibrant civic engagement that is essential for the functioning of democratic societies. These discussions not only hold the government accountable but also empower citizens to actively participate in the ongoing construction of their constitutional order.

The tension between stability and adaptability remains a central theme in constitutional critiques. The inclination towards constitutional stability is grounded in the need for legal certainty, predictability, and the protection of fundamental rights.

However, the evolving nature of societies demands a degree of flexibility in constitutional frameworks. The debates on formal amendments, judicial interpretation, and constitutional conventions reflect an ongoing negotiation between the necessity of a stable legal foundation and the imperative to respond to changing societal norms.

The role of the judiciary in constitutional systems emerges as a focal point in these discussions. Critiques of judicial decisions often revolve around questions of legitimacy, accountability, and the appropriate scope of judicial review. While the judiciary is entrusted with safeguarding constitutional values, ensuring that its authority aligns with democratic principles remains a constant challenge. The ongoing debates on the activism or restraint of the judiciary underscore the delicate balance that must be struck to preserve the integrity of constitutional democracies.

Constitutional critiques also highlight the interconnectedness of constitutional law with broader societal issues. Debates on social justice, equality, and minority rights reflect the evolving norms and values of contemporary societies. As constitutional systems grapple with historical injustices and systemic discrimination, these critiques propel constitutional discourse towards more inclusive and egalitarian frameworks. The ongoing dialogue on the intersection of constitutional principles with issues such as gender equality, LGBTQ+ rights, and environmental justice illustrates the constitutional system's responsiveness to the evolving understanding of human rights and dignity.

The global dimension of constitutional critiques underscores the interconnected nature of constitutional law in an increasingly interconnected world. Comparative analyses contribute to a richer understanding of constitutionalism, allowing legal scholars and practitioners to draw insights from diverse legal traditions. Debates on the influence of international law, human rights norms, and the challenges posed by emerging technologies reflect the shared challenges faced by constitutional systems across borders. The recognition of universal values and the adaptation of constitutional principles to address global issues underscore the collaborative nature of constitutional discourse on a global scale.

Technological advancements and their impact on constitutional principles emerge as a contemporary challenge that requires nuanced debates. The critiques surrounding issues of digital privacy, artificial intelligence, and the regulation of online spaces highlight the need for constitutional frameworks to evolve in tandem with technological progress. As societies grapple with the implications of the digital age, constitutional dialogues serve as a crucial forum for shaping the legal frameworks that govern these transformative technologies.

Environmental sustainability, an increasingly pressing concern, finds resonance in constitutional critiques. The debates surrounding the recognition of environmental rights, the duties of governments to protect ecological balance, and the role of citizens in environmental governance underscore the evolving understanding of the relationship between constitutional principles and ecological well-being. As constitutional systems engage with the imperative of environmental justice, these critiques contribute to the development of legal frameworks that reflect a heightened awareness of the interconnectedness between human rights and the health of the planet.

In conclusion, the tapestry of constitutional critiques and debates weaves together a narrative of dynamic engagement, reflective of the ever-evolving nature of constitutional law. From questions of constitutional design to the protection of individual liberties, from the role of the judiciary to the global dimensions of constitutionalism, these critiques serve as catalysts for introspection and improvement. Constitutional law, as a living and breathing discipline, relies on the continuous discourse that critiques generate to adapt to the challenges of each era.

As we reflect on the vast landscape traversed in this exploration, it becomes apparent that constitutional critiques are not merely exercises in questioning authority but profound reflections on the shared values that underpin constitutional democracies. They embody the ongoing endeavor to strike a delicate balance between stability and adaptability, between individual rights and collective interests, and between the timeless principles of justice and the evolving norms of contemporary societies.

The dialogues within constitutional law, as manifested in critiques and debates, resonate far beyond the confines of courtrooms and academic forums. They reverberate in the halls of legislatures, the chambers of judiciaries, and the collective consciousness of citizens. Constitutional critiques are the threads that knit together the fabric of democratic governance, ensuring that constitutional systems remain responsive to the aspirations, challenges, and ideals of the people they serve.

In this concluding reflection, we recognize that constitutional critiques are not a sign of weakness but a testament to the strength and vitality of constitutional democracies. The very act of questioning, debating, and challenging aspects of constitutional governance is an affirmation of the principles that underlie these systems. It is an acknowledgment that the pursuit of justice, equality, and the protection of fundamental rights is an ongoing journey-one that requires collective engagement, dialogue, and a commitment to the principles that form the bedrock of constitutional democracies.

As constitutional law continues to evolve in response to the complexities of the modern world, the critiques and debates encapsulated in this exploration provide a roadmap for future engagements. They invite scholars, practitioners, policymakers, and citizens to actively participate in the ongoing construction of constitutional systems that reflect the aspirations of diverse societies. In this spirit, the journey through constitutional critiques becomes not just a retrospective analysis but a forward-looking endeavor-one that invites continuous dialogue, introspection, and adaptation to the ever-changing landscapes of law, society, and governance.

Chapter 6

Contemporary Relevance and Challenges

In the intricate tapestry of constitutional law, the chapter on "Contemporary Relevance and Challenges" serves as a critical exploration of how constitutional principles navigate the complexities of the modern era. As societies evolve, so too does the role of the constitution, transforming it from a static legal document into a dynamic force that responds to the ever-shifting landscape of global, technological, and societal changes.

This chapter is an expedition into the heart of present-day constitutional discourse, probing the relevance of foundational principles in the face of unprecedented challenges. From the corridors of technological innovation to the arenas of social justice, the constitutional framework is continuously tested and adapted to meet the demands of a rapidly changing world.

As we embark on this journey, the chapter will unravel the constitutional implications of contemporary issues, dissecting the intricate interplay between the law and the pressing challenges of our time. It seeks not only to examine the doctrinal aspects but also to illuminate the broader context in which constitutional norms are applied and contested.

The following pages will scrutinize the impact of technological advancements on privacy rights, grapple with the delicate balance between national security imperatives and civil liberties, and explore the constitutional dimensions of environmental protection in the face of global climate crises. It will delve into the evolving landscape of equality and social justice, dissecting how the constitution responds to identity politics and the call for inclusivity.

Moreover, this chapter will unfold the constitutional dimensions of crisis response, probing the resilience of constitutional governance during times of emergency. It will survey global perspectives on constitutionalism, acknowledging that the challenges we face are not confined by borders but are part of a broader international conversation on rights, governance, and the rule of law.

In essence, the chapter is a testament to the adaptability of constitutional principles in an era characterized by rapid change and profound challenges. As we navigate the complexities of the present, the constitutional framework emerges not as a static set of rules but as a living, breathing entity that evolves to meet the aspirations and challenges of contemporary society. This exploration invites us to ponder the role of constitutional law as a guiding force in shaping our collective future.

6.1 Technological Advancements and Privacy Concerns

In the intricate tapestry of constitutional law, the interplay between technological advancements and privacy concerns unfolds as a profound chapter, intricately interwoven with the foundational principles of the Indian Constitution. This exploration delves into the transformative journey of the right to privacy, an integral facet of the basic structure doctrine, adapting to the complexities of an interconnected world.

The digital revolution has not merely streamlined our existence; it has woven an intricate tapestry of connectivity, innovation, and accessibility. Smartphones have become extensions of our identities, artificial intelligence permeates decision-making processes, and data analytics shapes our digital footprints. In this technologically advanced era, the contours of privacy, as safeguarded by the Constitution of India, are undergoing a profound evolution.

The Constitution, conceived in an era preceding the digital revolution, now finds itself navigating uncharted territories. The framers, in their sagacity, could not envision the complexities of the internet, biometric identification, or the sheer volume of personal data exchanged in the virtual realm. Courts grapple with the task of redefining privacy in a digital context, where traditional notions of physical intrusion give way to intangible aspects of life-digital communications, metadata, and virtual interactions.

K.S. Puttaswamy v. Union of India (2017) stands as a pivotal moment in this constitutional evolution. The Supreme Court's recognition of the right to privacy as a fundamental right under Article 21 marks a milestone. The canvas of privacy rights expands to encompass the digital trails individuals leave behind, prompting the judiciary to interpret constitutional protections in a manner that reflects the intricacies of contemporary life.

This narrative extends beyond courtrooms and legal doctrines into the essence of privacy as a fundamental right, grappling with philosophical questions that resonate with the tenets of the basic structure doctrine. In the digital age, where information is both a commodity and a form of social currency, privacy assumes a multifaceted character. The challenge is not merely legal; it is existential-a question of how our constitutional fabric weaves protections for the intangible aspects of our lives.

The convergence of public and private realms in the digital sphere presents a nuanced challenge. Social media platforms, e-commerce giants, and technology conglomerates amass vast troves of user data, challenging the traditional boundaries between government surveillance and private enterprise. In this landscape, the basic structure doctrine resonates in debates surrounding the commodification of personal information and the need for robust consent mechanisms.

As we peer into this digital frontier, we encounter not only legal intricacies but also ethical considerations that echo the constitutional ethos. Balancing the benefits of technological progress with the preservation of constitutional rights becomes a pressing concern. Here, the basic structure doctrine illuminates the path forward in crafting legal responses to the challenges posed by the digital age.

The narrative unfolds against a backdrop of global interconnectedness, raising questions of jurisdiction and international cooperation. Cross-border data flows, cloud computing, and the challenges of regulating global tech giants invite contemplation of the basic structure doctrine in a transnational context. The constitutional principles that form the bedrock of our legal system must adapt to the realities of a world where borders are porous, and digital interactions transcend geographical constraints.

The evolution of privacy rights in response to technological advancements becomes a testament to the resilience of constitutional principles. It is not a mere legal interpretation but a manifestation of the enduring spirit of the basic structure doctrine. The canvas of privacy rights expands and contracts, absorbing the nuances of technological progress, but the foundational principles enshrined in the Constitution remain steadfast.

In conclusion, the narrative of technological advancements and privacy concerns is not merely a subplot in the grand saga of constitutional law. It is a chapter that unravels the intricate threads of the basic structure doctrine, weaving together legal interpretations, ethical considerations, and the existential nature of privacy in the digital age. As we add these reflections to the pages of our constitutional discourse, the basic structure doctrine emerges as a guiding light, illuminating the path forward in a world where technology and constitutional principles dance in a delicate, ever- changing choreography.

6.2 National Security vs. Civil Liberties

In the intricate tapestry of constitutional law, the delicate dance between national security imperatives and the preservation of civil liberties emerges as a profound discourse within the framework of the Indian Constitution. This exploration delves into the nuanced balance required to uphold the constitutional fabric while safeguarding the nation from potential threats, and it is guided by the foundational principles encapsulated in the basic structure doctrine.

The constitutional landscape in India is a canvas painted with diverse challenges and competing interests. National security, an indispensable concern for any sovereign state, necessitates robust measures to ensure the safety and integrity of the nation. Conversely, civil liberties stand as the bedrock of a democratic society, safeguarding individual freedoms against potential overreach by the state.

The basic structure doctrine, a cornerstone of Indian constitutional jurisprudence, plays a pivotal role in navigating this complex terrain. The Preamble, Fundamental Rights, and the Directive Principles of State Policy collectively weave a constitutional tapestry that reflects not only the aspirations of a democratic society but also the imperatives of safeguarding national interests.

Critical milestones in this constitutional journey are marked by landmark cases such as ADM Jabalpur v. Shiv Kant Shukla (1976) and more recent judgments like K.S. Puttaswamy v. Union of India (2017). The former, a momentous but controversial decision, underscored the need for a nuanced understanding of the balance between individual rights and state authority during periods of emergency. The latter, on the other hand, asserted the inviolability of the right to privacy as an essential facet of personal liberty, even in the face of national security considerations.

As we delve into legislative measures and executive actions aimed at fortifying national security, the canvas broadens. Laws such as the Armed Forces (Special Powers) Act (AFSPA), the Unlawful Activities (Prevention) Act (UAPA), and the amendments to the National Investigation Agency (NIA) Act manifest the state's response to perceived threats. However, the challenge lies in ensuring that these measures, while instrumental in safeguarding the nation, do not trample upon the basic structure of the Constitution, particularly the cherished Fundamental Rights.

National security imperatives often collide with the ideals of transparency, accountability, and due process. The principles embedded in the Constitution demand that any abridgment of civil liberties for the sake of national security adheres to the tests of reasonableness, proportionality, and necessity. Here, the basic structure doctrine acts as a sentinel, guarding against the erosion of constitutional values in the face of exigencies.

The canvas deepens as we confront issues of surveillance, censorship, and the curtailment of freedoms in the name of national security. The right to privacy, freedom of expression, and the right to dissent are integral to the democratic ethos enshrined in the Constitution. Striking a balance between intelligence-gathering necessities and the preservation of individual liberties becomes a constitutional imperative, requiring a judicious and contextual application of the basic structure doctrine.

International perspectives further enrich the canvas, as global events shape the discourse on security and civil liberties. India's constitutional principles must resonate with evolving global standards while remaining rooted in the unique socio- cultural context. Here, the basic structure doctrine not only serves as a guide but also as a mirror reflecting the aspirations of a nation committed to democratic ideals.

In conclusion, the exploration of the interplay between national security and civil liberties within the framework of the basic structure doctrine is a journey through the soul of the Indian Constitution. It demands a constant reevaluation of the delicate balance between state power and individual freedoms. As we navigate this intricate terrain, the basic structure doctrine stands as a guardian, ensuring that the constitutional values endure even in the face of the complex challenges posed by the imperatives of national security.

6.3 Equality and Social Justice

The constitutional framework of India intricately weaves the principles of equality and social justice into its fabric, with the basic structure doctrine acting as a vigilant guardian. These principles find expression in the foundational provisions of the Constitution, judicial interpretations, legislative enactments, and societal endeavors, collectively shaping the nation's pursuit of a just and egalitarian society.

Constitutional Guarantees: At the core of this endeavor is Article 14, which assures every citizen equality before the law and equal protection of laws. This foundational principle lays the groundwork for a society where justice is dispensed impartially, irrespective of individual differences. Articles 15 and 16 further articulate the constitutional command against discrimination, fostering an environment where all citizens enjoy equal opportunities. The Constitution, cognizant of historical injustices, empowers the state through Articles 46 and 335 to adopt affirmative action, ensuring equitable participation for marginalized communities.

Judicial Sentinels of Equality: The judiciary, guided by the basic structure doctrine, has consistently interpreted the concept of equality expansively. Landmark cases, such as Kesavananda Bharati v. State of Kerala (1973), underscore that equality is not a mere formal concept but a substantive right ensuring fairness and justice. Judicial scrutiny of reservation policies, exemplified by cases like Indra Sawhney v. Union of India (1992), reflects a delicate balancing act, ensuring affirmative action is tailored to address specific inequalities. The right to equality is not merely a statutory right but a fundamental right, as seen in judicial pronouncements like Maneka Gandhi v. Union of India (1978).

Legislative Measures: Legislative interventions, fortified by the basic structure doctrine, have given life to constitutional imperatives. Acts like the Right to Education Act, 2009, and the Scheduled Castes and Scheduled Tribes (Prevention of Atrocities) Act, 1989, exemplify the commitment to inclusive development. Despite legislative frameworks, challenges persist in translating constitutional ideals into actionable realities. The basic structure doctrine serves as a guiding light, ensuring legislative measures are in harmony with overarching constitutional principles.

Intersectionality and Inclusivity: The intersectionality of equality is acutely observed in the realm of gender justice. The Constitution, through Articles 15(3) and 16(2), empowers the state to make special provisions for women, recognizing historical marginalization and fostering a more inclusive society. The canvas of social justice extends beyond binaries, embracing urban-rural divides. Policies such as the Mahatma Gandhi National Rural Employment Guarantee Act (MGNREGA) and schemes promoting rural development exemplify the commitment to inclusive development.

Challenges and Aspirations: Persistent challenges, especially in eradicating caste-based discrimination, demand sustained efforts. Judicial interventions, as seen in cases like State of Punjab v. Gurmit Singh (1996), emphasize the constitutional imperative of dismantling age-old hierarchies. The pursuit of social justice intertwines with the quest for economic equality. Policies aimed at uplifting the economically weaker sections must align with the basic structure doctrine, ensuring a nuanced approach to economic justice.

Global Perspectives on Social Justice: Global comparative analyses offer insights into different approaches to social justice. India's commitment to international human rights standards reflects a global perspective, ensuring that constitutional principles resonate on a broader stage. Participation in global dialogues on human rights places India within a broader framework. The constitutional tapestry, guided by the basic structure doctrine, ensures that the nation aligns with evolving global norms in the pursuit of social justice.

Conclusion: In conclusion, the constitutional tapestry of equality and social justice, guided by the principles of the basic structure doctrine, represents a perpetual aspiration for a society where every citizen is afforded dignity, fairness, and equal opportunities. The journey is dynamic, marked by judicial interpretations, legislative endeavors, and societal transformations, all converging towards the constitutional dream of a just, equitable, and inclusive India.

6.4 Environmental Law and Constitutional Rights

In the intricate landscape of Indian constitutional law, the interplay between environmental rights and the Constitution manifests a profound commitment to securing justice, liberty, equality, and fraternity. This constitutional foundation is encapsulated in the expansive interpretation of Article 21, where the right to life extends to encompass the right to a healthy environment. Judicial pronouncements, such as in Subhash Kumar v. State of Bihar (1991) and M.C. Mehta v. Union of India (1987), illuminate the constitutional significance of a clean and wholesome environment.

The transformative interpretation of Article 21 has propelled environmental rights to the forefront of constitutional discourse. Notably, in cases like M.C. Mehta v. Kamal Nath (1997), the Supreme Court unequivocally declared that a healthy environment is integral to the right to life. This shift represents a paradigmatic expansion of the constitutional guarantee, aligning it with the evolving understanding of human rights in the context of environmental jurisprudence.

Public Interest Litigation (PIL) emerges as a potent instrument in the realm of environmental activism, seamlessly aligning with the ethos of the basic structure doctrine. Landmark cases, including M.C. Mehta v. Union of India (1987) and Indian Council for Enviro-Legal Action v. Union of India (1996), underscore the transformative potential of PILs in addressing environmental concerns. The judiciary, guided by the basic structure doctrine, actively embraces PILs as vehicles for safeguarding environmental rights.

Legislative interventions, such as the Environment (Protection) Act, 1986, and the Water (Prevention and Control of Pollution) Act, 1974, form the legislative backbone for environmental governance. The constitutional touchstone, reinforced by the basic structure doctrine, ensures that legislative measures align with constitutional principles, fostering an environment where development coexists harmoniously with ecological sustainability.

India's participation in international agreements, guided by the basic structure doctrine, reflects a commitment to global environmental governance. Treaties like the Paris Agreement and the Montreal Protocol underscore India's resolve to address environmental challenges collaboratively. The judiciary, in interpreting international agreements, ensures that global commitments align with the constitutional ethos.

The environmental landscape in India presents a myriad of challenges, from deforestation to climate change impacts. Striking a balance between developmental imperatives and environmental preservation requires a delicate equilibrium. Judicial interventions, exemplified in cases like Vellore Citizens Welfare Forum v. Union of India (1996), highlight the judiciary's role in reconciling economic growth with ecological sustainability.

The judiciary, acting as the custodian of constitutional values, plays a pivotal role in environmental governance. Cases like M.C. Mehta v. Kamal Nath (1997) and Indian Council for Enviro-Legal Action v. Union of India (1996) showcase how the judiciary, guided by the basic structure doctrine, ensures that environmental considerations are woven into the fabric of decision-making processes.

Emerging trends, including the recognition of the 'Right to a Healthy Environment' as a fundamental right, reshape the contours of environmental law. Cases like Subhash Kumar v. State of Bihar (1991) and Rural Litigation and Entitlement Kendra v. State of U.P. (1985) underscore the transformative potential of environmental rights in shaping legal discourse.

In conclusion, the confluence of environmental law and constitutional rights forms a dynamic tapestry where the basic structure doctrine serves as a guiding beacon. The constitutional imperative to protect and preserve the environment is not a mere legal formality but an intrinsic commitment to securing the well-being of present and future generations. As the nation navigates the complex terrain of environmental governance, the constitutional canvas, illuminated by judicial wisdom and legislative foresight, charts a course towards a sustainable and harmonious coexistence of humanity and nature.

6.5 Global Perspectives on Constitutionalism

The historical roots of global constitutionalism can be traced back to ancient civilizations, where notions of governance, rule of law, and fundamental rights found expression in various forms. The Magna Carta of 1215 in England, often hailed as a foundational document in constitutional history, laid the groundwork for the principles of limited government and the rule of law. Subsequent milestones, including the English Bill of Rights (1689) and the American Constitution (1787), contributed to the global evolution of constitutional thought.

The Enlightenment era, with its emphasis on reason, individual rights, and representative government, played a pivotal role in shaping modern constitutionalism. Thinkers like John Locke, Montesquieu, and Rousseau laid the intellectual foundations for constitutional principles that would later influence the drafting of constitutions around the world. The American and French Revolutions in the late 18th century marked transformative moments in the global spread of constitutional ideals.

The aftermath of World War II witnessed a paradigm shift in the global understanding of constitutionalism, with a heightened focus on human rights. The Universal Declaration of Human Rights (1948) emerged as a landmark document, articulating a common set of rights that transcended national boundaries. The Nuremberg Trials further underscored the principle that individuals, including government officials, could be held accountable for human rights violations under international law.

The establishment of international organizations such as the United Nations (UN) and regional bodies like the European Union (EU) marked a concerted effort to promote collective security, cooperation, and the protection of fundamental rights. Treaties like the International Covenant on Civil and Political Rights (ICCPR) and the International Covenant on Economic, Social, and Cultural Rights (ICESCR) exemplify the global commitment to upholding a comprehensive range of human rights.

While the ideals of global constitutionalism have gained traction, challenges persist. The tension between state sovereignty and international law poses a perennial dilemma. Issues such as the enforcement of international judgments, accountability for human rights violations, and the role of powerful nations in shaping global governance frameworks underscore the complexities of a truly cosmopolitan constitutional order.

Constitutionalism manifests differently across regions, shaped by historical, cultural, and political contexts. The European tradition, characterized by supranational institutions and a strong commitment to human rights, contrasts with the federalist structure of the United States. Meanwhile, Asia, Africa, and Latin America each bring unique perspectives to the global constitutional discourse, influenced by their respective historical trajectories.

In the 21st century, the digital age has introduced new challenges to constitutionalism, with issues such as online privacy, cybersecurity, and the regulation of emerging technologies requiring innovative legal responses. The global community grapples with questions of climate change, migration, and public health, necessitating collaborative constitutional efforts to address these transnational issues.

Civil society plays a crucial role in advancing global constitutionalism. Non- governmental organizations (NGOs), advocacy groups, and international legal scholars contribute to the development and promotion of constitutional norms. The interconnectedness facilitated by globalization allows for the exchange of ideas and strategies to advance constitutional principles on a global scale.

In conclusion, global perspectives on constitutionalism reveal a complex tapestry of interconnected legal traditions, shared principles, and ongoing challenges. The historical roots of constitutionalism, the internationalization of human rights, and the diverse regional manifestations of constitutional principles collectively contribute to the rich fabric of global governance. As nations navigate the complexities of an interconnected world, the evolving landscape of global constitutionalism remains a testament to the enduring quest for justice, liberty, and equality across borders.

6.6 Crisis Response and Constitutional Governance

In times of crisis, the intricate balance between constitutional governance and crisis response becomes a focal point for nations grappling with unforeseen challenges. Whether facing natural disasters, public health emergencies, or geopolitical conflicts, the constitutional framework underpinning governance is tested. This exploration delves into the complexities of crisis response within the context of constitutional principles, examining the interplay between executive powers, civil liberties, and the imperative to safeguard the well-being of the populace.

Crisis response often necessitates swift and decisive action, requiring governments to deploy emergency measures that may temporarily expand executive powers. The tension between the need for expeditious action and the preservation of constitutional norms poses a delicate challenge. Historically, crises ranging from pandemics to armed conflicts have prompted legal scholars, policymakers, and jurists to grapple with questions of constitutional interpretation and the scope of executive authority.

Constitutional safeguards for civil liberties, such as freedom of movement, privacy, and assembly, may be subject to temporary limitations during crises. This raises profound questions about the delicate balance between individual rights and collective well-being. Striking this balance is essential to prevent the erosion of constitutional principles even in the face of urgent and compelling circumstances.

The legal framework governing states of emergency or martial law varies across jurisdictions, reflecting diverse constitutional traditions. Some constitutions explicitly define the conditions under which emergency powers can be invoked, while others rely on judicial review to ensure that executive actions during crises align with constitutional norms. The role of the judiciary in upholding constitutional principles during emergencies is pivotal, serving as a check on potential abuses of power.

The global response to the COVID-19 pandemic provides a contemporary example of the challenges inherent in crisis governance. Nations grappled with implementing public health measures, such as lockdowns and quarantine, that curtailed individual freedoms to curb the spread of the virus. The pandemic underscored the importance of clear legal frameworks that balance crisis response with the protection of fundamental rights.

In the realm of national security crises, governments often contend with the need to protect citizens from external threats while upholding constitutional values. The declaration of states of emergency, the suspension of certain legal protections, and the use of military forces are measures that may be employed in response to security challenges. The careful calibration of these responses is essential to prevent the overreach of executive power and the erosion of democratic norms.

Crisis response also invites considerations of intergovernmental cooperation and the role of international law. Transboundary crises, such as refugee flows, natural disasters, or pandemics, necessitate collaboration between nations. International legal frameworks, treaties, and conventions provide a basis for coordinated responses that respect the sovereignty and constitutional principles of involved states.

As societies evolve, so too must constitutional frameworks for crisis response. Advances in technology, changes in geopolitical landscapes, and emerging threats require ongoing adaptation of legal structures to ensure their relevance and effectiveness. Constitutional resilience in the face of crises requires not only legal acumen but also a commitment to upholding the foundational values that define a nation's governance.

In conclusion, crisis response and constitutional governance navigate a delicate equilibrium. The exigencies of crises demand agile and effective governance, yet the preservation of constitutional principles remains paramount. The challenges posed by crises prompt reflections on the nature of executive authority, the role of the judiciary, and the ongoing evolution of constitutional frameworks. As nations confront diverse crises in the 21st century, the fidelity to constitutional values becomes an indispensable compass, guiding societies through the storm while ensuring the enduring integrity of their governance structures.

6.7 Intersectionality and Identity Politics

The intricate interplay of intersectionality and identity politics represents a complex and evolving discourse within the broader framework of constitutionalism. As societies navigate issues of representation, social justice, and the acknowledgment of diverse identities, constitutional principles become a crucible for shaping policies that accommodate intersecting dimensions of individual experiences.

Understanding intersectionality is paramount in this context. Coined by legal scholar Kimberlé Crenshaw, the concept recognizes that individuals simultaneously occupy multiple social categories. These categories, including race, gender, class, sexuality, and ability, intersect in complex ways, influencing an individual's experiences, opportunities, and vulnerabilities. Intersectionality challenges simplistic, single-axis analyses, emphasizing the interconnected nature of social identities.

Identity politics, rooted in the assertion of political and social rights based on shared identities, plays a pivotal role in constitutional debates. Marginalized groups engage in identity politics to advocate for recognition, representation, and the rectification of historical injustices.

Constitutional frameworks become battlegrounds for securing legal protections and dismantling systemic barriers that perpetuate inequality.

Constitutions globally have evolved to incorporate anti-discrimination provisions aimed at addressing the intersectional dimensions of inequality. These provisions prohibit discrimination based on race, gender, religion, sexual orientation, and other grounds. Courts are tasked with interpreting and applying these laws in ways that recognize and remedy the specific challenges faced by individuals at the intersections of multiple identities.

Issues of gender and sexual identity exemplify the intersectional nature of struggles for recognition and rights. LGBTQ+ individuals, especially those from marginalized racial or ethnic backgrounds, often contend with compounded forms of discrimination. Constitutional battles related to marriage equality, anti-discrimination laws, and transgender rights showcase the intersectional dimensions of identity politics within the legal sphere.

The intersection of race and ethnicity with other identity markers amplifies challenges faced by minority communities. Indigenous peoples, for instance, navigate a complex intersection of racial, cultural, and land rights issues. Constitutional recognition of indigenous rights becomes a critical aspect of fostering social justice and redressing historical injustices.

Class intersects with various identity markers, influencing access to economic opportunities and resources. Constitutional discussions on economic rights and wealth distribution often intersect with considerations of race, gender, and other identities. Addressing economic inequality requires an intersectional approach that acknowledges the diverse factors shaping disparities.

The intersectionality of disability with other identities is crucial in shaping inclusive policies. Constitutional guarantees of equal protection and accommodation become essential for individuals navigating the intersection of disability with race, gender, or other identity markers. The fight for disability rights within constitutional frameworks underscores the interconnected nature of identity politics.

While intersectionality and identity politics contribute to a more comprehensive understanding of social issues, they are not without challenges and critiques. Debates arise around the potential for identity politics to be exclusionary or to essentialize identities. Balancing the pursuit of justice for specific groups with a broader commitment to inclusivity poses inherent tensions.

Intersectionality and identity politics take on diverse expressions in different cultural and global contexts. Constitutional approaches to recognizing and addressing intersectional issues vary, reflecting the unique histories, legal traditions, and cultural landscapes of individual nations.

Constitutional courts play a pivotal role in shaping jurisprudence on intersectionality and identity politics. Landmark cases often set precedents for recognizing the rights of individuals at the intersections of multiple identities. Judicial interpretations influence the trajectory of social justice movements and the evolution of constitutional principles.

In conclusion, the nexus of intersectionality and identity politics profoundly influences constitutionalism and legal frameworks. The recognition of individuals as multifaceted beings with intersecting identities challenges traditional legal paradigms. As constitutional democracies grapple with the imperative of fostering inclusivity and dismantling systemic inequalities, the lens of intersectionality provides a critical perspective for navigating the complexities of identity politics. Constitutional principles, when informed by an intersectional understanding, become powerful tools for advancing justice, equity, and the protection of the diverse identities that constitute the fabric of society.

6.8 Conclusion

In conclusion, the exploration of intersectionality and identity politics with in the realm of constitutionalism unveils a rich tapestry of complexities and challenges. This discourse, rooted in the acknowledgment of diverse and intersecting identities, has profound implications for constitutional principles, legal frameworks, and the pursuit of a more inclusive and equitable society.

The understanding of intersectionality, as articulated by Kimberlé Crenshaw, provides a crucial lens through which to appreciate the multifaceted nature of individual experiences. No longer can social categories be neatly compartmentalized; instead, they intersect and intertwine, shaping the lived realities of individuals in profound ways. This nuanced understanding challenges traditional legal paradigms that often rely on single-axis analyses, encouraging a more holistic and inclusive approach.

Identity politics, a natural response to historical marginalization, emerges as a powerful force within constitutional debates. Groups advocating for recognition and rights based on shared identities utilize constitutional frameworks as platforms for justice. The constitutional arena becomes a dynamic space where struggles for representation, acknowledgment, and the rectification of historical injustices play out.

Constitutions globally have responded to the call for inclusivity by incorporating anti-discrimination provisions. These provisions, addressing a spectrum of identity markers, stand as testament to the commitment of constitutional democracies to redress historical and systemic inequalities. Courts, entrusted with interpreting and applying these provisions, bear the responsibility of recognizing and remedying the specific challenges faced by individuals navigating the intersections of multiple identities.

In navigating the contemporary landscape, constitutional law faces multifaceted challenges that demand nuanced legal responses. This chapter aims to provide insights into the ongoing discourse and underscore the adaptability of constitutional principles in addressing the complexities of the present era.

Issues such as gender and sexual identity, race and ethnicity, economic status, disability, and indigenous rights highlight the intricate interplay of identity politics within constitutional contexts. Landmark cases often set precedents, shaping jurisprudence that recognizes the rights of individuals at these intersections. These cases become pivotal in advancing the cause of justice, dismantling systemic barriers, and affirming the constitutional principles of equality and nondiscrimination.

However, the discourse on intersectionality and identity politics is not without challenges and critiques. Debates surrounding potential exclusionary tendencies or essentialization of identities underscore the delicate balance needed in navigating the complexities of constitutional recognition. Striking a balance between pursuing justice for specific groups and maintaining a commitment to broader inclusivity poses ongoing challenges.

The global perspectives on intersectionality and identity politics highlight the contextual variations in constitutional approaches. Legal traditions, cultural landscapes, and historical backgrounds influence the ways in which nations grapple with issues of recognition and justice. Constitutional courts, as custodians of justice, play a pivotal role in shaping the trajectory of social justice movements and contributing to the evolution of constitutional principles.

In essence, the exploration of intersectionality and identity politics within constitutionalism reveals an ongoing and transformative journey. It underscores the imperative for constitutional democracies to evolve continually, adapting to the changing dynamics of societal norms, values, and identities. As we navigate the complexities of the intersectional terrain, constitutional principles, informed by an understanding of diverse identities, become powerful instruments for fostering justice, equity, and the protection of the myriad identities that constitute the vibrant mosaic of society. The journey towards a more inclusive constitutionalism is an ongoing endeavor, propelled by a commitment to recognizing the dignity and rights of all individuals, regardless of where they reside within the intricate web of intersecting identities.

Chapter 7

Comparative Perspectives

7.1 Introduction to Comparative Analysis

Embarking on the exploration of the Basic Structure Doctrine through comparative analysis unveils a complex terrain, where legal, historical, and socio-political dimensions intersect. As scholars and jurists delve into this multifaceted realm, the methodological approach plays a pivotal role. Comparative analysis is not a one-size-fits-all endeavor; instead, it demands a nuanced understanding of the 'whys' behind legal patterns and the 'hows' of constitutional evolution.

One approach to comparative analysis involves a meticulous examination of case law. Through this lens, scholars dissect judgments, identify legal reasoning, and understand the judicial philosophies that underpin decisions related to the Basic Structure Doctrine. Case law provides a window into the evolution of constitutional principles, offering insights into the principles upheld or challenged in different jurisdictions.

Another avenue for exploration is an in-depth analysis of constitutional texts. Unraveling the explicit or implicit recognition of the basic structure within these foundational documents provides a unique perspective. Comparative scrutiny of constitutional provisions sheds light on how different jurisdictions embed the Basic Structure Doctrine in their constitutional frameworks.

A socio-legal approach becomes imperative to fully comprehend comparative dimensions. Societal dynamics, including public attitudes, political climates, and historical legacies, influence judicial decisions. Understanding the interplay between legal principles and broader societal contexts is essential to appreciating why certain constitutional interpretations gain prominence in some jurisdictions while facing resistance in others.

Challenges abound in the realm of comparative analysis. Superficial comparisons risk oversimplification, potentially missing the intricacies that define each jurisdiction's approach to the Basic Structure Doctrine. Language, cultural context, and legal traditions add layers of complexity, requiring a methodological approach that appreciates the multidimensional nature of comparative analysis.

Legal pluralism further complicates the landscape. The coexistence of multiple legal systems within a single jurisdiction demands a nuanced exploration of how the Basic Structure Doctrine intersects with indigenous legal traditions or religious legal systems. Comparative analysis within legal pluralism necessitates a delicate balance, recognizing that constitutional interpretations may vary across these diverse legal frameworks.

The significance of historical context cannot be overstated. For postcolonial nations, the Basic Structure Doctrine carries the imprint of struggles for independence, the framing of new constitutions, and the desire to prevent future erosions of fundamental principles. Historical narratives shape why certain constitutional principles gain prominence or face resistance, providing a lens through which to understand the evolution of the Basic Structure Doctrine in different jurisdictions.

Navigating these methodological challenges requires a scholarly rigor that appreciates the rich tapestry of narratives, historical contexts, and legal pluralism. Comparative analysis within the Basic Structure Doctrine is not a mere academic exercise; it is a journey into the heart of constitutional thought globally. The exploration goes beyond legal divergences, uncovering shared challenges, and revealing the intricate intersections of constitutional principles across diverse legal frameworks.

7.2 Historical Development of Constitutional Doctrines

Exploring the historical development of constitutional doctrines provides a panoramic view of the evolution of legal principles that shape the foundations of governance.

This journey transcends borders and delves into the rich tapestry of narratives, jurisprudential philosophies, and societal dynamics that have influenced constitutional thought over centuries.

Early Constitutional Ideals

The roots of constitutionalism can be traced back to ancient civilizations where rudimentary forms of governance existed. Ancient legal codes, such as the Code of Ur-Nammu in Mesopotamia or the Twelve Tables in Ancient Rome, reflected early attempts to codify laws and establish a semblance of constitutional order. These foundational documents laid the groundwork for later constitutional developments.

Medieval Influences

The medieval period witnessed the emergence of charters and agreements that sought to limit the powers of monarchs and protect the rights of subjects. The Magna Carta of 1215 in England is a landmark example, representing a contractual limitation on the authority of the monarch and establishing the principle that even rulers were bound by the law. This marked a crucial shift in the relationship between rulers and the ruled, setting the stage for the development of constitutional doctrines.

The Renaissance and Enlightenment

The Renaissance and Enlightenment periods ushered in an era of intellectual ferment, challenging traditional notions of authority and advocating for the protection of individual rights. Thinkers like John Locke and Montesquieu articulated theories of government that emphasized the social contract, separation of powers, and the inherent rights of individuals. These ideas laid the groundwork for constitutional principles that would later shape modern democracies.

American Revolution and Constitutionalism

The American Revolution of 1776 was a watershed moment in the history of constitutional development. The United States' Declaration of Independence articulated the idea that governments derive their just powers from the consent of the governed, echoing Locke's social contract theory. The U.S. Constitution, drafted in 1787, became a model for constitutional design, incorporating separation of powers, checks and balances, and a bill of rights.

19th Century Constitutionalism

The 19th century witnessed the spread of constitutional ideals across Europe and Latin America. The Napoleonic Code in France, the German Confederation's constitutional experiments, and Latin American independence movements all reflected a growing recognition of constitutional principles. The notion of constitutionalism as a bulwark against arbitrary rule gained prominence.

Post-World War II Constitutionalism

The aftermath of World War II saw a global resurgence of constitutionalism as nations sought to rebuild and establish democratic governance. The Universal Declaration of Human Rights in 1948 signaled a commitment to protecting fundamental human rights on an international scale. In Europe, the formation of the European Union and the European Convention on Human Rights marked significant steps towards regional constitutional cooperation.

Contemporary Challenges and Innovations

The 20th and 21st centuries brought new challenges and innovations to constitutional doctrines. The rise of globalization, the proliferation of human rights discourse, and technological advancements have necessitated a reevaluation of constitutional principles. Issues such as privacy rights in the digital age, environmental concerns, and the intersection of constitutional law with international law have become focal points of contemporary constitutional development.

Judicial Activism and Interpretation

The role of judiciaries in interpreting and shaping constitutional doctrines has become increasingly prominent. Judicial activism, where courts actively interpret and enforce constitutional provisions, has been a defining feature of constitutional development in many jurisdictions. Landmark decisions have expanded the scope of constitutional rights and addressed pressing societal issues.

Conclusion

The historical development of constitutional doctrines is a testament to the ever-evolving nature of governance and the persistent quest for justice, rights, and democratic principles. From ancient codes to modern constitutional democracies, this journey reflects the collective human endeavor to establish frameworks that uphold the dignity and freedoms of individuals within a structured legal order. As we navigate the complexities of contemporary constitutional challenges, understanding this historical trajectory provides valuable insights into the enduring principles that underpin constitutional thought worldwide.

7.3 Basic Structure Doctrine in Different Jurisdictions

Examining the Basic Structure Doctrine across different jurisdictions offers a fascinating exploration into how constitutional principles evolve within diverse legal frameworks. From India to Germany, South Africa to Bangladesh, the Basic Structure Doctrine manifests itself in unique ways, shaped by historical contexts, legal traditions, and societal dynamics.

India: Pioneering the Basic Structure Doctrine

The genesis of the Basic Structure Doctrine can be traced to India, where the Supreme Court, in the landmark case of Kesavananda Bharati v. State of Kerala (1973), articulated the idea that while Parliament has the power to amend the constitution, it cannot alter its basic structure. The Court, through a series of decisions, identified certain essential features that form the core of the Indian Constitution. These include the supremacy of the Constitution, the republican and democratic form of government, the secular character of the Constitution, federalism, and the separation of powers.

The Indian experience with the Basic Structure Doctrine has been dynamic, with the judiciary actively interpreting and applying these principles to safeguard constitutional integrity. The doctrine has played a crucial role in preventing arbitrary amendments that could undermine the foundational values of the Constitution.

Germany: Balancing Constitutional Identity

In Germany, the concept of the Basic Structure Doctrine finds resonance in the idea of "eternity clauses" within the Basic Law (Grundgesetz). These clauses explicitly declare certain constitutional principles, like human dignity and federalism, as unamendable. The German Constitutional Court, while not explicitly adopting the term "Basic Structure Doctrine," has affirmed the idea that amendments should not undermine the essential principles of the constitution.

The German approach reflects a delicate balance between the need for constitutional flexibility and the imperative to protect core constitutional values. The notion of eternity clauses sets boundaries on the power of amendment, ensuring that fundamental principles remain inviolable.

South Africa: Constitutional Supremacy and Transformative Constitutionalism

In post-apartheid South Africa, the Basic Structure Doctrine takes the form of constitutional supremacy and transformative constitutionalism. The Constitutional Court, in the case of Doctors for Life International v. Speaker of the National Assembly (2006), emphasized that constitutional amendments must adhere to the foundational values of the constitution, particularly the Bill of Rights. This approach aligns with the transformative constitutionalism that seeks to address historical injustices and transform society.

The South African experience highlights the role of the judiciary in upholding the constitutional vision of a just and inclusive society. The Basic Structure Doctrine, in this context, becomes a tool for ensuring that amendments contribute to, rather than undermine, the transformative goals of the constitution.

Bangladesh: The Evolving Landscape

In Bangladesh, the Basic Structure Doctrine has emerged through judicial interpretations that emphasize the supremacy of the constitution. The case of Anwar Hossain Chowdhury v. Bangladesh (1989) marked a significant moment when the Supreme Court declared certain fundamental principles, including democracy and the separation of powers, as part of the basic structure.

The Bangladeshi experience reflects the evolving nature of the Basic Structure Doctrine, with the judiciary adapting it to the constitutional context of the country. As in India, the doctrine serves as a check on arbitrary amendments that could compromise the foundational values of the constitution.

Comparative Analysis: Themes and Variations

Across these jurisdictions, common themes emerge. The Basic Structure Doctrine is often invoked to prevent amendments that would alter the essential features of the constitution. Constitutional supremacy and the protection of fundamental rights are recurring themes, reflecting a commitment to upholding core constitutional values.

However, variations exist in the way each jurisdiction defines its basic structure. While India explicitly identifies certain features, Germany relies on eternity clauses, and South Africa emphasizes transformative constitutionalism. These differences reflect the unique historical and legal contexts within which these doctrines operate.

Challenges and Critiques

The application of the Basic Structure Doctrine is not without challenges and critiques. Questions arise about the role of the judiciary in determining the basic structure, potential judicial overreach, and the need for a more democratic process in constitutional amendments. Critics argue that a rigid Basic Structure Doctrine could impede legitimate constitutional changes.

Conclusion

Exploring the Basic Structure Doctrine in different jurisdictions reveals a dynamic interplay between constitutional principles, legal traditions, and societal aspirations. Whether explicitly recognized or implicitly embedded, the doctrine serves as a safeguard against arbitrary amendments and a protector of core constitutional values. As legal systems continue to evolve, the Basic Structure Doctrine remains a crucial tool for ensuring that constitutional amendments align with the enduring principles that form the bedrock of democratic governance.

7.4 Impact on Legal Systems

The Basic Structure Doctrine has a profound impact on legal systems across the globe, influencing constitutional governance, judicial roles, and the interpretation of fundamental legal principles.

Judicial Activism and Constitutional Adjudication

In jurisdictions recognizing the doctrine, courts play a pivotal role in interpreting and safeguarding the basic structure. This shift towards an activist judiciary is evident in landmark decisions where courts actively engage in reviewing legislative actions and constitutional amendments to ensure compliance with the basic structure.

Constitutional Limitations on Amendment Powers

The Basic Structure Doctrine imposes limitations on the amendment powers of legislative bodies. In countries where this doctrine is embraced, the legislature's authority to alter fundamental aspects of the constitution is circumscribed. This limitation ensures that the core values and principles enshrined in the constitution remain resilient to arbitrary changes, offering a form of constitutional stability.

Protection of Fundamental Rights

An inherent impact of the Basic Structure Doctrine is the protection and preservation of fundamental rights. By identifying certain features as part of the basic structure, courts establish a benchmark for evaluating the constitutionality of legislative actions. This, in turn, safeguards individual rights and liberties, preventing their erosion through amendments that may run counter to the constitutional ethos.

Ensuring Constitutional Consistency

The doctrine acts as a check against inconsistencies within the constitution. By delineating the basic structure, courts create a framework for internal coherence.

Amendments that deviate from this framework risk being declared unconstitutional, ensuring that the constitution maintains a consistent and harmonious character.

Role in Constitutional Interpretation

The Basic Structure Doctrine influences the methodology of constitutional interpretation. Courts, in their quest to preserve the basic structure, engage in interpretative exercises that go beyond the literal text of the constitution. This dynamic approach to constitutional interpretation allows for a more context-sensitive understanding of constitutional provisions.

Balancing Democracy and Constitutionalism

The impact of the Basic Structure Doctrine extends to the delicate balance between democracy and constitutionalism. While upholding democratic principles, the doctrine serves as a safeguard against majoritarian excesses that might undermine the foundational values of the constitution. It establishes a framework where democratic governance coexists with the protection of constitutional fundamentals.

Evolution of Constitutional Jurisprudence

The recognition of the Basic Structure Doctrine contributes to the evolution of constitutional jurisprudence. Landmark cases that define and refine the contours of the basic structure become pivotal in shaping legal thought and influencing subsequent decisions. This evolution reflects the adaptability of legal systems to changing societal norms and challenges.

Impact on Legal Education and Scholarship

The doctrine's impact extends to legal education and scholarship, fostering a deeper understanding of constitutional principles. Law schools and scholars engage in the analysis of cases related to the basic structure, contributing to the broader discourse on constitutional law. The doctrine becomes a subject of academic inquiry, influencing the curriculum and shaping the perspectives of future legal practitioners.

International Influence

In an era of global interconnectedness, the impact of the Basic Structure Doctrine goes beyond national borders. Jurisdictions that recognize and apply this doctrine contribute to a broader international conversation on constitutional governance. Comparative constitutional law studies benefit from insights gained through the examination of how different legal systems grapple with preserving their basic structures.

Challenges and Criticisms

While the impact is substantial, the Basic Structure Doctrine is not without its challenges and criticisms. Some argue that it can lead to judicial overreach, potentially undermining the democratic will of the people. Others contend that the inherent vagueness of identifying the basic structure may give courts excessive discretion.

Conclusion

The impact of the Basic Structure Doctrine on legal systems is multifaceted, influencing the judiciary, constitutional interpretation, legislative powers, and the broader legal landscape. As this doctrine continues to evolve and adapt to changing societal contexts, its impact on legal systems will remain a central theme in constitutional discourse worldwide.

7.5 Divergence and Convergence

The Basic Structure Doctrine's influence on legal systems globally unfolds through a nuanced tapestry of divergence and convergence. This dynamic interplay reflects the diverse ways in which different jurisdictions interpret and apply the doctrine, contributing to the evolution of constitutional governance.

Judicial Approaches

Within the realm of constitutional interpretation, there exists a divergence in judicial approaches. Some jurisdictions adopt a broad and flexible interpretation of the basic structure, allowing for a dynamic response to societal changes. In contrast, others may adhere to a more rigid and narrow approach, emphasizing the original intent of the constitution's framers. These divergent approaches underscore the inherent flexibility or rigidity in applying the Basic Structure Doctrine.

Impact on Legislative Powers

The Basic Structure Doctrine's impact on legislative powers exhibits both convergence and divergence. In jurisdictions where the doctrine is embraced, there is a convergence in limiting the powers of legislatures to amend foundational aspects of the constitution. However, the specific limitations and the extent to which legislative powers are curtailed may vary, leading to divergent outcomes in different legal systems.

Protection of Fundamental Rights

Convergence emerges in the realm of protecting fundamental rights. The identification of certain principles as part of the basic structure often aligns with the global consensus on fundamental rights. However, the divergence lies in the specific rights considered fundamental and the scope of protection afforded to them. Some jurisdictions may prioritize social and economic rights, while others may place a greater emphasis on civil and political rights.

Institutional Dynamics

Divergence becomes apparent in the institutional dynamics shaped by the Basic Structure Doctrine. The role assigned to the judiciary in safeguarding the basic structure varies across jurisdictions. Some legal systems witness an active and interventionist judiciary, while others may adopt a more restrained approach, deferring to the legislative or executive branches. These institutional dynamics contribute to the divergent paths in the application of the doctrine.

Adaptation to Social Context

Convergence and divergence intertwine in how legal systems adapt the Basic Structure Doctrine to their social contexts. While there is a shared recognition of the need for adaptability, the specific features identified as part of the basic structure may diverge based on cultural, historical, and social considerations. The doctrine's resonance with the prevailing societal ethos contributes to both convergence in recognizing its relevance and divergence in its specific application.

International Dialogue

The Basic Structure Doctrine fosters convergence in international legal dialogue. Jurisdictions engaging with the doctrine contribute to a shared understanding of constitutional principles, influencing global constitutional discourse. However, divergence arises as legal systems navigate their unique historical and political landscapes, incorporating the doctrine into their constitutional fabric in distinct ways.

Challenges and Responses

Divergence is evident in the challenges posed to legal systems by the Basic Structure Doctrine. Different jurisdictions grapple with challenges such as balancing judicial review with democratic principles, defining the scope of the basic structure, and addressing criticisms of judicial overreach. Responses to these challenges vary, reflecting the unique legal, political, and cultural contexts of each jurisdiction.

Conclusion

The Basic Structure Doctrine, with its convergence and divergence, enriches the global constitutional landscape. As legal systems navigate the intricate dynamics of interpretation, application, and adaptation, the doctrine becomes a catalyst for both shared principles and diverse expressions of constitutional governance. The interplay of convergence and divergence underscores the dynamic and evolving nature of the Basic Structure Doctrine across jurisdictions.

7.6 Judicial Activism and Restraint

The role of the judiciary in interpreting and applying the Basic Structure Doctrine gives rise to a nuanced interplay between judicial activism and restraint. This dynamic relationship shapes the judiciary's approach to constitutional matters and influences the broader legal landscape.

Judicial Activism

In jurisdictions recognizing the Basic Structure Doctrine, instances of judicial activism are notable. Judicial activism refers to a proactive role assumed by the judiciary in interpreting and safeguarding constitutional principles. Courts engaging in judicial activism often assert themselves as guardians of the basic structure, actively reviewing legislative actions and amendments to ensure alignment with constitutional fundamentals.

Expansive Interpretation

Judicial activism manifests in the form of expansive interpretation. Courts, when adopting an activist stance, may interpret constitutional provisions liberally to protect and promote the values identified as part of the basic structure. This approach allows for a dynamic and evolving understanding of constitutional principles in response to changing societal dynamics.

Protection of Fundamental Rights

One hallmark of judicial activism within the Basic Structure Doctrine is the heightened protection of fundamental rights. Activist courts are more inclined to scrutinize legislation that may infringe upon individual rights, ensuring that any encroachment is justified within the parameters of the basic structure. This proactive protection of rights contributes to a robust human rights jurisprudence.

Striking Down Legislation

Courts engaging in judicial activism are more likely to strike down legislation that runs afoul of the basic structure. This involves the court declaring a law unconstitutional and, in some cases, prescribing remedies or guidelines for legislative redress. The willingness to strike down legislation underscores the judiciary's commitment to upholding constitutional principles.

Policy Formulation

Judicial activism extends to policy formulation, where courts actively participate in shaping public policy. Activist judges may go beyond the traditional adjudicatory role and provide directives or recommendations to address societal issues. This involvement in policy matters reflects a belief in the judiciary's capacity to contribute to broader social transformation.

Judicial Restraint

Conversely, judicial restraint represents a more cautious and deferential approach by the judiciary. Courts practicing restraint refrain from actively intervening in legislative and executive domains unless there is a clear violation of constitutional principles. Restraint acknowledges the importance of democratic processes and the separation of powers.

Limiting Judicial Review

Judicial restraint involves limiting the scope of judicial review, particularly concerning legislative acts. Courts may defer to the legislative branch, recognizing its prerogative to make policy decisions. This approach is rooted in a belief that unelected judges should exercise restraint to respect the democratic will of elected representatives.

Preserving Legislative Autonomy

Restraint entails preserving legislative autonomy unless there is a manifest constitutional violation. Courts exercising restraint are less likely to strike down legislation and may adopt a deferential attitude towards legislative choices. This approach seeks to strike a balance between judicial review and the principle of separation of powers.

Balancing Act

The interplay between judicial activism and restraint constitutes a delicate balancing act. Courts must navigate the tension between upholding constitutional principles and respecting democratic processes. Striking the right balance ensures that the judiciary plays a meaningful role in safeguarding the basic structure without unduly encroaching on the powers of the legislative and executive branches.

Conclusion

The nuanced relationship between judicial activism and restraint within the Basic Structure Doctrine reflects the judiciary's evolving role in constitutional governance. Whether leaning towards activism or restraint, courts contribute to the ongoing dialogue on the interpretation and preservation of constitutional principles. This dynamic interplay is a defining feature of the judiciary's engagement with the Basic Structure Doctrine across diverse legal systems.

7.7 Comparative Case Studies

Examining the application of the Basic Structure Doctrine across different jurisdictions unveils a rich tapestry of experiences and outcomes. Comparative case studies illuminate how distinct legal systems grapple with constitutional challenges and engage with the foundational principles identified as part of the basic structure.

United States

In the United States, the concept of a basic structure is implicit rather than explicitly outlined in the Constitution. The Supreme Court, through landmark decisions like Marbury v. Madison (1803) and Brown v. Board of Education (1954), has played a crucial role in interpreting and safeguarding constitutional principles. The U.S. judiciary's approach, characterized by a strong tradition of judicial review, reflects a commitment to upholding the Constitution's fundamental tenets.

Germany

Germany's Basic Law (Grundgesetz) serves as a unique case study in post-war constitutionalism. The German Federal Constitutional Court has actively engaged in shaping the basic structure through decisions like the Lüth case (1958) and the Maastricht Treaty case (1993). The German approach emphasizes the protection of human dignity and places constitutional values at the core of judicial review, showcasing a commitment to learning from historical mistakes.

South Africa

The post-apartheid South African Constitution introduces an explicit and expansive list of foundational values. The Constitutional Court, in cases like Certification of the Constitution of the Republic of South Africa (1996), has employed a transformative approach. This approach involves interpreting the basic structure in a manner that addresses historical injustices and promotes social and economic transformation, illustrating a unique socio-legal dynamic.

India

India's Basic Structure Doctrine, originating in Kesavananda Bharati v. State of Kerala (1973), represents a pivotal case study. The Indian judiciary has actively shaped and expanded the basic structure through subsequent decisions like Minerva Mills Ltd. v. Union of India (1980) and Waman Rao v. Union of India (1981). The doctrine's application in diverse contexts, including federalism, secularism, and social justice, underscores its adaptability to India's socio-political landscape.

United Kingdom

The United Kingdom, lacking a written constitution, navigates constitutional principles through statutes and common law. The concept of a basic structure is implicit, and the judiciary relies on legal conventions and principles. Decisions like Anisminic Ltd. v. Foreign Compensation Commission (1969) exemplify the UK courts' commitment to upholding the rule of law, contributing to an evolving constitutional landscape.

Brazil

Brazil's Supreme Federal Court has grappled with the basic structure through landmark decisions like the Case of the Closure of the Brazilian Communist Party (1981). The Brazilian approach emphasizes the supremacy of the Constitution and the judiciary's role as the ultimate interpreter of constitutional principles, showcasing a commitment to constitutionalism in the face of political challenges.

Conclusion

Comparative case studies highlight the diversity and adaptability of the Basic Structure Doctrine across legal systems. Each jurisdiction's unique historical, cultural, and political context shapes the doctrine's interpretation and application. Understanding these diverse experiences contributes to a more nuanced appreciation of how the basic structure functions as a dynamic and context-specific constitutional principle globally.

7.8 Influence on Constitutional Amendments

The Basic Structure Doctrine profoundly influences the process of amending constitutions in jurisdictions that recognize its existence. Constitutional amendments are a critical aspect of legal evolution, and the application of the Basic Structure Doctrine introduces a layer of complexity and scrutiny to these transformative processes.

Limitations on Amendment Power

One of the key implications of the Basic Structure Doctrine is the imposition of limitations on the power to amend the constitution. The judiciary, acting as the guardian of the basic structure, asserts the authority to review and potentially invalidate constitutional amendments that violate or seek to alter the fundamental principles identified as part of the basic structure.

Judicial Review of Amendments

Courts in jurisdictions adhering to the Basic Structure Doctrine engage in rigorous judicial review when assessing the validity of constitutional amendments. The review involves an examination of whether the proposed amendment infringes upon the core principles integral to the constitutional framework. Courts may strike down amendments that are deemed incompatible with the basic structure, ensuring a consistent adherence to constitutional fundamentals.

Identifying the Basic Structure

One of the challenges in cases involving constitutional amendments is the determination of what constitutes the basic structure. The judiciary plays a crucial role in identifying and delineating these core principles. This process involves a nuanced analysis of the constitution's text, historical context, and evolving societal values to ascertain the foundational elements that must remain inviolable.

Balancing Constitutional Rigidity and Flexibility

The Basic Structure Doctrine introduces a delicate balance between constitutional rigidity and flexibility. While the doctrine aims to safeguard core principles from arbitrary changes, it also acknowledges the need for constitutional adaptability. Courts must navigate this balance judiciously, ensuring that the basic structure remains resilient while allowing for legitimate and necessary constitutional amendments.

Evolution of Basic Structure

The concept of the basic structure is not static; it evolves over time. Courts must grapple with the challenge of interpreting the basic structure in the context of contemporary issues and changing societal norms. The dynamic nature of the basic structure requires courts to adopt a forward-looking approach that accommodates evolving constitutional values.

Political and Legal Debates

The Basic Structure Doctrine often triggers significant political and legal debates when constitutional amendments are proposed. These debates revolve around the scope of the basic structure, the role of the judiciary, and the balance between democratic principles and constitutional constraints. The resolution of these debates shapes the trajectory of constitutional amendments and influences the broader discourse on constitutionalism.

Preserving Constitutional Identity

A central aim of the Basic Structure Doctrine in the context of constitutional amendments is to preserve the constitutional identity. Courts endeavor to prevent amendments that could fundamentally alter the character of the constitution or undermine its core principles. This preservation of constitutional identity ensures continuity in the constitutional order while allowing for meaningful and principled changes.

Conclusion

The influence of the Basic Structure Doctrine on constitutional amendments reflects a commitment to maintaining the constitutional order's integrity and coherence. Courts, through judicious judicial review, contribute to the ongoing dialogue on constitutional evolution, ensuring that amendments align with the enduring principles encapsulated in the basic structure. This intricate interplay between constitutional amendments and the Basic Structure Doctrine shapes the legal and political landscape in jurisdictions where this doctrine holds sway.

7.9 Public Perception and Reception

The Basic Structure Doctrine, as a constitutional principle, exerts a profound impact on public perception and reception. Its application in judicial decisions and its interaction with societal dynamics contribute to shaping how the doctrine is perceived by the public and how it, in turn, influences broader attitudes towards constitutional governance.

Public Awareness and Education

The recognition and understanding of the Basic Structure Doctrine among the general public play a pivotal role in shaping its reception. Legal literacy campaigns, educational initiatives, and public discourse contribute to raising awareness about the doctrine's existence, significance, and the role it plays in safeguarding constitutional principles. A well-informed public is more likely to appreciate the doctrine's importance in upholding the constitutional framework.

Media Representation

The media's role in disseminating information about legal concepts, including the Basic Structure Doctrine, significantly influences public perception. News coverage, legal analyses, and commentary shape the narrative surrounding the doctrine. Media outlets contribute to framing discussions about judicial decisions that involve the basic structure, influencing how the public perceives the doctrine's impact on governance and constitutional values.

Public Trust in the Judiciary

The application of the Basic Structure Doctrine by the judiciary can impact public trust in the legal system. Decisions that demonstrate the judiciary's commitment to upholding constitutional principles, even in the face of political or societal pressures, enhance public trust. Conversely, perceptions of judicial overreach or inconsistency may lead to skepticism about the doctrine's effectiveness.

Political Narratives

Political actors often engage with the Basic Structure Doctrine in shaping their narratives and garnering public support. Debates in political arenas, legislative discussions, and political campaigns may involve references to the basic structure to underscore a commitment to constitutional principles or challenge specific policies. The political discourse contributes to public perceptions of the doctrine's relevance and impact on governance.

Challenges to Legitimacy

Controversial applications of the Basic Structure Doctrine may lead to challenges regarding the legitimacy of judicial decisions. Public debates may arise over the perceived role of the judiciary in shaping policy outcomes. Balancing the doctrine's role with democratic governance and the will of the people is a nuanced challenge, and public reactions to such debates can influence the doctrine's acceptance.

Social Movements and Activism

Social movements and activist initiatives that align with or challenge the Basic Structure Doctrine contribute to public discourse. Movements advocating for constitutional values may view the doctrine as a bulwark against potential infringements, while dissenting voices may critique it as hindering democratic decision-making. These dynamics shape the public's stance on the doctrine.

Cultural and Societal Shifts

Cultural and societal shifts over time can impact how the Basic Structure Doctrine is received. Evolving social norms, generational changes, and cultural transformations influence perspectives on constitutional principles. The doctrine's resonance with contemporary values and its adaptability to societal shifts contribute to its enduring relevance.

Public Perceptions of Justice

The Basic Structure Doctrine's impact on justice and fairness is integral to public perceptions. Instances where the doctrine is applied to rectify historical injustices or protect marginalized communities may enhance its image as a tool for justice. Conversely, concerns about the doctrine impeding certain policy goals may lead to divergent views on its role in promoting justice.

Conclusion

The interplay between the Basic Structure Doctrine and public perception is a multifaceted dynamic that reflects the broader relationship between constitutional principles and societal attitudes. Public awareness, media representation, political narratives, and societal movements collectively contribute to how the doctrine is perceived and received. Recognizing and understanding these dynamics is crucial for assessing the doctrine's impact on the broader fabric of constitutional governance.

7.10 Future Trends and Comparative Prospects

The Basic Structure Doctrine, as a cornerstone of constitutional jurisprudence, not only shapes the present legal landscape but also holds significant implications for future trends and offers insights into comparative constitutional developments across jurisdictions.

Continued Evolution of Basic Structure

The trajectory of the Basic Structure Doctrine suggests that its evolution is an ongoing process. Courts grapple with emerging constitutional challenges, technological advancements, and shifting societal paradigms. The doctrine's continued evolution will likely be influenced by these factors, ensuring its adaptability to the changing dynamics of governance.

Impact on Constitutional Design

The influence of the Basic Structure Doctrine extends to its impact on future constitutional designs. Jurisdictions considering constitutional reforms or drafting new constitutions may look to the basic structure as a guiding principle to safeguard fundamental values. The doctrine's recognition may influence the drafting process, leading to the incorporation of explicit provisions protecting the constitutional core.

Global Diffusion of Basic Structure Principles

The Basic Structure Doctrine, originally developed in specific jurisdictions, has the potential to influence constitutional thinking globally. As legal scholars and practitioners study its applications and implications, the principles underlying the basic structure may find resonance in the constitutional frameworks of other nations. Comparative analyses and cross-jurisdictional studies contribute to the global diffusion of basic structure principles.

Challenges to Global Constitutionalism

The doctrine's influence on future trends includes its potential role in addressing challenges to global constitutionalism. As nations grapple with issues such as populism, authoritarianism, and threats to democratic governance, the basic structure can serve as a bulwark against constitutional erosion. Comparative experiences may guide countries in navigating these challenges while preserving constitutional values.

Technological and Socioeconomic Considerations

Future trends in constitutional law will inevitably be shaped by technological advancements and socioeconomic developments. The Basic Structure Doctrine, when confronted with issues arising from technological innovations or economic transformations, will play a crucial role in ensuring that constitutional principles are resilient and adaptable. Courts may be called upon to interpret the basic structure in light of these evolving dynamics.

Judicial Activism vs. Restraint

The ongoing debate between judicial activism and restraint will continue to influence the trajectory of the Basic Structure Doctrine. Courts will grapple with the delicate balance between safeguarding constitutional principles and respecting democratic processes. The doctrinal approach taken by judiciaries will set precedents for future cases, impacting the broader discourse on the role of the judiciary in constitutional governance.

Human Rights and Basic Structure

The intersection between human rights and the Basic Structure Doctrine will be a focal point for future constitutional developments. Courts may increasingly interpret the basic structure in alignment with evolving human rights standards, ensuring that constitutional protections remain consistent with international norms. This alignment contributes to the global discourse on constitutional rights and freedoms.

Comparative Constitutional Case Studies

As nations engage in comparative constitutional case studies, the Basic Structure Doctrine will serve as a benchmark for assessing the robustness of constitutional frameworks. Comparative analyses will explore how different jurisdictions navigate constitutional challenges, providing valuable insights into the strengths and limitations of the basic structure as a constitutional safeguard.

Preserving Constitutional Identity

The doctrine's role in preserving constitutional identity will be pivotal in future constitutional trends. Courts will be tasked with discerning the essential features that define a nation's constitutional identity and ensuring their protection. The doctrine's application will contribute to the preservation of diverse constitutional identities in the face of global and domestic pressures.

Conclusion

The Basic Structure Doctrine's influence on future trends and its comparative prospects underscore its enduring significance in the realm of constitutional law. As nations grapple with evolving challenges, the basic structure serves as a lodestar for preserving constitutional values, fostering global constitutional dialogue, and contributing to the ongoing development of constitutional jurisprudence. Its impact will reverberate across jurisdictions, offering valuable lessons for the future of constitutional governance.

The exploration of the Basic Structure Doctrine's influence on future trends and its comparative prospects reveals a dynamic and multifaceted impact on constitutional jurisprudence. As a foundational principle, the doctrine extends its reach beyond immediate legal considerations, shaping the trajectory of constitutional development in a global context.

The doctrine's continued evolution emerges as a central theme, reflecting its adaptability to contemporary challenges and changing societal dynamics. Courts across jurisdictions grapple with the nuanced interplay between the basic structure and emerging issues, showcasing the doctrine's resilience in addressing novel constitutional questions. The ongoing evolution of the basic structure reaffirms its relevance as a living constitutional concept.

Influencing constitutional design emerges as a significant dimension of the basic structure's impact on future trends. Nations contemplating constitutional reforms or embarking on the creation of new constitutions are likely to draw inspiration from the basic structure as a safeguard for fundamental values. This influence on constitutional design underscores the doctrine's role as a guiding principle in shaping the constitutional foundations of diverse legal systems.

The global diffusion of basic structure principles emerges as a key theme, highlighting the doctrine's potential to transcend national boundaries. Comparative constitutional studies and cross-jurisdictional analyses contribute to the dissemination of basic structure concepts, fostering a shared understanding of constitutional safeguards. The doctrine's principles become part of a broader global constitutional discourse, enriching the exchange of ideas and experiences.

Addressing challenges to global constitutionalism emerges as a critical aspect of the basic structure's influence on future trends. In an era marked by threats to democratic governance, authoritarianism, and populism, the doctrine stands as a bulwark against constitutional erosion. Its principles offer a principled response to challenges faced by constitutional democracies worldwide, providing a blueprint for upholding constitutional values.

The interplay between the basic structure and technological advancements, socioeconomic considerations, and the delicate balance between judicial activism and restraint further shapes the trajectory of future trends. Courts find themselves at the intersection of constitutional principles and the evolving dynamics of modern society, navigating complex legal terrain with an eye on preserving constitutional integrity.

Human rights, an essential component of constitutional discourse, intersect with the basic structure, contributing to a rights-based interpretation of constitutional principles. The alignment of the basic structure with evolving human rights standards underscores its role in ensuring constitutional protections that resonate with international norms.

As nations engage in comparative constitutional case studies, the Basic Structure Doctrine emerges as a benchmark for assessing the robustness of constitutional frameworks. These comparative analyses provide valuable insights into how different jurisdictions navigate constitutional challenges, contributing to the global discourse on constitutional rights and freedoms.

Preserving constitutional identity emerges as a pivotal theme, with the doctrine playing a crucial role in discerning and protecting the essential features that define a nation's constitutional identity. This emphasis on preserving diverse constitutional identities contributes to the richness of global constitutionalism, ensuring that constitutional principles remain reflective of the unique historical, cultural, and social contexts of each nation.

In conclusion, the Basic Structure Doctrine's influence on future trends and its comparative prospects transcends the confines of legal doctrine. It resonates as a dynamic force shaping the constitutional landscape globally, contributing to the ongoing dialogue on constitutional governance, rights, and the delicate balance between judicial oversight and democratic processes. As the basic structure continues to evolve, its legacy becomes intertwined with the shared aspirations for constitutional order and justice across diverse legal systems.

Chapter 8

Future Horizons: The Evolving Canvas

8.1 Introduction to Future Trends

The canvas of constitutional law is continuously evolving, painted by the brushstrokes of legal minds, societal shifts, and global dynamics. As we stand on the threshold of the future, anticipating the trends that will shape constitutional governance becomes a fascinating endeavor. The following exploration delves into the nuanced interplay of various factors that will likely influence the trajectory of constitutional law in the coming years.

At the heart of future trends is the digital revolution, which has permeated every facet of modern life. The advent of technology brings both promise and peril to constitutional frameworks. The challenges of balancing technological advancements with individual rights, particularly in the realms of privacy, artificial intelligence, and cybersecurity, will undoubtedly occupy a central place in future constitutional discourse. The evolving jurisprudence on digital rights will be pivotal in defining the parameters of freedom and security in an interconnected world.

Globalization, with its intricate web of economic, political, and cultural interdependencies, casts a long shadow over constitutional considerations. As nations become increasingly interconnected, constitutional law must grapple with the complexities of transnational issues. The harmonization of legal standards and the recognition of universal human rights present both opportunities and challenges, necessitating a delicate balance between national sovereignty and international cooperation.

Environmental sustainability emerges as a pressing concern that will shape the future contours of constitutional law. The imperative to address climate change and ecological degradation demands innovative legal solutions. Constitutional frameworks will likely be challenged to integrate principles of environmental justice, sustainability, and the protection of future generations into their foundational principles.

The social fabric of societies is evolving, marked by changing norms, demographics, and expressions of identity. Constitutional law, therefore, must be adaptive and responsive to shifting societal values. Issues related to gender equality, LGBTQ+ rights, and cultural diversity will likely occupy the forefront of constitutional debates, pushing for a more inclusive and egalitarian legal landscape.

Economic dynamics, characterized by globalization and rapid technological advancements, pose intricate challenges for constitutional governance. The future will witness constitutional courts engaging with questions of economic justice, fair distribution of resources, and the regulation of emerging economic paradigms. Striking a balance between fostering economic growth and ensuring equitable distribution of benefits will be a delicate task.

In the realm of governance, questions of accountability, transparency, and the role of constitutional institutions will continue to be pivotal. Constitutional frameworks must evolve to meet the expectations of citizens in an era where public participation and scrutiny are facilitated by digital communication. The future will likely see constitutional innovations aimed at enhancing democratic practices and safeguarding against abuses of power.

As we peer into the future, the role of constitutional courts in interpreting foundational principles gains paramount importance. The judiciary's ability to adapt and respond to emerging challenges will determine the resilience and relevance of constitutional governance. The delicate dance between judicial activism and restraint will continue to define the judiciary's role in shaping legal landscapes.

In conclusion, the introduction to future trends sets the stage for a comprehensive exploration of the multifaceted challenges and opportunities that lie ahead. The canvas of constitutional law, ever receptive to the brushstrokes of societal evolution, awaits the hands of those who will craft its next chapters. The following chapters will delve deeper into specific themes, unraveling the intricate tapestry of constitutional governance in the unfolding landscape of the future.

8.2 Technology and Constitutional Governance

In the 21st century, the rapid advancement of technology has ushered in an era of unprecedented challenges and opportunities for constitutional governance. As societies become increasingly reliant on digital infrastructure and emerging technologies, constitutional frameworks must grapple with the intricate interplay between technological innovation and fundamental principles of governance. This exploration delves into the multifaceted dimensions of technology's impact on constitutional governance.

One of the pivotal areas where technology intersects with constitutional principles is in the realm of privacy. The ubiquity of digital devices and the vast collection of personal data raise profound questions about the scope of privacy protections. Constitutional courts worldwide are faced with the task of interpreting existing legal frameworks in the context of evolving surveillance technologies, biometric data collection, and the expansive reach of digital communication platforms. Striking a balance between ensuring individual privacy rights and addressing legitimate security concerns poses a complex challenge for constitutional adjudication.

Artificial Intelligence (AI) emerges as a transformative force that permeates various facets of governance. From automated decision-making in administrative processes to predictive algorithms in criminal justice systems, the impact of AI on constitutional principles is profound. Constitutional courts are tasked with scrutinizing the constitutionality of AI applications, especially concerning issues of due process, accountability, and the potential for discriminatory outcomes. As AI continues to evolve, the legal framework must adapt to safeguard individual rights and prevent the entrenchment of algorithmic biases.

The digital realm also introduces novel challenges to freedom of expression and information. Constitutional courts grapple with issues of online censorship, disinformation, and the regulation of digital platforms. Balancing the imperative of preserving democratic discourse with the need to curb harmful content presents a delicate task. The evolving jurisprudence on digital rights plays a crucial role in defining the contours of freedom of expression in the digital age.

Cybersecurity considerations add another layer of complexity to constitutional governance. As nations navigate the challenges of protecting critical infrastructure and national security in cyberspace, constitutional frameworks must adapt to address the novel threats posed by cyber-attacks. The role of constitutional courts in adjudicating cases related to cybersecurity measures, surveillance laws, and the protection of digital infrastructure becomes increasingly vital.

The rise of digital currencies and blockchain technology introduces new dimensions to constitutional considerations, especially in the realm of economic governance. Constitutional courts may find themselves adjudicating cases related to the regulation of cryptocurrencies, the impact of blockchain on financial systems, and the protection of economic rights in the digital economy. As financial transactions become increasingly digitized, constitutional frameworks must evolve to ensure the stability and fairness of economic systems.

Emerging technologies such as biotechnology, nanotechnology, and neurotechnology pose unique challenges to constitutional governance. Questions related to bodily autonomy, genetic privacy, and the ethical implications of scientific advancements require constitutional courts to navigate uncharted legal territory. The evolving jurisprudence in these domains will shape the boundaries of constitutional rights concerning human dignity and bodily integrity.

In conclusion, the intersection of technology and constitutional governance presents a dynamic landscape where traditional principles must adapt to the complexities of the digital age. Constitutional courts play a central role in defining the parameters of individual rights, democratic governance, and the rule of law in the face of technological advancements. As societies grapple with the transformative effects of technology, constitutional frameworks become the crucial canvas upon which the future of governance is painted.

8.3 Artificial Intelligence and Legal Systems

The advent of Artificial Intelligence (AI) has ushered in a paradigm shift in legal systems across the globe, posing profound challenges and opportunities. As legal scholars and practitioners grapple with the integration of AI into various facets of the legal landscape, constitutional considerations become paramount. This exploration delves into the multifaceted impact of AI on legal systems, examining how it intersects with the foundational principles enshrined in the Indian Constitution.

One of the key areas where AI transforms legal systems is in the realm of judicial decision-making. Automated tools and predictive algorithms are increasingly utilized to assist judges in legal research, case analysis, and even in predicting case outcomes. The introduction of AI in the judiciary raises questions about the right to a fair trial, due process, and the accountability of automated decision-making systems. Constitutional courts must navigate the delicate balance between leveraging AI for efficiency and ensuring that the rights of individuals are not compromised in the process.

AI applications extend beyond the judiciary to the realm of legal research and analysis. Legal professionals increasingly rely on AI-powered tools for contract review, legal research, and document analysis. While these technologies enhance efficiency, they also prompt constitutional considerations regarding the right to legal representation and access to justice. Constitutional frameworks must evolve to accommodate the ethical and legal implications of AI tools in legal practice.

In the criminal justice system, AI is employed for predictive policing, risk assessment, and even sentencing recommendations. The use of algorithms in these contexts raises fundamental questions about fairness, transparency, and potential biases embedded in the data on which AI systems are trained. Constitutional principles of equality before the law, protection against discrimination, and the right to a fair trial necessitate a careful examination of the ethical and legal implications of AI in criminal justice.

The integration of AI in administrative agencies and regulatory bodies also has constitutional implications. Automated decision-making in areas such as immigration, benefits allocation, and regulatory compliance requires scrutiny to ensure that constitutional rights, such as the right to be heard and the right to appeal, are not undermined. The principle of administrative fairness becomes particularly crucial as AI systems play a role in shaping individual rights and entitlements.

As AI technologies advance, concerns about data privacy and protection gain prominence. The use of AI often involves extensive data collection and analysis, raising questions about informational self-determination and the right to privacy. Constitutional frameworks must grapple with the challenges posed by AI-driven surveillance, data profiling, and the potential misuse of personal information.

Moreover, AI's impact on legal education and the practice of law necessitates a reevaluation of constitutional principles related to the right to education and the right to engage in the legal profession. The integration of AI tools in legal curricula and practice introduces new considerations regarding the skills and competencies required of legal professionals in the digital age.

In conclusion, the intersection of AI and legal systems marks a transformative moment in the evolution of constitutional governance. As AI becomes an integral part of the legal landscape, constitutional courts play a pivotal role in ensuring that the principles enshrined in the Indian Constitution adapt to safeguard individual rights, uphold the rule of law, and foster a legal system that is just, transparent, and accountable. The canvas of constitutional principles must be expansive enough to encompass the complexities introduced by AI, ensuring that technology serves as a tool for justice rather than a challenge to constitutional values.

8.4 Environmental Law in the 21st Century

The 21st century presents unprecedented challenges to the global environment, necessitating a reevaluation of legal frameworks to address ecological concerns. Environmental law, in its evolution, intersects with constitutional principles to navigate the delicate balance between developmental imperatives and the imperative to protect the environment. This exploration delves into the multifaceted dimensions of environmental law in the contemporary era, examining its symbiotic relationship with constitutional governance in the context of the Indian Constitution's basic structure doctrine.

One of the central tenets of environmental law is the recognition of the right to a healthy environment as a fundamental right. Constitutional courts play a pivotal role in interpreting and safeguarding this right, ensuring that citizens are entitled to live in an environment that is conducive to their well-being. The evolving jurisprudence around the right to a healthy environment encompasses issues such as access to clean air, water, and a sustainable ecosystem, with constitutional principles guiding the interpretation of statutory provisions and executive actions.

As environmental challenges become increasingly global, the concept of intergenerational equity gains prominence within constitutional considerations. Intergenerational equity posits that the present generation has a responsibility to preserve the environment for the benefit of future generations. Constitutional frameworks must grapple with the temporal dimensions of environmental protection, ensuring that decisions made today do not compromise the rights and interests of future generations. This principle becomes a vital thread woven into the fabric of the basic structure doctrine, reflecting the timeless commitment to environmental sustainability.

The intersection of environmental law and economic development raises intricate constitutional considerations. While development is essential for societal progress, it must not come at the cost of irreversible environmental degradation. Constitutional courts are called upon to adjudicate cases that involve striking a balance between economic development and environmental protection. This involves interpreting constitutional provisions related to the right to livelihood, property, and economic freedoms, ensuring that sustainable development becomes a guiding principle within the constitutional framework.

The principle of 'public trust doctrine' is another cornerstone of environmental law that implicates constitutional principles. This doctrine asserts that certain natural resources are held in trust by the government for the benefit of the public. Constitutional courts play a vital role in upholding and interpreting the public trust doctrine, ensuring that natural resources are utilized sustainably and that the government acts as a custodian rather than a proprietor of these resources.

In the international arena, environmental law intersects with constitutional governance through treaties and agreements that address transboundary environmental issues. Constitutional principles guide the incorporation of international obligations into domestic law, ensuring coherence and consistency in addressing global environmental challenges. The doctrine of 'common but differentiated responsibilities,' embedded in many international environmental agreements, reflects the application of constitutional principles to global environmental governance, recognizing the varied capacities and historical contributions of nations.

The evolving jurisprudence on the 'precautionary principle' within environmental law adds another layer to constitutional considerations. This principle asserts that in the face of uncertainty or lack of scientific consensus, actions that may harm the environment should be approached with caution. Constitutional courts are tasked with interpreting and applying the precautionary principle to balance scientific evidence, societal needs, and environmental protection, thereby embodying the precautionary approach within the constitutional fabric.

The role of environmental impact assessment (EIA) processes also implicates constitutional principles. Constitutional courts often scrutinize EIAs to ensure that proposed projects adhere to environmental norms and safeguard the rights of affected communities. This involves interpreting constitutional principles related to public participation, environmental justice, and the right to information.

Furthermore, the recognition of biodiversity as an integral part of the environment adds nuance to constitutional considerations. Constitutional courts must interpret provisions related to biodiversity conservation, taking into account the interconnectedness of ecosystems and the protection of diverse species. This involves weaving biodiversity conservation into the constitutional canvas, acknowledging its intrinsic value and its importance for ecological balance.

In conclusion, the canvas of environmental law in the 21st century is intricately woven into the fabric of constitutional governance. Constitutional principles guide the interpretation and application of environmental norms, ensuring that the right to a healthy environment is upheld, intergenerational equity is respected, and sustainable development becomes a guiding ethos. As environmental challenges persist and intensify, constitutional courts continue to play a central role in navigating the evolving landscape, adapting constitutional principles to address the imperatives of ecological preservation and environmental justice. The synergy between environmental law and the basic structure doctrine reflects a commitment to fostering a harmonious relationship between human activities and the natural world.

8.5 Globalization and Constitutionalism

The phenomenon of globalization has ushered in an era of interconnectedness and interdependence among nations, fundamentally altering the landscape in which constitutional governance operates. This section explores the intricate relationship between globalization and constitutionalism, examining how the principles of the basic structure doctrine resonate within the context of a rapidly globalizing world.

Constitutionalism traditionally finds its roots in the idea that governmental authority should be bound by a fundamental law or constitution, ensuring the protection of individual rights and the limitation of state power. As nations become increasingly integrated into the global fabric, constitutional principles are subjected to new dynamics, necessitating a reevaluation of their scope and application.

One of the primary challenges posed by globalization to constitutional governance lies in the tension between national sovereignty and international obligations. Constitutional courts grapple with interpreting and harmonizing constitutional provisions with treaties and agreements entered into on the international stage. The basic structure doctrine serves as a guiding light, helping courts navigate the delicate balance between preserving the essence of the constitution and aligning with the demands of a globalized world.

The expansion of transnational trade, finance, and communication has led to a convergence of legal and regulatory frameworks across borders. Constitutional principles are invoked to ensure that such convergence does not undermine domestic legal safeguards and the protection of individual rights. The basic structure doctrine becomes a crucial tool in this regard, providing a framework to assess whether global norms align with the core principles enshrined in the constitution.

Globalization brings forth new challenges to individual rights, particularly in the realm of privacy and data protection. The proliferation of digital technologies and cross-border data flows necessitates constitutional scrutiny to safeguard citizens from potential infringements. Constitutional courts, guided by the basic structure doctrine, must adapt and interpret privacy rights in the context of evolving technological landscapes, ensuring that constitutional protections remain robust even in the face of global technological advancements.

Moreover, the economic dimensions of globalization prompt constitutional courts to assess the impact of global economic forces on domestic socioeconomic rights. The basic structure doctrine becomes a touchstone for evaluating whether economic policies and international agreements adhere to constitutional imperatives of social justice, equality, and the protection of vulnerable populations.

In the realm of environmental governance, globalization introduces challenges and opportunities. Constitutional principles guide the interpretation of environmental rights in the context of global environmental agreements, ensuring that the constitution remains a steadfast protector of the right to a healthy environment even as environmental challenges cross borders.

The role of constitutional courts in addressing global challenges such as climate change is critical. The basic structure doctrine provides a lens through which courts can evaluate the constitutionality of government actions or omissions concerning environmental policies with global implications. This involves an expansive interpretation of constitutional provisions to accommodate the imperative of protecting the environment for current and future generations.

Constitutionalism, when viewed through the lens of the basic structure doctrine, is not static but evolves in response to the demands of a globalized world. The constitutional canvas adapts to encompass new challenges and opportunities, ensuring that the timeless principles of justice, liberty, equality, and fraternity continue to resonate even in a global context. As constitutional courts navigate the complexities of globalization, the basic structure doctrine serves as a compass, guiding them to preserve the foundational principles that constitute the constitutional soul while embracing the transformative forces of a globalized era.

8.6 Constitutional Responses to Public Health Crises

In recent times, the global community has witnessed the profound impact of public health crises, with events such as pandemics challenging the fabric of constitutional governance. This section delves into the constitutional responses to public health crises, exploring how the basic structure doctrine guides nations in navigating the complex intersection of public health, individual rights, and governmental powers.

Public health crises, epitomized by pandemics like the COVID-19 outbreak, present constitutional dilemmas that require swift and decisive responses. The basic structure doctrine, as a foundational principle of constitutional interpretation, plays a pivotal role in ensuring that these responses adhere to the core values enshrined in the constitution.

One of the primary challenges is the balance between protecting public health and safeguarding individual liberties. Constitutional courts are tasked with assessing the constitutionality of emergency measures that may restrict fundamental rights such as freedom of movement, assembly, and privacy. The basic structure doctrine becomes a touchstone for determining the proportionality and necessity of these measures in the face of a public health emergency.

Emergency powers invoked by governments during a public health crisis must withstand constitutional scrutiny. The basic structure doctrine guides courts in evaluating whether these powers align with the constitutional framework and whether they respect the principles of separation of powers and the rule of law. This ensures that even in times of crisis, the constitutional order remains resilient and that extraordinary measures do not become a pretext for the erosion of democratic values.

Moreover, public health responses often involve resource allocation, policy decisions, and vaccination campaigns. Constitutional principles, under the guidance of the basic structure doctrine, are invoked to ensure that such measures are equitable, non- discriminatory, and in line with the constitutional imperative of promoting the welfare of all citizens.

The role of constitutional courts extends beyond individual rights to encompass broader questions of governance and accountability. The basic structure doctrine provides a framework for assessing whether government actions during a public health crisis adhere to the principles of transparency, accountability, and the protection of vulnerable populations.

In the context of federal systems, public health responses may involve coordination and collaboration between different levels of government. The basic structure doctrine guides courts in delineating the boundaries of federal and state powers, ensuring a harmonious interplay between the tiers of government while upholding the constitutional division of powers.

As public health crises transcend borders, constitutional responses must also consider international obligations and cooperation. The basic structure doctrine facilitates the incorporation of global health norms into domestic constitutional frameworks, emphasizing the interconnectedness of constitutional governance in the face of shared health challenges.

In conclusion, the constitutional responses to public health crises underscore the adaptability of constitutional principles guided by the basic structure doctrine. As nations grapple with the evolving landscape of public health emergencies, constitutional courts play a crucial role in upholding the integrity of the constitution and ensuring that responses to crises reflect a commitment to democratic values, human rights, and the overall well-being of society.

8.7 Inclusive Constitutionalism

In the contemporary discourse of constitutional law, the concept of inclusive constitutionalism has emerged as a guiding principle, reflecting the dynamic nature of constitutional interpretation and the imperative to accommodate diverse voices within the constitutional framework. Grounded in the basic structure doctrine, this section explores the nuances of inclusive constitutionalism and its relevance in fostering a more equitable and participatory democratic order.

At its core, inclusive constitutionalism recognizes that constitutional governance extends beyond a legal framework to encompass a broader societal ethos. It acknowledges the diversity inherent in society, whether it be in terms of culture, religion, gender, or socio-economic status, and seeks to weave these diverse threads into the fabric of constitutional democracy.

The basic structure doctrine acts as a lodestar for inclusive constitutionalism by setting the foundational values and principles that must be respected in any constitutional arrangement. The doctrine implies a commitment to justice, liberty, equality, and fraternity, which inherently presupposes an inclusive approach that accommodates the interests and rights of all individuals, irrespective of their background.

One of the primary considerations in the context of inclusive constitutionalism is the recognition and protection of minority rights. The basic structure doctrine guides constitutional courts in ensuring that the rights of minority communities are not subsumed by majoritarian impulses. This involves safeguarding cultural and religious freedoms, linguistic diversity, and other facets that contribute to the rich tapestry of a pluralistic society.

Inclusive constitutionalism also intersects with social justice, as enshrined in the Directive Principles of State Policy. The basic structure doctrine mandates that any constitutional interpretation must align with the commitment to socio-economic justice. This involves addressing historical inequalities and ensuring that the benefits of constitutional governance reach marginalized and vulnerable sections of society.

Gender justice is another crucial aspect of inclusive constitutionalism. The basic structure doctrine, through its commitment to equality, calls for dismantling patriarchal norms and structures that perpetuate discrimination. Courts guided by the basic structure doctrine have played a pivotal role in advancing gender equality jurisprudence, recognizing the importance of inclusive gender perspectives in constitutional interpretation.

The participatory dimension of inclusive constitutionalism emphasizes the involvement of citizens in the democratic process. The basic structure doctrine reinforces the democratic ethos by ensuring that constitutional amendments or legal provisions do not undermine the democratic foundations themselves. Inclusivity implies not only protection from discrimination but active participation in shaping the constitutional narrative.

Moreover, inclusive constitutionalism extends to accommodating the rights of persons with disabilities, LGBTQ+ communities, and other historically marginalized groups. The basic structure doctrine, as a living principle, evolves to incorporate contemporary understandings of human rights and inclusivity, challenging legal norms that perpetuate exclusion.

In conclusion, inclusive constitutionalism, rooted in the basic structure doctrine, embodies the constitutional commitment to pluralism, diversity, and justice. It stands as a bulwark against exclusionary tendencies, fostering a constitutional order that reflects the aspirations and rights of all citizens. As the constitutional canvas expands to embrace diverse perspectives, inclusive constitutionalism remains a beacon guiding the trajectory of constitutional evolution.

8.8 Human Rights in the Digital Age

The rapid evolution of technology has ushered in an era where the digital landscape profoundly influences various facets of human life, including governance, communication, and individual rights. Understanding the implications of this digital transformation within the framework of human rights is essential, especially in the context of the basic structure doctrine of the Indian Constitution.

The digital age has witnessed an unprecedented expansion of information and communication technologies, presenting both opportunities and challenges to the protection of human rights. The basic structure doctrine, acting as a guiding principle, necessitates an exploration of how constitutional values intersect with the digital realm, ensuring that the essence of fundamental rights is not diluted in the face of technological advancements.

One critical dimension is the right to privacy, a fundamental right implicitly protected by the basic structure doctrine. The digital age has brought about concerns related to mass surveillance, data breaches, and the commodification of personal information. Courts guided by the basic structure doctrine must grapple with defining the contours of privacy in the digital sphere, striking a balance between individual freedoms and legitimate state interests.

Freedom of expression, another cornerstone of democratic societies enshrined in the basic structure doctrine, encounters new challenges in the digital age. The interconnectedness of global communication platforms raises questions about the regulation of online speech, content moderation, and the potential for censorship. Courts are tasked with adapting constitutional principles to ensure that the right to free expression remains robust in the digital public square.

The right to access information, integral to a vibrant democracy, takes on new dimensions in the digital age. As information becomes increasingly digitized and accessible online, the basic structure doctrine compels constitutional courts to consider how the right to information can be effectively protected and promoted in a technologically advanced society.

Furthermore, the digital age presents challenges to the right to equality, as disparities in access to technology may exacerbate existing socio-economic inequalities. The basic structure doctrine, with its commitment to socio-economic justice, requires constitutional courts to scrutinize digital policies to ensure that they do not perpetuate or deepen existing divides.

Issues of digital citizenship and participation also come to the forefront. The basic structure doctrine emphasizes the participatory nature of democracy, and as such, constitutional courts must consider how the digital realm can be democratized, ensuring that all citizens have an equal opportunity to engage in the digital discourse.

Moreover, the impact of artificial intelligence (AI) on human rights poses intricate questions. The basic structure doctrine, by emphasizing the protection of human dignity, prompts constitutional courts to evaluate the ethical implications of AI systems, particularly in areas such as automated decision-making, algorithmic bias, and the potential infringement on individual autonomy.

In conclusion, the intersection of human rights and the digital age necessitates a nuanced exploration within the purview of the basic structure doctrine. Courts guided by this constitutional principle must navigate the complexities of the digital landscape, ensuring that fundamental rights remain resilient and adaptive to the evolving challenges posed by technology. The canvas of human rights, as envisaged by the basic structure doctrine, extends to the digital realm, demanding thoughtful and principled adjudication in the face of technological advancements.

8.9 Constitutional Governance in Times of Crisis

The basic structure doctrine of the Indian Constitution stands as a robust framework, guiding the nation's governance even in times of crisis. As the constitutional canvas encounters various crises, ranging from public health emergencies to national security threats, the doctrine's relevance becomes particularly pronounced.

One of the fundamental aspects is the preservation of democratic values during crises. The basic structure doctrine, rooted in democratic principles, asserts that even in times of emergency, constitutional governance must be upheld. The doctrine acts as a shield against arbitrary exercises of power, ensuring that the principles of separation of powers and rule of law remain intact.

During public health crises, such as the ongoing global pandemic, the basic structure doctrine compels constitutional authorities to strike a delicate balance between public health imperatives and individual rights. The right to life, a core aspect protected by the doctrine, necessitates measures that protect public health without unduly infringing on individual liberties. Courts, guided by the doctrine, must scrutinize emergency measures to ensure they are proportionate, necessary, and in compliance with constitutional values.

National security crises present another dimension where the basic structure doctrine plays a pivotal role. While acknowledging the state's duty to protect its citizens, the doctrine emphasizes that such measures should not compromise the democratic fabric. Constitutional courts, applying the basic structure doctrine, are tasked with reviewing emergency powers, ensuring they are exercised within the constitutional framework, preventing abuses that might erode democratic principles.

The doctrine's role in upholding federalism becomes particularly crucial during crises. The balance of power between the center and the states, an inherent part of the basic structure, ensures that emergency measures do not undermine the federal structure of the Constitution. Courts, as custodians of the basic structure, play a crucial role in adjudicating disputes arising from the distribution of powers during crises.

The principle of judicial review, a cornerstone of the basic structure, gains prominence during crises. Constitutional courts are entrusted with the responsibility of reviewing executive actions, ensuring they align with constitutional norms. The doctrine acts as a check on overreach, reinforcing the idea that even in times of crisis, constitutional limitations on state power must be upheld.

Moreover, the basic structure doctrine incorporates principles of inclusivity and social justice. In times of crisis, vulnerable communities are often disproportionately affected. The doctrine demands that emergency responses consider the impact on marginalized groups, preventing discriminatory measures and promoting an inclusive approach.

In conclusion, the basic structure doctrine of the Indian Constitution remains a guiding light even in the darkest hours of crisis. Its principles of democracy, rule of law, federalism, and individual rights provide a compass for constitutional governance. Courts, as the guardians of the constitution, play a vital role in upholding the basic structure and ensuring that even in times of crisis, the constitutional fabric remains resilient and unwavering.

8.10 Constitutionalism and Social Justice

The intersection of constitutionalism and social justice lies at the heart of the basic structure doctrine of the Indian Constitution. As the constitutional canvas unfolds, the doctrine's commitment to fostering a just and equitable society becomes increasingly significant.

At its core, constitutionalism refers to the adherence to constitutional principles and the rule of law. In the context of social justice, constitutionalism serves as a powerful tool for addressing systemic inequalities. The basic structure doctrine, with its emphasis on fundamental rights, equality, and justice, becomes a guiding force in shaping a society that upholds the dignity and rights of every individual.

One of the primary ways the basic structure doctrine contributes to social justice is through the protection and enforcement of fundamental rights. The doctrine recognizes certain rights as inviolable and inherent to human dignity. These include the right to equality, right to life and personal liberty, and the right to freedom from discrimination. Courts, acting as custodians of the basic structure, play a crucial role in interpreting and expanding these rights to address evolving social challenges.

Equality, a foundational principle embedded in the basic structure, is a key driver for social justice. The doctrine mandates that the state ensures equal protection of laws and prohibits discrimination on various grounds, including caste, religion, gender, and more. Courts, through their interpretations guided by the basic structure, have played a pivotal role in dismantling discriminatory practices and promoting a more inclusive and egalitarian society.

Moreover, the basic structure doctrine recognizes the importance of affirmative action in rectifying historical injustices. The reservation policies, particularly for marginalized communities, find constitutional validation within the framework of the basic structure. This affirmative action aligns with the broader goal of social justice by addressing historical inequalities and providing opportunities for marginalized sections of society.

The doctrine's commitment to social justice is also evident in its recognition of economic and social rights. While not expressly enumerated as fundamental rights, the basic structure acknowledges the importance of socio-economic justice. Courts, interpreting the doctrine, have expanded the scope of these rights, emphasizing the state's duty to ensure the well-being of all citizens, especially those on the margins of society.

Environmental justice, a contemporary aspect of social justice, finds resonance within the basic structure doctrine. The right to a clean and healthy environment is integral to the right to life, and the doctrine recognizes the interconnectedness of environmental well-being and social justice. Courts, relying on the basic structure, have intervened to protect the environment and ensure intergenerational equity.

In conclusion, the marriage of constitutionalism and social justice within the framework of the basic structure doctrine reflects a commitment to building a society that is not only governed by the rule of law but is also characterized by fairness, equality, and inclusivity. As the constitutional canvas continues to evolve, the basic structure doctrine stands as a bulwark against social injustices, guiding the nation towards a more equitable and just future.

8.11 Constitutional Challenges Posed by Biotechnology

The infusion of biotechnology into various facets of life has presented novel challenges to the constitutional fabric of India. As the basic structure doctrine weaves through the complexities of this technological frontier, it confronts profound questions related to privacy, human dignity, and the equilibrium between scientific advancements and constitutional values.

One of the primary constitutional challenges arising from biotechnology pertains to the right to privacy. The basic structure doctrine, as interpreted by the judiciary, recognizes the right to privacy as a fundamental right intrinsic to the right to life and personal liberty. Biotechnological innovations, such as genetic testing and profiling, raise concerns about the potential intrusion into an individual's genetic information. Courts, while upholding the right to privacy, face the delicate task of balancing scientific progress with the protection of personal autonomy.

Furthermore, the basic structure doctrine's commitment to human dignity is tested by advancements like gene editing and cloning. The ethical implications of altering the fundamental genetic makeup of individuals or creating life through artificial means challenge established norms of dignity and the sanctity of life. Courts, guided by the basic structure, must navigate these uncharted waters to ensure that biotechnological interventions adhere to constitutional principles.

The intersection of biotechnology and constitutionalism also brings to the fore questions of equality. Access to biotechnological advancements, such as assisted reproductive technologies, may create disparities among different sections of society. The basic structure doctrine, with its emphasis on equal protection of laws, requires a nuanced examination of how these technologies are distributed and made available to all, irrespective of socio-economic considerations.

Environmental concerns arising from biotechnology, such as genetically modified organisms (GMOs), pose challenges to the basic structure's commitment to environmental justice. The potential impact of biotechnological interventions on biodiversity, ecosystems, and the right to a healthy environment necessitates a constitutional scrutiny of regulatory frameworks to ensure they align with the principles enshrined in the basic structure.

The dynamic nature of biotechnological innovations also raises questions about legal frameworks' adaptability, challenging the constitutional principles of legal certainty and predictability. The basic structure doctrine, while recognizing the need for legal evolution, requires a delicate balance to ensure that constitutional values remain steadfast even as the legal landscape transforms.

In conclusion, the constitutional challenges posed by biotechnology underscore the adaptability and resilience of the basic structure doctrine. As the canvas of constitutionalism expands to encompass the frontiers of biotechnology, the judiciary, guided by the principles of the basic structure, must navigate these challenges to uphold individual rights, preserve human dignity, and maintain the delicate balance between scientific progress and constitutional values.

8.12 The Role of International Law in National Constitutions

The interplay between international law and national constitutions represents a crucial dimension in the evolving canvas of constitutionalism. As the basic structure doctrine guides the interpretation of the Indian Constitution, the integration of international legal principles raises intricate questions about the relationship between domestic sovereignty and global legal norms.

At the heart of this intersection lies the principle of constitutional supremacy. The basic structure doctrine underscores the paramount authority of the Indian Constitution, recognizing it as the supreme law of the land. However, the incorporation of international law into national constitutions challenges this supremacy by introducing a layer of legal obligations emanating from global treaties and conventions.

One aspect of this relationship revolves around the incorporation of international treaties into domestic law. While the basic structure doctrine enshrines the supremacy of the Constitution, it does not preclude the incorporation of international treaties, provided they align with the constitutional framework. Courts, guided by the basic structure, are tasked with harmonizing international commitments with domestic constitutional values.

The constitutional interpretation also grapples with the concept of customary international law. As the basic structure doctrine evolves, courts are confronted with the challenge of discerning customary norms that may not be explicitly codified in treaties. The delicate balance between recognizing evolving customary norms and upholding constitutional principles requires a nuanced approach, ensuring that international legal developments do not compromise the core tenets of the basic structure.

Human rights, a focal point of international law, present both challenges and opportunities for constitutional interpretation. The basic structure doctrine's commitment to fundamental rights aligns with the international human rights framework. However, divergences may emerge, requiring the judiciary to navigate between constitutional imperatives and international obligations, ensuring a cohesive and principled approach.

The principle of sovereign equality, embedded in international law, also resonates with the basic structure doctrine's commitment to federalism. As international legal norms influence areas traditionally within the domain of states, such as environmental protection or human rights, courts must uphold federal principles while acknowledging the interconnectedness of global challenges.

Furthermore, the basic structure doctrine invites a critical examination of the executive's role in treaty-making and international agreements. The constitutional framework provides for the executive's authority to enter into treaties, but the basic structure requires that such engagements align with constitutional principles. Judicial review becomes a crucial mechanism to ensure the executive's adherence to the basic structure while navigating international commitments.

In conclusion, the role of international law in national constitutions, viewed through the lens of the basic structure doctrine, demands a delicate balance. As the constitutional canvas expands to accommodate global norms, courts must harmonize international legal obligations with the foundational principles of the Indian Constitution. The basic structure, as a guiding brushstroke, ensures that the integration of international law enriches rather than compromises the constitutional ethos.

8.13 Constitutional Governance in Multi-Cultural Societies

The canvas of constitutional governance takes on a distinctive hue in multi-cultural societies, reflecting the diverse tapestry of identities, beliefs, and traditions. In the context of the basic structure doctrine within the Indian Constitution, the constitutional commitment to unity in diversity resonates, and the governance of a multi-cultural society requires careful calibration to uphold the principles of justice, liberty, equality, and fraternity.

One of the key challenges lies in crafting a constitutional framework that accommodates and celebrates cultural diversity without compromising the foundational principles. The basic structure doctrine, as the guiding brushstroke, underscores the importance of protecting fundamental rights, ensuring that no community or individual is marginalized on the grounds of cultural differences.

Language, as a cultural marker, occupies a significant space in multi-cultural societies. The basic structure doctrine's emphasis on preserving linguistic diversity aligns with the constitutional vision of India as a linguistically pluralistic nation. Constitutional governance, guided by the basic structure, must safeguard linguistic rights, ensuring that linguistic minorities have the freedom to preserve and promote their languages.

Religious diversity, a defining feature of multi-cultural societies, poses intricate challenges and opportunities. The basic structure doctrine, with its commitment to secularism, necessitates a constitutional order that ensures the equal protection of the rights of individuals from all religious communities. The judiciary, interpreting the basic structure, becomes the custodian of religious freedom, ensuring that no community faces discrimination based on its faith.

The principle of affirmative action, embedded in the basic structure through reservations, assumes added significance in multi-cultural societies. Constitutional governance must address historical injustices and socio-economic disparities among different cultural communities, striving to achieve a more equitable society without compromising meritocracy.

The role of local self-governance, as articulated in the basic structure, becomes crucial in multi-cultural settings. Empowering local communities to participate in decision-making processes ensures that governance reflects the unique needs and aspirations of diverse cultural groups. It fosters a sense of belonging and ownership, aligning with the constitutional vision of participatory democracy.

Moreover, the recognition of customary laws and practices within the broader legal framework becomes imperative. The basic structure doctrine, while upholding the primacy of the Constitution, acknowledges the importance of respecting cultural traditions that are not in conflict with fundamental rights. Striking a balance between cultural autonomy and constitutional principles becomes a delicate but necessary task for constitutional governance.

In conclusion, constitutional governance in multi-cultural societies, under the guiding light of the basic structure doctrine, demands an intricate dance between unity and diversity. The constitution, as a living document, must evolve to accommodate the dynamic expressions of culture while safeguarding the core principles that define the nation. The basic structure doctrine, as the constitutional compass, ensures that the governance of multi-cultural societies remains rooted in justice, liberty, equality, and fraternity.

8.14 Education and Constitutional Literacy

In the vast canvas of constitutional governance, education emerges as a pivotal brushstroke, shaping the contours of a nation's democratic fabric. Within the realm of the basic structure doctrine of the Indian Constitution, the role of education becomes even more significant, acting as both a means and an end to uphold and perpetuate the constitutional values of justice, liberty, equality, and fraternity.

The constitutional imperative to provide free and compulsory education for all children up to the age of fourteen, as envisaged in Article 21A, aligns seamlessly with the basic structure doctrine. The judiciary, as the custodian of the constitution, has reiterated that education is not just a directive principle but an inherent part of the right to life and dignity.

This interpretation ensures that education is not seen in isolation but as an integral component of the constitutional framework.

Moreover, the constitutional commitment to promoting scientific temper, humanism, and the spirit of inquiry and reform (Article 51A) underscores the transformative role education can play in shaping an enlightened citizenry. The basic structure doctrine, by emphasizing the importance of informed and participative citizens, envisages education as a tool for nurturing critical thinking and civic responsibility.

Constitutional literacy, an extension of general education, becomes crucial in the context of the basic structure doctrine. It involves imparting knowledge about the constitution, its principles, and the rights and duties it bestows upon citizens. The judiciary, in various pronouncements, has highlighted the need for constitutional literacy to empower individuals to assert their rights and hold the government accountable.

The recognition of diversity within the educational landscape is another facet that aligns with the basic structure doctrine. The constitution, through Article 30, safeguards the rights of religious and linguistic minorities to establish and administer educational institutions of their choice. This protection ensures that the educational sector reflects the pluralistic ethos of the nation.

However, challenges persist in achieving the constitutional vision of a robust and inclusive education system. Disparities in access to quality education, particularly along socio-economic lines, create fault lines that need urgent attention. The basic structure doctrine, by emphasizing egalitarian principles, calls for affirmative action to bridge these gaps and ensure that education becomes a leveller rather than a source of inequality.

In contemporary times, the integration of technology in education also assumes constitutional significance. The basic structure doctrine, though crafted in a pre- digital era, provides a flexible framework that accommodates technological advancements in the field of education. The right to education, when interpreted in consonance with the basic structure, extends to encompass the right to quality digital education for all.

In conclusion, the nexus between education and the basic structure doctrine is a dynamic and evolving one. Education serves not just as a means for personal growth but as a cornerstone for the preservation and perpetuation of constitutional values. As the basic structure doctrine continues to guide the nation's legal and constitutional evolution, education remains a potent instrument for realizing its aspirations and fostering an enlightened citizenry committed to the ideals of the Indian Constitution.

8.15 The Future of Judicial Activism

In the evolving narrative of constitutional governance shaped by the basic structure doctrine, the role of judicial activism has been both a subject of praise and critique. As we contemplate the future of judicial activism within the contours of this doctrine, it becomes imperative to decipher the trajectory, challenges, and potential transformations that lie ahead.

Judicial activism, as a concept, refers to the proactive role of the judiciary in interpreting and enforcing the constitution, often going beyond traditional notions of adjudication. The basic structure doctrine, with its roots in landmark cases like Kesavananda Bharati v. State of Kerala, has served as a touchstone for judicial activism in India. The doctrine inherently underscores the judiciary's duty to preserve and protect the core values enshrined in the Constitution.

Looking forward, the future of judicial activism lies at the crossroads of striking a delicate balance between the judiciary's interventionist role and the principle of separation of powers. As the judiciary navigates this path, one cannot ignore the inherent tension that sometimes arises between the judiciary and other branches of government. The basic structure doctrine, acting as a guiding force, emphasizes that while activism is warranted to safeguard constitutional principles, it should not transgress the bounds of institutional equilibrium.

One aspect that is likely to shape the future of judicial activism is the adaptation of constitutional principles to contemporary challenges. The basic structure doctrine, by its very nature, allows for a dynamic interpretation of the constitution, taking into account societal changes and emerging issues. The judiciary, in its activist role, is poised to respond to novel constitutional questions brought about by technological advancements, social transformations, and global developments.

Furthermore, the evolving nature of fundamental rights within the basic structure provides a canvas for judicial activism to address pressing concerns of individual liberties and social justice. The judiciary's proactive engagement with issues such as right to privacy, environmental protection, and economic rights has been a hallmark of its activist stance. The future promises a continued exploration of these frontiers, with the judiciary acting as a vanguard for expanding the canvas of constitutional rights.

However, challenges loom on the horizon. The delicate interplay between activism and restraint requires a nuanced approach. Striking down legislative enactments or executive actions under the basic structure doctrine should be guided by a judicious assessment of constitutional imperatives and democratic principles. Overreaching judicial activism, divorced from constitutional moorings, could potentially undermine the very principles it seeks to protect.

In the future, the judiciary's role in interpreting the basic structure may witness varied perspectives and interpretations. The dialogue between the judiciary, legal scholars, and the public will shape the contours of this discourse. The basic structure doctrine, acting as a lodestar, encourages a robust and participative engagement that ensures the judiciary remains true to its constitutional mandate.

In conclusion, the future of judicial activism within the framework of the basic structure doctrine holds promise for the continued evolution of constitutional governance in India. As the judiciary grapples with emerging challenges and opportunities, its commitment to preserving the foundational principles of the Constitution will be crucial in shaping a future where justice, liberty, equality, and fraternity are not just ideals but lived realities for every citizen.

8.16 Constitutional Amendments and Flexibility

In the intricate web of constitutional governance, the power to amend the constitution stands as a testament to the flexibility inherent in its design. The basic structure doctrine, a cornerstone of constitutional interpretation, has delineated the boundaries within which this flexibility operates. As we delve into the realm of constitutional amendments, it is imperative to understand the interplay between the need for adaptability and the preservation of the constitutional core.

Constitutional amendments serve as the lifeblood of any vibrant democracy, providing the legal means to adjust to changing circumstances and societal expectations. The framers of the Indian Constitution, cognizant of the evolving nature of governance, incorporated Article 368, which outlines the procedure for amending the constitution. However, the power to amend is not boundless, as elucidated by the basic structure doctrine.

The doctrine, articulated in Kesavananda Bharati v. State of Kerala (1973), asserts that while the constitution is amenable to change, certain fundamental features are beyond the reach of the amending power. These fundamental features, comprising the basic structure, are considered inviolable and form the bedrock of constitutional identity. The judiciary, acting as the guardian of the constitution, is entrusted with the task of delineating the contours of this basic structure.

The concept of the basic structure provides a safeguard against arbitrary and capricious amendments that may undermine the essence of the constitution. It places a check on transient majoritarian impulses that could potentially erode the foundational principles of justice, liberty, equality, and fraternity. The judiciary's role in ensuring the sanctity of the basic structure underscores its commitment to upholding constitutional values.

As we peer into the future, the question of constitutional amendments and flexibility takes center stage. The evolving socio-political landscape and global dynamics necessitate a certain degree of adaptability. The basic structure doctrine, while imposing limitations, also offers a framework for discerning the permissible boundaries of constitutional change.

A nuanced understanding of constitutional flexibility must acknowledge the delicate balance between stability and dynamism. Excessive rigidity can render a constitution obsolete, unable to respond to the evolving needs of society. On the other hand, unchecked flexibility may lead to the dilution of foundational principles, compromising the very essence of constitutional governance.

The role of constitutional amendments in the future will be shaped by the judiciary's interpretation of the basic structure and its responsiveness to contemporary challenges. As new issues emerge, from technological advancements to changing social norms, the need for judicious constitutional adaptations will become increasingly apparent.

In conclusion, the interplay between constitutional amendments and the basic structure doctrine reflects the essence of constitutional governance in India. The delicate equilibrium between continuity and change, stability and flexibility, is a testament to the foresight of the framers. The journey ahead requires a thoughtful navigation of this balance, ensuring that the constitutional edifice stands firm while accommodating the evolving aspirations of a dynamic society.

8.17 E-Governance and Constitutional Governance

In the age of technological acceleration, the advent of E-Governance has emerged as a transformative force, reshaping the contours of public administration and citizen- state interactions. As we navigate the intricacies of this digital frontier, the confluence of E-Governance and Constitutional Governance becomes a focal point for examination within the framework of the basic structure doctrine.

The integration of technology in governance holds the promise of efficiency, transparency, and accessibility. Digital platforms, encompassing a spectrum from online services to data-driven decision-making, have the potential to streamline bureaucratic processes and enhance citizen participation. However, this technological evolution raises pertinent questions about its compatibility with the foundational principles enshrined in the constitution.

The fundamental tenets of the basic structure doctrine, as delineated by judicial pronouncements, provide a lens through which we can scrutinize the impact of E-Governance on Constitutional Governance. The principles of justice, liberty, equality, and fraternity must not be compromised in the pursuit of administrative expediency. The question arises: How can the infusion of technology align with constitutional values, ensuring that the benefits of E-Governance are harnessed without sacrificing the core essence of the constitution?

One facet of this discussion pertains to the protection of individual privacy-a right now recognized as intrinsic to the right to life and personal liberty. The digital footprint created through E-Governance initiatives raises concerns about the potential intrusion into citizens' private spheres. The Supreme Court, in Justice K.S. Puttaswamy (Retd.) v. Union of India (2017), underscored the importance of protecting informational privacy as an essential facet of personal autonomy. As we navigate the terrain of E-Governance, finding the delicate balance between technological advancement and privacy safeguards becomes imperative.

Another dimension of this discourse involves the inclusivity of E-Governance initiatives. The constitution's commitment to equality necessitates that technological advancements do not inadvertently exclude sections of society. Accessibility challenges, the digital divide, and disparities in technological literacy must be addressed to ensure that E-Governance becomes a tool for social empowerment rather than a source of marginalization.

The efficacy of E-Governance in upholding the rule of law is also a critical consideration. The digital transformation of legal processes, while promising efficiency and accessibility, must not compromise the principles of procedural fairness and natural justice. The integrity of legal proceedings and the protection of due process rights remain paramount.

Looking ahead, the compatibility of E-Governance with the basic structure of the constitution will be contingent on the evolution of legal frameworks, robust data protection measures, and the judiciary's vigilance in safeguarding constitutional values. The adaptation of governance to technological advancements should occur within the broader contours of justice, liberty, equality, and fraternity.

In conclusion, E-Governance, while presenting unprecedented opportunities for administrative efficiency, necessitates a nuanced examination within the constitutional framework. The basic structure doctrine acts as a lodestar, guiding the assimilation of technology into governance while ensuring the enduring principles of the constitution remain unscathed. As India strides into a digital future, the synergy between E-Governance and Constitutional Governance holds the key to a resilient, transparent, and just administrative apparatus.

8.18 Constitutional Rights in the Cyber Age

In the era of rapid technological evolution, the advent of the Cyber Age has introduced novel challenges and opportunities to the landscape of constitutional rights. As we navigate this digital frontier, the intersection of constitutional principles with the intricacies of the Cyber Age becomes a crucial area of exploration within the purview of the basic structure doctrine.

One of the primary considerations is the safeguarding of individual privacy in the virtual realm. The constitutionally guaranteed right to privacy, as enshrined in landmark judgments like Justice K.S. Puttaswamy (Retd.) v. Union of India (2017), assumes heightened significance in the age of ubiquitous digital communication and data exchange. The interplay between the right to privacy and the expansive reach of cyberspace necessitates a reevaluation of legal standards and protections to ensure the constitutional integrity of individuals remains intact.

The right to freedom of expression, a cornerstone of democratic societies, also undergoes a transformative shift in the Cyber Age. Social media platforms and online forums have become digital town squares where citizens exercise their right to express opinions and dissent. The challenge lies in striking a balance between the free flow of information and curbing the potential misuse of these platforms for hate speech, misinformation, or cyberbullying. Constitutional rights, while adaptable, must find equilibrium in the dynamic cyber landscape.

The right to equality takes center stage as the digital divide poses challenges to equitable access to technological resources. Bridging this gap becomes imperative to ensure that all citizens can participate meaningfully in the digital discourse and benefit from technological advancements. The basic structure doctrine's commitment to justice and equality resonates in the pursuit of digital inclusion as an essential facet of constitutional governance.

The Cyber Age also presents novel dimensions to the right to liberty and due process. Concerns around online surveillance, cybercrimes, and the balance between national security imperatives and individual liberties demand nuanced legal frameworks. The judiciary, guided by the principles of the basic structure doctrine, plays a pivotal role in delineating the contours of constitutional rights in the cyber realm.

As we contemplate the constitutional implications of the Cyber Age, it becomes apparent that the basic structure doctrine provides a stable foundation for this exploration. The enduring principles of justice, liberty, equality, and fraternity act as guiding principles in adapting constitutional rights to the digital paradigm. Judicial interpretation and legislative measures must align with these principles to ensure that the constitutional fabric remains resilient in the face of technological advancements.

In conclusion, Constitutional Rights in the Cyber Age demands a nuanced understanding of the interplay between technology and constitutional values. As India strides into an increasingly digitized future, the basic structure doctrine stands as a sentinel, ensuring that the constitutional rights of citizens evolve without compromising the essence of justice, liberty, equality, and fraternity.

8.19 The Role of Constitutional Courts in Shaping the Future

In the grand tapestry of constitutional governance, the role of constitutional courts emerges as a crucial thread, weaving together the intricate balance of power, protection of individual rights, and the preservation of the basic structure of the constitution. As we navigate the challenges and opportunities presented by the evolving landscape, constitutional courts stand as sentinels, interpreting the constitution and shaping the contours of our democratic framework.

One of the primary functions of constitutional courts is the interpretation of the constitution, a task laden with profound implications for the basic structure doctrine. The judiciary, as the ultimate arbiter of constitutional meaning, ensures the continued relevance of constitutional principles to contemporary challenges. Landmark decisions, such as Kesavananda Bharati v. State of Kerala (1973), have established the doctrine that no amendment can alter the basic structure of the constitution. This not only serves as a testament to the resilience of constitutional values but also underscores the pivotal role of constitutional courts in upholding the foundational principles.

The commitment to justice, liberty, equality, and fraternity, embedded in the basic structure doctrine, finds expression in the jurisprudence crafted by constitutional courts. Through their judgments, these courts not only interpret laws but also become architects of societal change. Cases related to social justice, environmental protection, and individual freedoms become milestones that chart the path of the nation's constitutional evolution.

The principle of checks and balances is intrinsic to constitutional governance, and constitutional courts play a crucial role in ensuring this equilibrium. Through their power of judicial review, these courts scrutinize legislative and executive actions, ensuring that they align with the constitutional blueprint. The judicial interpretation of laws in light of the basic structure doctrine becomes a bulwark against potential overreach by other branches of government, safeguarding the delicate balance envisioned by the framers.

Constitutional courts also grapple with complex questions arising from technological advancements, societal transformations, and global interconnectedness. Issues like privacy in the digital age, the balance between national security and civil liberties, and the ethical implications of biotechnological advancements all fall within the purview of judicial scrutiny. The basic structure doctrine serves as a guiding beacon, ensuring that the principles it embodies adapt to the changing times without compromising their essence.

The evolving role of constitutional courts is not without challenges. Striking a delicate balance between interpretation and restraint, ensuring judicial independence, and addressing the growing caseload pose formidable tasks. Yet, it is precisely in navigating these challenges that the resilience of constitutional courts in shaping the future is demonstrated.

In conclusion, The Role of Constitutional Courts in Shaping the Future underscores the pivotal position these institutions occupy in the constitutional framework. As guardians of the basic structure doctrine, constitutional courts act as custodians of constitutional values, ensuring their continuity and relevance in a dynamic world. Through their judgments and interpretations, these courts sculpt the constitutional narrative, contributing to the ever-unfolding story of justice, liberty, equality, and fraternity.

8.20 Conclusion: Navigating the Evolving Constitutional Landscape

As we traverse the diverse terrain of constitutional governance, marked by the enduring principles encapsulated in the basic structure doctrine, the journey unveils a dynamic tapestry woven with the threads of justice, liberty, equality, and fraternity. The constitutional landscape, ever-evolving and responsive to the pulsating rhythm of societal progress, reflects the resilience of a constitutional order rooted in the wisdom of the framers.

The foundational principles enshrined in the basic structure doctrine serve as the North Star, guiding constitutional interpretation and judicial deliberation. Justice H.R. Khanna's eloquent words in Kesavananda Bharati v. State of Kerala (1973) resonate across time, emphasizing the inviolable nature of certain principles that form the bedrock of our constitutional ethos. It is within this framework that we navigate the complexities of a changing world, where technological advancements, societal shifts, and global interconnections present both challenges and opportunities.

Constitutional evolution, as witnessed through the lens of landmark cases and the expansive jurisprudence of constitutional courts, is not merely a legal phenomenon but a reflection of societal aspirations and values. The judiciary's role as the interpreter and guardian of the constitution extends beyond the confines of courtrooms, influencing the very fabric of our democratic existence.

The chapters preceding this conclusion have meticulously explored the multifaceted dimensions of the basic structure doctrine. From its conceptual underpinnings to its manifestation in landmark cases, from global perspectives on constitutional principles to contemporary challenges and future horizons, each facet contributes to a nuanced understanding of constitutional governance.

In the intricate dance between tradition and progress, the basic structure doctrine emerges as a fulcrum that maintains equilibrium. Its interpretation requires a delicate choreography, where judicial wisdom and societal needs dance in harmony. The anticipation of challenges, aspirations for socio-economic justice, and global influences underscore the need for a contextual and forward-looking approach.

As we reflect on the dynamics of constitutional evolution, it becomes apparent that the basic structure doctrine is not a static relic but a living doctrine that breathes life into the constitution. The judiciary, as the custodian of this doctrine, bears the responsibility of ensuring its adaptive resonance with the ever-changing socio- political milieu.

Navigating the evolving constitutional landscape demands a judicious blend of continuity and change. The resilience of the basic structure doctrine lies in its ability to absorb and reflect the aspirations of successive generations, ensuring that the constitutional promise remains vibrant and relevant. The judicial interpretative process becomes a bridge between the intent of the framers and the exigencies of contemporary challenges.

In conclusion, this journey through the nuanced realms of constitutional philosophy, global influences, foundational principles in action, and the intricate dance between tradition and progress converges in a profound realization. The basic structure doctrine, far from being a legal abstraction, is the beating heart of our constitutional democracy, pulsating with the vitality of justice, liberty, equality, and fraternity. As we navigate the evolving constitutional landscape, the basic structure doctrine stands as a testament to the enduring power of constitutional ideals, guiding our path into an uncertain but hopeful future.

Chapter 9

Conclusion

9.1 Summary of Key Findings

In summarizing the key findings of your book on the Basic Structure Doctrine, it is crucial to distill and synthesize the main insights, arguments, and revelations that the readers have encountered throughout the chapters. The following is an extensive summary, providing a comprehensive overview of the book's central findings:

The Basic Structure Doctrine, as explored in this book, represents a profound and enduring facet of the Indian constitutional landscape. Through a meticulous examination of historical developments, constitutional principles, and global perspectives, the book endeavors to unravel the intricate layers of this doctrine and shed light on its significance in shaping the constitutional narrative of India.

At its core, the Basic Structure Doctrine is a guiding light that illuminates the fundamental tenets of the Indian Constitution. This doctrine, articulated and refined through landmark judicial pronouncements, serves as a bulwark against arbitrary amendments and ensures the preservation of the constitution's foundational values. The journey through the contextualization of this doctrine has traversed historical milestones, juridical interpretations, and societal transformations.

One of the salient findings of this exploration is the dynamic interplay between the Basic Structure Doctrine and the broader canvas of constitutional governance. The doctrine acts as a vanguard, safeguarding not only individual rights but also the delicate equilibrium between different organs of the state. It stands as a testament to the resilience and adaptability of the Indian Constitution in the face of evolving challenges.

Comparative insights drawn from constitutional jurisprudence across the globe reveal the universal relevance of the Basic Structure Doctrine. Its echoes can be discerned in constitutional frameworks of various nations, contributing to a global discourse on the protection of core constitutional principles. The book strives to underscore the interconnectedness of constitutional ideologies and the potential cross-pollination of legal thought.

Judicial activism and restraint emerge as crucial facets of the Basic Structure Doctrine's application. The judiciary's role in interpreting and expanding constitutional principles shapes the contours of governance and the protection of individual freedoms. This book contends that a judicious balance between activism and restraint is essential for maintaining the doctrine's integrity and relevance.

Public perception and legitimacy constitute another critical dimension explored in the book. The acceptance and understanding of the Basic Structure Doctrine among the populace play a pivotal role in sustaining the legitimacy of judicial decisions. However, the book acknowledges the challenges and debates surrounding public acceptance, emphasizing the need for transparent communication and civic engagement.

Looking forward, the book anticipates future horizons in constitutional law and governance. The Basic Structure Doctrine is poised to play a pivotal role in addressing emerging challenges such as technological advancements, environmental concerns, and societal shifts. The book calls for proactive measures to enhance constitutional literacy and awareness, envisioning an informed citizenry capable of contributing meaningfully to constitutional debates.

In conclusion, this extensive exploration of the Basic Structure Doctrine encapsulates a profound journey through constitutional principles, legal philosophy, and the socio- political tapestry of India. The summary underscores the enduring relevance of this doctrine as a cornerstone of constitutional governance, providing readers with a nuanced understanding of its evolution, impact, and potential trajectories in the future.

9.2 Relevance to Contemporary Challenges

The relevance of the Basic Structure Doctrine to contemporary challenges is a testament to its enduring significance in navigating the complex landscape of constitutional governance. As we delve into the intricacies of this doctrine, it becomes evident that its adaptability and resilience make it a linchpin in addressing the multifaceted challenges posed by the evolving socio-political, technological, and environmental dynamics of the 21st century.

In the realm of technological advancements, the Basic Structure Doctrine assumes a critical role in safeguarding individual privacy and civil liberties. The exponential growth of digital technologies has ushered in an era where the boundaries between the public and private spheres are increasingly blurred. The doctrine's emphasis on protecting the essential features of the constitution becomes particularly pertinent in the context of ensuring that technological advancements do not infringe upon the foundational principles enshrined in the constitution.

Privacy concerns, exacerbated by the pervasive influence of digital technologies, underscore the need for a robust constitutional framework. The Basic Structure Doctrine, with its emphasis on protecting fundamental rights, acts as a bulwark against any encroachment on individual privacy. As the digital landscape continues to evolve, the doctrine provides a principled foundation for adjudicating the delicate balance between technological progress and the preservation of constitutional values.

Furthermore, the intersectionality of issues such as national security and civil liberties necessitates a nuanced approach embedded in constitutional principles. The Basic Structure Doctrine serves as a guiding framework in navigating this intricate terrain, ensuring that measures taken in the name of national security do not compromise the essential features of the constitution. The evolving nature of security threats demands a constitutional response that is both adaptive and principled, a balance that the Basic Structure Doctrine seeks to maintain.

In grappling with questions of equality and social justice, the doctrine emerges as a touchstone for progressive constitutional interpretation. The evolving understanding of equality in the 21st century, encompassing issues of gender, sexuality, and socio-economic disparities, requires a constitutional framework that reflects the evolving values of a democratic society. The Basic Structure Doctrine, with its commitment to preserving the core principles of justice and equality, provides a robust foundation for addressing these contemporary challenges.

Environmental law, in the context of constitutional rights, underscores the interconnectedness of human rights and ecological well-being. The Basic Structure Doctrine, when applied to environmental jurisprudence, reinforces the idea that a sustainable and ecologically balanced environment is intrinsic to the overarching constitutional scheme. As climate change and environmental degradation emerge as pressing concerns, the doctrine provides a constitutional lens through which to address these challenges.

In conclusion, the Basic Structure Doctrine remains an indispensable tool in navigating the complexities of contemporary challenges. Its adaptability to address issues ranging from technological advancements to environmental concerns underscores its enduring relevance. As India and the world grapple with unprecedented transformations, the doctrine stands as a beacon, guiding constitutional interpretations that balance tradition and progress, stability and change. It is through a steadfast commitment to the principles embedded in the Basic Structure Doctrine that constitutional governance can effectively respond to the intricate challenges of the present and future.

9.3 Impact on Governance and Rights

The impact of the Basic Structure Doctrine on governance and rights is a multifaceted exploration of its profound influence on the functioning of the Indian constitutional system. This doctrine, emanating from landmark judicial pronouncements, has reverberated through the corridors of power, shaping governance structures and delineating the contours of fundamental rights.

At its core, the Basic Structure Doctrine serves as a constitutional sentinel, guarding against arbitrary exercises of power by the executive and legislative branches. The doctrine, rooted in the interpretation of Article 21 and other fundamental rights, imposes limitations on the government's ability to transgress the essential features of the constitution. This has profound implications for governance, injecting a degree of constitutional discipline that prevents overreach and preserves the delicate balance of power envisioned by the framers.

One of the pivotal arenas where the impact of the doctrine is palpable is in safeguarding fundamental rights. The doctrine acts as a bulwark against legislative or executive actions that may impinge upon the core values enshrined in the constitution. Whether it be issues of individual liberty, freedom of expression, or right to equality, the Basic Structure Doctrine serves as a constitutional touchstone, ensuring that these rights remain inviolable even in the face of evolving societal norms and challenges.

The interplay between the Basic Structure Doctrine and the concept of separation of powers is crucial in understanding its impact on governance. By delineating the contours of essential features, the doctrine reinforces the separation of powers as a foundational principle. The judiciary, as the custodian of the constitution, exercises the power of judicial review to scrutinize legislative and executive actions, ensuring that they align with the basic structure. This dynamic interaction contributes to a system of checks and balances, fostering good governance and preventing the concentration of power in any one branch.

In the context of federalism, the Basic Structure Doctrine plays a pivotal role in maintaining the delicate equilibrium between the center and the states. It prevents amendments that alter the federal structure, thus preserving the intended distribution of powers between different levels of government. This impact resonates in governance practices, ensuring that the federal character of the Indian state endures, providing flexibility without compromising the foundational principles.

Moreover, the doctrine's impact extends to issues of social justice and affirmative action. It influences policies and legislations that seek to address historical inequalities and discrimination, guiding the state in formulating measures that are consistent with the principles embedded in the Basic Structure. As governance grapples with the complexities of a diverse and pluralistic society, the doctrine offers normative guidance, reinforcing the commitment to justice and equality.

The impact of the Basic Structure Doctrine on governance and rights is a narrative of constitutional resilience and adaptability. It underscores the enduring relevance of a doctrine conceived in response to the challenges of its time. As the constitutional landscape continues to evolve, the doctrine stands as a testament to the enduring values that shape governance and rights in the Indian context. Its impact is not confined to a particular era but resonates through the annals of constitutional history, leaving an indelible mark on the trajectory of governance and individual rights in India.

9.4 Comparative Insights

Comparative insights into the Basic Structure Doctrine provide a valuable lens through which the unique features and dynamics of the Indian constitutional experiment can be understood and contextualized within the broader global legal landscape. As we delve into this comparative exploration, it becomes evident that the Basic Structure Doctrine is not merely a doctrinal innovation confined to Indian jurisprudence but is part of a broader conversation on constitutionalism, judicial review, and the limitations of state power.

In examining constitutional systems across various jurisdictions, one cannot escape the realization that the concept of an unamendable or basic structure is not universal.

While some legal systems explicitly recognize such limitations on constitutional amendments, others rely on different mechanisms to ensure the integrity of their foundational legal documents. Comparative constitutional analysis allows us to appreciate the diversity of approaches employed by different nations in grappling with questions of constitutional identity and resilience.

The United States, for instance, relies heavily on a system of judicial review, wherein the judiciary, through the power of judicial review established in Marbury v. Madison (1803), interprets the constitution and has the authority to strike down legislation inconsistent with its provisions. This is distinct from the Indian approach, which, through the Basic Structure Doctrine, grants the judiciary the power to review and potentially invalidate constitutional amendments themselves. The comparison sheds light on the nuanced ways in which different legal systems reconcile the tension between constitutional change and constitutional identity.

In Germany, the Basic Law (Grundgesetz) establishes the eternity clause, prohibiting amendments that undermine the principles of human dignity, democracy, the rule of law, the federal state, and the separation of powers. This constitutional safeguard, akin to the spirit of the Basic Structure Doctrine, showcases the global resonance of protecting fundamental values from constitutional overhauls.

The Canadian Charter of Rights and Freedoms, embedded within the Constitution Act, 1982, acts as a guardian of fundamental rights. While Canada lacks an explicit basic structure doctrine, the Charter's entrenched protection of certain rights and freedoms from legislative interference shares similarities with the Indian approach.

South Africa, post-apartheid, presents an intriguing case. The transformative constitution adopted in 1996, with its Bill of Rights, displays parallels to India's constitutional journey. Both nations grapple with issues of historical injustice, and their constitutional frameworks reflect a commitment to addressing social inequalities.

These comparative insights highlight the adaptability of constitutional principles across diverse legal cultures. The Basic Structure Doctrine, while uniquely Indian in its origin, taps into a broader global conversation on constitutionalism, democratic governance, and the role of the judiciary in safeguarding fundamental values.

Moreover, comparative analysis extends beyond specific legal provisions to encompass broader constitutional traditions. The Westminster system, prevalent in countries like the United Kingdom, Australia, and Canada, contrasts with the presidential system found in the United States. These structural differences contribute to distinct approaches to constitutional governance and the protection of fundamental rights.

In essence, the Basic Structure Doctrine invites us to engage in a global conversation about the foundational principles that underpin constitutional democracies. Through comparative insights, we glean a deeper understanding of how different legal systems navigate the tensions between constitutional change and the preservation of core values. It emphasizes that while constitutionalism may manifest differently across jurisdictions, the underlying quest for justice, equality, and protection of individual rights resonates universally.

9.5 Public Perception and Legitimacy

Public perception and legitimacy constitute critical dimensions in assessing the impact of the Basic Structure Doctrine within the Indian constitutional framework. The judiciary, as the custodian of the constitution, relies on public trust and legitimacy to ensure the effective implementation of its decisions. Examining the intricate relationship between public perception, judicial legitimacy, and the Basic Structure Doctrine unveils a complex interplay that shapes the constitutional landscape.

Public Perception and Judicial Decision-Making

Public perception of the judiciary plays a pivotal role in shaping the legitimacy of its decisions. In the context of the Basic Structure Doctrine, the judiciary's assertion of the power to review and strike down constitutional amendments necessitates a delicate balance between judicial independence and public acceptance.

The Kesavananda Bharati case (1973), which gave birth to the Basic Structure Doctrine, was a watershed moment in Indian constitutional history. The judiciary's intervention in determining the limits of constitutional amendments was a bold step that sought to protect the core values of the constitution. However, such interventions have not always been universally embraced, and public reactions have varied.

Public perception is often influenced by the perceived alignment of judicial decisions with societal values and expectations. While some decisions may be celebrated as guardianship of constitutional principles, others may be met with skepticism, particularly when they touch upon contentious issues or challenge popular sentiment.

Media Influence and Public Opinion

Media plays a crucial role in shaping public perception of judicial decisions. The coverage, framing, and interpretation of judicial rulings contribute significantly to how these decisions are perceived by the general public. The media's role as an intermediary between the judiciary and the public is instrumental in determining the narrative around judicial legitimacy.

For instance, landmark cases involving the Basic Structure Doctrine have garnered extensive media coverage, influencing public discourse and opinions. The media's ability to simplify legal complexities and convey judicial decisions in a comprehensible manner impacts public understanding and, consequently, perception.

Challenges in Maintaining Legitimacy

Maintaining judicial legitimacy poses challenges, especially when decisions are perceived as conflicting with popular mandates or political ideologies. Cases involving constitutional amendments, which lie at the heart of the Basic Structure Doctrine, often trigger debates about the judiciary's role vis-à-vis elected representatives.

Critics argue that an unelected judiciary should exercise restraint and avoid entering the domain of political decisions. The legitimacy of the judiciary's intervention in constitutional matters is contingent on its ability to articulate its reasoning, assuage public concerns, and demonstrate a commitment to constitutional values.

Public Understanding of the Basic Structure Doctrine

The intricacies of constitutional law, especially a doctrine as nuanced as the Basic Structure, may not always be fully comprehensible to the general public. Bridging the gap between legal intricacies and public understanding is crucial for maintaining legitimacy.

Efforts by the judiciary to enhance legal literacy through mechanisms like public interest litigation (PIL) and outreach programs contribute to fostering a better understanding of constitutional principles. Public engagement, dialogues, and educational initiatives play a role in demystifying legal concepts and reinforcing the importance of the Basic Structure Doctrine in upholding constitutional integrity.

Impact of Controversial Decisions

Controversial decisions, particularly those with far-reaching implications for governance and societal norms, can significantly impact public perception. For instance, cases involving interpretations of the Basic Structure Doctrine that touch upon issues like secularism, individual rights, or federalism may spark divergent reactions.

The Emergency period in India (1975-1977) witnessed a suspension of fundamental rights and a strained relationship between the judiciary and the executive. The judiciary's response during this period, including the Habeas Corpus case, contributed to shaping public perception about the role of the judiciary as a protector of individual liberties.

Role of Judicial Independence

Judicial independence is a cornerstone of judicial legitimacy. The judiciary's ability to act independently, free from undue influence or pressure, is vital for public trust. The Basic Structure Doctrine, by its very nature, requires the judiciary to exercise independence in determining the constitution's fundamental tenets.

Instances where the judiciary has demonstrated independence in challenging the government's actions or interpreting the constitution have bolstered public confidence. On the contrary, any perception of compromise on judicial independence may erode trust in the institution.

Public Engagement in Judicial Appointments

The process of judicial appointments also influences public perception. Transparency, fairness, and inclusivity in the appointment of judges contribute to enhancing the judiciary's legitimacy. Public confidence in the judiciary is intricately linked to the belief that judges are appointed based on merit, integrity, and a commitment to upholding constitutional values.

The National Judicial Appointments Commission (NJAC) case (2015) exemplifies the significance of public engagement in decisions affecting the judiciary. The Supreme Court's decision striking down the NJAC Act and upholding the collegium system reflected a judicial assertion aimed at safeguarding judicial independence and preserving the constitutional framework.

International Perspectives on Judicial Legitimacy

Understanding public perception and legitimacy requires a broader lens that considers international perspectives. Comparative analyses of how judiciaries in other democracies navigate similar challenges offer valuable insights. For instance, the U.S. Supreme Court's landmark decisions on issues like abortion, affirmative action, and marriage equality highlight the complex relationship between judicial decisions and public acceptance.

In the global context, international human rights tribunals and courts face challenges related to their legitimacy. Public skepticism regarding decisions perceived as infringing on national sovereignty or cultural values underscores the universal nature of the interplay between public perception and judicial legitimacy.

Conclusion

Public perception and legitimacy are integral aspects of the Basic Structure Doctrine's impact on the Indian constitutional landscape. The judiciary's role in safeguarding constitutional principles, while simultaneously aligning with public expectations, necessitates a delicate balance. The evolving nature of societal norms, political ideologies, and the media landscape underscores the importance of maintaining an open dialogue between the judiciary and the public. As the Basic Structure Doctrine continues to shape constitutional discourse, ensuring public trust and legitimacy remains paramount for a resilient constitutional democracy.

9.6 Future Horizons

The exploration of future horizons concerning the Basic Structure Doctrine unveils a dynamic canvas shaped by evolving societal, technological, and global trends. As the doctrine continues to be a cornerstone of India's constitutional jurisprudence, its trajectory extends beyond the present, resonating with the challenges and opportunities that lie ahead.

1. Technological Advancements and Constitutional Governance

The advent of advanced technologies, including artificial intelligence, blockchain, and quantum computing, poses unprecedented challenges and opportunities for constitutional governance. As these technologies redefine communication, privacy, and state-citizen interactions, the judiciary's role in safeguarding constitutional values becomes increasingly complex. The Basic Structure Doctrine may find new dimensions in addressing issues related to digital rights, data protection, and the ethical use of emerging technologies.

2. Artificial Intelligence and Legal Systems

Artificial intelligence (AI) is poised to revolutionize legal systems globally. The incorporation of AI in legal processes, from legal research to predictive analytics, raises questions about the impact on judicial decision-making. The judiciary's role in ensuring fairness, transparency, and accountability in AI-driven legal proceedings will likely become a focal point. The Basic Structure Doctrine may need to adapt to these technological shifts to uphold constitutional principles in the digital age.

3. Environmental Law in the 21st Century

Environmental challenges, including climate change and biodiversity loss, are expected to intensify in the coming decades. The Basic Structure Doctrine, with its emphasis on protecting the environment as part of the basic structure, may play a pivotal role in shaping legal responses to environmental crises. As the judiciary grapples with intricate environmental issues, the doctrine's application may evolve to address emerging ecological concerns and promote sustainable development.

4. Globalization and Constitutionalism

Globalization continues to influence legal and constitutional frameworks. The Basic Structure Doctrine, originally rooted in national constitutional principles, may need to

navigate the complexities of a globalized world. The interplay between domestic constitutional norms and international obligations, trade agreements, and human rights conventions may redefine the scope and applicability of the doctrine on a global scale.

5. Constitutional Responses to Public Health Crises

The COVID-19 pandemic has underscored the need for robust constitutional responses to public health emergencies. The Basic Structure Doctrine may need to adapt to situations where fundamental rights are temporarily restricted to address public health concerns. Balancing individual liberties with collective well-being presents a nuanced challenge, and the judiciary's role in ensuring constitutional resilience during health crises will be a critical aspect of future constitutional governance.

6. Inclusive Constitutionalism

Inclusivity and diversity are integral to constitutional governance. The Basic Structure Doctrine's application may expand to address issues related to social justice, minority rights, and the inclusion of marginalized communities. The judiciary's commitment to inclusive constitutionalism may shape future interpretations of the doctrine, reflecting an evolving societal consciousness.

7. Human Rights in the Digital Age

As the digital age progresses, safeguarding human rights in online spaces becomes paramount. The Basic Structure Doctrine's relevance may extend to protect individual freedoms in the digital realm, addressing challenges such as online privacy, freedom of expression, and protection against algorithmic biases. Judicial interventions in shaping the contours of digital human rights will likely shape the doctrine's trajectory.

8. Constitutional Governance in Times of Crisis

Unforeseen crises, whether environmental, economic, or geopolitical, may test the resilience of constitutional governance. The Basic Structure Doctrine's ability to provide a stable framework during turbulent times may become a defining factor in ensuring constitutional order. Judicial decisions in times of crisis will shape perceptions of the doctrine's efficacy in upholding constitutional values under challenging circumstances.

9. Constitutional Challenges Posed by Biotechnology

Advancements in biotechnology, including gene editing and genetic engineering, present ethical and legal challenges. The Basic Structure Doctrine's application may extend to address questions of bioethics, individual autonomy, and the constitutional implications of biotechnological innovations. The judiciary's role in striking a balance between scientific progress and constitutional safeguards will influence the doctrine's evolution.

10. Role of Constitutional Courts in Shaping the Future

The role of constitutional courts in shaping the future cannot be overstated. As guardians of the constitution, the judiciary's decisions will continue to shape the trajectory of constitutional governance. The Basic Structure Doctrine, as a guiding principle, will likely be invoked to address emerging constitutional issues, ensuring the enduring relevance of its core principles.

In conclusion, the future horizons of the Basic Structure Doctrine are intricately tied to the evolving dynamics of society, technology, and the global landscape. As the judiciary grapples with unprecedented challenges and opportunities, the doctrine's adaptability and resilience will be tested. The interplay between constitutional principles, societal expectations, and global shifts will define the doctrine's role in navigating the complex terrain of constitutional governance in the years to come.

9.7 Educational and Awareness Initiatives

The future horizons of the Basic Structure Doctrine unfold with a nuanced tapestry, encapsulating the symbiotic relationship between constitutional principles and the ever-evolving facets of societal, technological, and global dynamics. As we gaze into the constitutional landscape of the future, several key dimensions emerge, each contributing to the ongoing narrative of the doctrine's significance and adaptability.

1. Technological Advancements and Constitutional Governance

In the coming decades, the rapid progression of technology is poised to reshape the contours of constitutional governance. Artificial intelligence, blockchain, and quantum computing, among other advancements, introduce unprecedented challenges and possibilities. The Basic Structure Doctrine, deeply rooted in safeguarding constitutional values, must navigate these uncharted waters. As technology permeates every facet of life, the doctrine may find itself grappling with questions of digital rights, privacy in the age of surveillance, and the ethical implications of emerging technologies.

2. Artificial Intelligence and Legal Systems

The integration of artificial intelligence into legal systems is a paradigm shift that demands careful consideration. As algorithms and machine learning algorithms play an increasing role in legal proceedings, the judiciary's role in maintaining transparency, fairness, and accountability becomes crucial. The Basic Structure Doctrine, with its commitment to upholding constitutional values, may be invoked to ensure that the introduction of AI aligns with the principles of justice, equality, and due process.

3. Environmental Law in the 21st Century

Environmental challenges are expected to intensify, necessitating a robust legal response. The Basic Structure Doctrine, with its inherent commitment to environmental protection as a fundamental tenet, may evolve to address contemporary ecological concerns. The judiciary's role in interpreting and applying the doctrine will likely extend to complex issues such as climate change, conservation of biodiversity, and sustainable development.

4. Globalization and Constitutionalism

In an increasingly interconnected world, the impact of globalization on constitutionalism is undeniable. The Basic Structure Doctrine, traditionally rooted in national contexts, may need to adapt to the dynamics of a globalized legal landscape. The interplay between domestic constitutional norms and international legal obligations, trade agreements, and human rights conventions may redefine the doctrine's applicability on a global scale.

5. Constitutional Responses to Public Health Crises

The ongoing COVID-19 pandemic underscores the need for agile constitutional responses to public health emergencies. The Basic Structure Doctrine, while upholding fundamental rights, may also need to contend with situations where temporary restrictions become necessary for the greater good. Balancing individual liberties with collective well-being poses a nuanced challenge, and the doctrine's application may need to evolve to address unforeseen health crises.

6. Inclusive Constitutionalism

Inclusivity and diversity are foundational to constitutional governance. The Basic Structure Doctrine may expand its scope to address issues related to social justice, minority rights, and the inclusion of marginalized communities. As societal norms progress, the doctrine's application may reflect an evolving consciousness, fostering a more inclusive constitutional framework.

7. Human Rights in the Digital Age

As individuals increasingly navigate the digital realm, safeguarding human rights online becomes imperative. The Basic Structure Doctrine, committed to protecting fundamental rights, may extend its reach to address challenges in the digital age. Questions of online privacy, freedom of expression, and protection against algorithmic biases may become focal points for the judiciary, invoking the doctrine to ensure the preservation of individual liberties.

8. Constitutional Governance in Times of Crisis

Unforeseen crises, whether environmental, economic, or geopolitical, test the mettle of constitutional governance. The Basic Structure Doctrine's ability to provide stability and guidance during turbulent times is crucial. Judicial decisions during crises will shape perceptions of the doctrine's efficacy in upholding constitutional values under challenging circumstances.

9. Constitutional Challenges Posed by Biotechnology

Biotechnological advancements present ethical and legal challenges that require careful consideration. The Basic Structure Doctrine may extend its purview to address questions of bioethics, individual autonomy, and the constitutional implications of biotechnological innovations. The judiciary's role in navigating the ethical dimensions of scientific progress will influence the doctrine's trajectory.

10. Role of Constitutional Courts in Shaping the Future

The centrality of constitutional courts in shaping the future cannot be overstated. As interpreters and guardians of the constitution, the judiciary's decisions will continue to shape the trajectory of constitutional governance. The Basic Structure Doctrine, as a guiding principle, will be invoked to address emerging constitutional issues, ensuring the enduring relevance of its core principles.

In essence, the future horizons of the Basic Structure Doctrine are entwined with the evolving fabric of societal, technological, and global shifts. As we peer into the unknown, the doctrine stands as a sentinel, adapting to new challenges while steadfastly upholding the constitutional values that form the bedrock of India's democratic ethos. The journey ahead is dynamic and uncertain, but the principles embedded in the Basic Structure Doctrine provide a compass, guiding constitutional governance through the uncharted territories of the future.

9.8 Educational and Awareness Initiatives

Educational and Awareness Initiatives hold the key to fostering a deeper understanding of the Basic Structure Doctrine among the populace, ensuring that constitutional principles become ingrained in the collective consciousness. In the evolving landscape of constitutional governance, the role of educational initiatives becomes pivotal in disseminating knowledge, promoting civic awareness, and nurturing a sense of constitutional responsibility among citizens.

The Basic Structure Doctrine, as a cornerstone of constitutional jurisprudence, necessitates a concerted effort to demystify its complexities and significance. Educational programs aimed at schools, colleges, and civic institutions can play a transformative role in achieving this objective. Through a comprehensive curriculum that integrates constitutional studies, students can develop a nuanced understanding of the doctrine's historical context, its evolution through landmark cases, and its enduring impact on India's constitutional framework.

Awareness initiatives, including workshops, seminars, and public lectures, serve as crucial platforms for engaging citizens in informed discussions about the Basic Structure Doctrine. These forums provide an opportunity to explore the doctrine's application in contemporary scenarios, fostering a dialogue between legal scholars, policymakers, and the general public. By demystifying legal concepts and making constitutional principles accessible, these initiatives contribute to a more informed and active citizenry.

The media, including print, electronic, and digital platforms, also plays a significant role in disseminating information about the Basic Structure Doctrine. Educational content, documentaries, and interviews with legal experts can enhance public awareness and provide insights into the doctrine's relevance in shaping the country's constitutional identity. Collaborations between legal scholars and media outlets can bridge the gap between legal intricacies and public comprehension, ensuring that constitutional discourse remains accessible.

In the digital age, leveraging online platforms for educational and awareness initiatives becomes imperative. E-learning modules, webinars, and interactive resources can reach a broader audience, transcending geographical constraints. Social media, with its pervasive reach, offers a dynamic space for sharing bite-sized information, infographics, and engaging content that captures the essence of the Basic Structure Doctrine.

Furthermore, integrating constitutional literacy into broader civic education programs can empower individuals to actively participate in democratic processes. Understanding the implications of the Basic Structure Doctrine equips citizens to critically evaluate legal developments, engage in informed public discourse, and advocate for constitutional values. This, in turn, strengthens the foundations of a vibrant and participative democracy.

Educational and awareness initiatives also serve as a bulwark against misinformation and misconceptions surrounding the Basic Structure Doctrine. By fostering a culture of constitutional literacy, these initiatives contribute to a more enlightened citizenry capable of discerning the constitutional implications of legal and political developments.

In conclusion, Educational and Awareness Initiatives emerge as catalysts for nurturing a constitutional ethos within society. By imparting knowledge, fostering dialogue, and instilling a sense of constitutional responsibility, these initiatives fortify the Basic Structure Doctrine's role as a guiding principle in India's constitutional journey. As educational programs and awareness campaigns continue to evolve, they contribute to the enduring legacy of the Basic Structure Doctrine, ensuring that its principles resonate with every citizen, transcending legal circles to become an integral part of the nation's civic consciousness.

9.9 Challenges and Opportunities

Challenges and Opportunities in the context of the Basic Structure Doctrine present a nuanced landscape that demands careful consideration. The doctrine, while serving as a bulwark for constitutional principles, confronts multifaceted challenges that necessitate proactive responses. Simultaneously, these challenges give rise to opportunities for refinement, adaptation, and the continuous evolution of constitutional governance.

One of the foremost challenges lies in the interpretation and delineation of the Basic Structure. As the doctrine relies on judicial interpretation, varying perspectives among jurists may lead to ambiguity, leaving room for debate and potential inconsistencies in its application. Striking a delicate balance between the need for a flexible constitutional framework and the imperative of maintaining constitutional sanctity poses an ongoing challenge.

The evolving nature of society and its dynamics presents another challenge. The Basic Structure Doctrine was conceptualized in a different era, and its application to contemporary issues requires a judicious approach. Emerging technologies, socio-economic shifts, and cultural transformations pose challenges to adapting a doctrine crafted in the past to the complexities of the present. Balancing tradition with progress remains a perpetual challenge.

Judicial activism, while instrumental in upholding constitutional values, also raises concerns about the separation of powers. Striking a balance between the judiciary's role as the guardian of the constitution and the executive and legislative branches' autonomy poses an ongoing challenge. Overreaching judicial interventions may inadvertently impact the delicate equilibrium envisioned by the framers of the constitution.

Opportunities, however, emerge amidst these challenges. The dynamism of the Basic Structure Doctrine allows for its reinterpretation in light of contemporary needs. Courts have the opportunity to adapt the doctrine to address new challenges and ensure its relevance in a rapidly changing world. Legal scholars and practitioners can contribute to this ongoing dialogue, providing nuanced perspectives to refine and reinforce the doctrine.

In the realm of constitutional amendments, the challenges posed by evolving societal needs present opportunities for thoughtful revisions. While preserving the core principles of the Basic Structure, amendments can enhance its applicability to current realities, ensuring that the constitution remains a living document capable of addressing the evolving needs of the nation.

Public awareness and engagement, facilitated through educational initiatives, offer an opportunity to foster a deeper understanding of the Basic Structure Doctrine. As citizens become more informed about the constitutional intricacies, they can actively participate in the discourse surrounding its application, contributing to a more robust constitutional culture.

The challenge of striking a balance between individual rights and societal interests presents an opportunity for a nuanced exploration of constitutional values. Courts have the opportunity to refine the contours of the Basic Structure in cases that involve competing rights, ensuring that constitutional protections are harmonized with the collective welfare.

The intersectionality of challenges and opportunities requires a holistic approach to constitutional governance. Legal practitioners, scholars, and policymakers must collaboratively navigate these complexities, leveraging challenges as opportunities for growth and refinement. By fostering a culture of dialogue, adaptability, and continuous learning, the Basic Structure Doctrine can evolve organically, ensuring its resilience in the face of contemporary challenges.

In conclusion, the challenges and opportunities surrounding the Basic Structure Doctrine offer a dynamic terrain for constitutional discourse. As the doctrine grapples with the complexities of a changing society, there exists the potential for growth, adaptation, and the reaffirmation of constitutional values. Recognizing these challenges as opportunities for refinement ensures that the Basic Structure Doctrine remains a robust foundation for India's constitutional journey, capable of withstanding the test of time.

9.10 Closing Thoughts

In reflecting upon the extensive exploration of the Basic Structure Doctrine and its multifaceted dimensions, it becomes evident that this constitutional principle stands as a cornerstone in the edifice of India's legal landscape. The journey through the intricacies of this doctrine has unraveled its significance, challenges, and transformative potential in shaping the constitutional ethos.

At its core, the Basic Structure Doctrine emerges as a sentinel guarding the foundational values of the Indian Constitution. Its evolution mirrors the Republic's journey, offering resilience and adaptability in the face of changing times. As the custodian of constitutional morality, the doctrine manifests the framers' intent to create a living, breathing constitution capable of withstanding the tests of time.

The constitutional journey has witnessed the doctrine's role in protecting individual rights, upholding democratic principles, and acting as a bulwark against arbitrary state action. The judiciary, through its interpretative prowess, has sculpted the doctrine into a dynamic force, responsive to the evolving needs of society.

However, traversing the contours of the Basic Structure Doctrine reveals a complex interplay of challenges. The fine balance between judicial review and the principle of separation of powers requires continuous recalibration. The challenges of interpretation, ambiguity, and the doctrine's application to contemporary issues necessitate a delicate judicial dance.

Yet, within these challenges lie opportunities for growth and refinement. The Basic Structure Doctrine invites a continuous dialogue, not only within the judiciary but also among legal scholars, policymakers, and the public. The challenges posed by societal evolution and technological advancements serve as catalysts for a more profound understanding and application of constitutional principles.

In this journey, educational initiatives become crucial in fostering constitutional literacy and awareness. As citizens become more cognizant of their constitutional rights and responsibilities, the Basic Structure Doctrine transforms from a legal concept into a shared societal value, collectively upheld and protected.

The future horizons of the Basic Structure Doctrine hold promises of adaptability, inclusivity, and a harmonious balance between tradition and progress. As the constitutional landscape continues to evolve, the doctrine's relevance and resilience are contingent upon the collective commitment to constitutional values.

The Basic Structure Doctrine, while rooted in Indian jurisprudence, echoes universal principles of constitutionalism. Its exploration transcends geographical boundaries, inviting comparative analyses, critical debates, and collaborative efforts to fortify constitutional governance worldwide.

In conclusion, the Basic Structure Doctrine stands not only as a legal concept but as a testament to India's constitutional journey. It symbolizes the aspirations of a nation striving for justice, liberty, equality, and fraternity. As the constitutional saga unfolds, the Basic Structure Doctrine remains a guiding light, steering the course of India's constitutional governance with unwavering commitment and enduring relevance.

9.11 Call to Action

In concluding this comprehensive exploration of the Basic Structure Doctrine, it is imperative to transition from the realm of theoretical understanding to a practical call for action. The insights garnered from dissecting the doctrine and its multifaceted impacts on constitutional governance lay the foundation for a proactive engagement with the evolving constitutional landscape.

First and foremost, there is a pressing need for continued scholarly inquiry and research into the intricacies of the Basic Structure Doctrine. As the legal and societal landscape undergoes dynamic shifts, it is crucial for scholars, jurists, and legal practitioners to remain at the forefront of intellectual discourse. This calls for sustained efforts in uncovering new dimensions, emerging challenges, and potential advancements in constitutional jurisprudence.

Simultaneously, the call to action extends to the legal fraternity, policymakers, and the broader public. An informed and engaged citizenry is the bedrock of a vibrant democracy. Legal literacy campaigns, seminars, and public discussions centered around the Basic Structure Doctrine can empower individuals to comprehend the nuances of constitutional principles and their impact on governance.

Judicial activism and advocacy also emerge as potent avenues for channeling the principles of the Basic Structure Doctrine into tangible outcomes. Courts, as custodians of the constitution, play a pivotal role in interpreting and safeguarding its fundamental tenets. Legal challenges, public interest litigations, and strategic litigation can be employed to test the constitutional validity of laws and policies, ensuring their alignment with the basic structure.

The call to action further extends to the legislative domain. Policymakers and legislators are urged to approach constitutional amendments with a discerning eye, considering the potential implications on the basic structure. Public participation in the legislative process is pivotal, emphasizing the importance of inclusive governance that respects the foundational principles of the constitution.

Educational initiatives form a linchpin in this call to action. Integrating constitutional studies into academic curricula at various levels, fostering legal literacy programs, and utilizing digital platforms for disseminating legal knowledge are critical steps. This proactive educational approach ensures that future generations are equipped with a nuanced understanding of constitutional essentials.

Moreover, fostering an environment of open dialogue and debate is essential. Civil society organizations, think tanks, and advocacy groups can serve as catalysts for these discussions. Platforms for informed debates on constitutional principles, public forums, and policy dialogues contribute to the shaping of a collective consciousness that appreciates the significance of the Basic Structure Doctrine in preserving democratic ideals.

International collaboration and comparative constitutional studies also feature prominently in the call to action. Learning from global experiences, engaging with international legal frameworks, and contributing to the global discourse on constitutionalism can provide valuable insights and perspectives that enrich the understanding of the Basic Structure Doctrine.

As we heed this call to action, it is essential to recognize that the Basic Structure Doctrine is not a static concept but an evolving principle that adapts to the changing needs of society. Embracing this dynamism and committing to the principles of justice, equality, and constitutionalism, we embark on a collective journey towards a robust and resilient constitutional future.

Bibliography

1. G.N. Singh-Landmark of Indian Constitutional and National Development.
2. Report of the Joint Parliamentary Committee, Vol. 1.
3. M.V. Pylee-Constitutional History of India.
4. Constituent Assembly Debate, Vol. 4.
5. K.C. Wheare-Federal Government (4th Ed., 1963).
6. A.V. Dicey-The Law of the Constitution (10th ed.).
7. State of West Bengal v. Union of India, AIR 1963 SC 1241.
8. Jennings-Some Characterstics of the Indian Constitution.
9. Re, Kerala Education Bill, AIR 1958 SC 956.
10. V.N. Shukla-Constitution of India (1969).
11. M.P. Jain-Indian Constitutional Law (3rd Ed., 1978).
12. V.G. Ramchandran-1958 (SCJ).
13. Constituent Assembly Debates, Vol. XI.
14. Constituent Assembly Debates, Vol. VIII.
15. Bowie and Friedrich-Studies in Federalism.
16. Constituent Assembly Debates, Vol. VI.
17. The Constitution (61st Amendment) Act, 1989.

18. Ram Jawaya v. State of Punjab, AIR 1955 SC 549.
19. Bhim Singh v. Union of India, (2010) 5 SCC 538.
20. Minerva Mills v. Union of India, (1980) 3 SCC 625.
21. Indira Nehru Gandhi v. Raj Narain, AIR 1975 SC 2299.
22. Supreme Court Advocates on Record Association v. Union of India, 2015 AIR SCW 260.
23. Keshavanand Bharti v. State of Kerala, AIR 1973 SC 1461.
24. E.S. Crown-Essay on the Judicial Review in Encyclopaedia of Social Sciences, Vol. VIII.
25. Basu's Commentaries on Constitution of India, Vol. I.
26. State of Bihar v. Bihar Distillery Ltd, AIR 1997 SC 1511.
27. State of M.P. v. Rakesh Kohli, AIR 2012 SC 2351.
28. Union of India v. S.K. Sharma, AIR 2015 SC 246.
29. Madras Bar Association v. Union of India, AIR 2015 SC 1571.
30. Kerala Bar Hotels Association v. State of Kerala, AIR 2016 SC 163.
31. Census Commissioner v. R. Krishnamurthy, (2015) 2 SCC 796.
32. Tamil Nadu Pollution Control Board v. Sterilo Industries (I) Ltd., AIR 2019 SC 1074.
33. I.C. Golak Nath v. State of Punjab, AIR 1967 SC 1643.
34. Sir Alladi Krishnaswami-Constituent Assembly Debates, Vol. 10.
35. Basu-Introduction to the Constitution of India, (3rd Ed., 1954).
36. Buckingham & Carnatic Co. Ltd. v. Venkatiah, AIR 1964 SC 1272.
37. M.K. Gandhi-India of My Dreams.
38. V.S. Deahpande-Rights and and duties under the Indian constitution, (15 JILI 1973).
39. Draft Constitution 21.2.1948.

40. Constituent Assembly Debates, Vol. 7.

41. State Bank of India v. Santosh Gupta, AIR 2017 SC 25.

42. State of Tamil Nadu v. State of Kerala, AIR 2014 SC 2407.

43. Babuial v. State of Bombay, AIR 1960 SC 51.

44. Ram Kishore v. Union of India, AIR 1966 SC 644.

45. Surinder Singh v. Engineer-in-Chief, CPWD, AIR 1986 SC 584.

46. Jaipal v. State of Haryana, AIR 1988 SC 1504.

47. State of U.P. v. J.P. Chaurasia, AIR 1989 SC 19.

48. Harbans Lal v. State of Himachal Pradesh, AIR 1989 SC 459.

49. U.P. Raja Sahakari Bhoomi Vikas Bank v. Its Workmen, AIR 1990 SC 495.

50. Punjab State Electricity Board v. Thana Singh, AIR 2019 SC 354.

51. Praga Tools Corpn. v. Imanual, AIR 1969 Sc 1306.

52. Som Prakash v. Union of India, AIR 1981 SC 212.

53. Narinder v. Lt. Governor, (1971) II SCWR 651 (657).

54. Govinda Menon v. Union of India, AIR 1967 Sc 1.

55. East India Commercial Co. v. Collector of Customs, AIR 1962 SC 1893.

56. Sewpujanrai v. Collector of Customs, AIR 1958 SC 845.

57. Cf. Manak Lal v. Prem Chand, AIR 1957 SC 425.

58. Bidi Supply Co. v. Union of India, (1956) SCR 267.

59. Prov. of Bombay v. Khusaldas, (1950) SCR 621.

60. Radheshyam v. State of M.P., AIR 1959 SC 107.

61. Dantuluri Ram Raju v. State of A.P., (1972) 1 SCC 421.

62. "The Constitution of India" by Dr. B.R. Ambedkar.

63. "Our Constitution: An Introduction to India's Constitution and Constitutional Law" by Subhash C. Kashyap.

64. "Indian Polity" by M. Laxmikanth.

65. "Introduction to the Constitution of India" by D.D. Basu.

66. "The Framing of India's Constitution: Select Documents" by Granville Austin.

67. "Constitutional History of India: 1600-1935" by Arthur Berriedale Keith.

68. "The Oxford Handbook of the Indian Constitution" edited by Sujit Choudhry, Madhav Khosla, and Pratap Bhanu Mehta.

69. "The Indian Constitution: Cornerstone of a Nation" by Granville Austin.

70. "Making of India's Constitution" by A. Subbarao.

71. "Working a Democratic Constitution: A History of the Indian Experience" by Granville Austin.

72. "Making of India's Constitution: Select Documents" by B. Shiva Rao.

73. "The Constitution of India: A Politico-Legal Study" by M. P. Jain.

74. "The Indian Constitution: Miracle, Surrender, Hope" by Rajeev Dhavan.

75. "The Making of the Indian Constitution: A Case Study of Benegal Narsing Rau" by G. Austin and David Butler.

76. "The Oxford Companion to Politics in India" edited by Niraja Gopal Jayal and Pratap Bhanu Mehta.

77. "The Constitution of India: Select Issues" by Austin Granville and Jayan Nayar.

78. "The Founding Moment: Constitutional Philosophy in the Radical Enlightenment" by Ganesh Sitaraman.

79. "India's Founding Moment: The Constitution of a Most Surprising Democracy" by Madhav Khosla.

80. "Indian Constitution: Documents and Interpretations" edited by S. K. Verma.

81. "The Indian Constitution: A Very Short Introduction" by Madhav Khosla.

82. "Constitutional Law of India" by J.N. Pandey.

83. "The Indian Constitution and Social Revolution: Right to Property Since Independence" by Uday Mehta.

84. "Making of the Constitution of India: A Critical Analysis of the Constituent Assembly Debates" by Subhash C. Kashyap.

85. "Constitutional History of India: Ancient and Modern" by K.P. Jayaswal.

86. "The Indian Constitution: A Case Study of Backward Classes" by P.S. Krishnan.

87. "Working a Democratic Constitution: The Indian Experience" by G. Austin.

88. "The Constitution of India: A Contextual Analysis" by Arun K. Thiruvengadam.

89. "The Indian Constitution: Oxford India Short Introductions" by Madhav Khosla.

90. "Beyond a Billion Ballots: Democratic Reforms for a Resurgent India" by Vinay Sahasrabuddhe.

91. "The Indian Parliament: A Critical Appraisal" by Sudha Pai.

92. "Indian Constitution: Text and Context" by Prathama Banerjee.

93. "Legislative Procedures in the Parliament of India" by V.N. Shukla.

94. "Parliamentary Procedure in India" by S.C. Kashyap.

95. "India's Living Constitution: Ideas, Practices, Controversies" by Zoya Hasan and Eswaran Sridharan.

96. "Women and the Constitution of India: A Selective, Annotated Bibliography" by Usha Iyer.

97. "Federalism in India: Origin and Development" by Kochicheril R. Chandy.

98. "The Indian Constitution: A Critical Appraisal" by S.S. Rana.

99. "The Judiciary and Governance in India: Judicial Activism and Public Interest Litigation" by Sudha Pai.

100. "Equality, Inequality, and the Law: Global Contexts, Local Realities" edited by Upendra Baxi, et al.

101. "India's Silent Revolution: The Rise of the Low Castes in North Indian Politics" by Christophe Jaffrelot.

102. "The Indian Parliament and Democratic Transformation" by S. N. Sadasivan.

103. "The Indian Constitution: Its Provisions and Flexibilities" by K. K. Mathew.

104. "Parliamentary Diplomacy in India" by C. V. Narasimhan.

105. "The Administrative Law" by M.P. Jain.

106. "Constitutional Law of India" by J.N. Pandey.

107. "The Indian Constitution: A Critical Appraisal" by S.S. Rana.

108. "The Working of the Indian Constitution: A Centenary and Comparative Analysis" edited by Arun K. Thiruvengadam.

109. "Indian Constitution at Work" by Granville Austin.

110. "Parliamentary Diplomacy in India" by C.V. Narasimhan.

111. "Environmental Law and Policy in India: Cases, Materials, and Statutes" by Shyam Divan and Armin Rosencranz.

112. "Federalism in India: Origin and Development" by Kochicheril R. Chandy.

113. "The Constitution of India: Select Issues" by Austin Granville and Jayan Nayar.

114. "India's Constitution: Roots, Values and Challenges" by Subhash C. Kashyap.

115. "India's Living Constitution: Ideas, Practices, Controversies" by Zoya Hasan and Eswaran Sridharan.

116. "Supreme Court of India: The Beginnings" by George H. Gadbois Jr.

117. "The Constitution of India: As Amended by the Constitution (Ninety-Eighth Amendment) Act, 2012" by Universal Law Publishing Co.

118. "The Supreme Court in a Parliamentary Democracy: Judicial Review and Its Limits" by Upendra Baxi.

119. "The Indian Parliament and Democratic Transformation" by S. N. Sadasivan.

120. "The Indian Constitution and Social Revolution: Right to Property Since Independence" by Uday Mehta.

121. "Understanding the Constitution of India" by Vandana Ramanna.

122. "The Law of the Constitution of India" by V.N. Shukla.

123. "The Indian Judiciary: A Tribute" by M.C. Setalvad.

124. "Parliamentary Control over Public Expenditure: An Inquiry" by V. Krishna Rao.

125. "The Indian Constitution: A Dossier" edited by Rajeev Dhavan.

www.ingramcontent.com/pod-product-compliance
Lightning Source LLC
LaVergne TN
LVHW061539070526
838199LV00077B/6841